Introduction to the Devout Life

By St. Francis of Sales

Edited by Anthony Uyl

Devoted Publishing
Woodstock, Ontario, 2017

Introduction to the Devout Life
By St. Francis of Sales (1567-1622)
Edited by Anthony Uyl

This English edition first published 1891

**What kind of philosophies do you have?
Let us know!**

Contact us at: devotedpub@hotmail.com
Visit our shop on Facebook: @DevotedPublishing

Published in Woodstock, Ontario, Canada 2017

For bulk educational rates, please contact us at the above email address.

ISBN: 978-1-77356-030-4

Table of Contents

Preface by the Author

DEAR reader, I request you to read this Preface for your own satisfaction as well as mine.

The flower-girl Glycera was so skilled in varying the arrangement and combination of her flowers, that out of the same kinds she produced a great variety of bouquets; so that the painter Pausias, [1] who sought to rival the diversity of her art, was brought to a standstill, for he could not vary his painting so endlessly as Glycera varied her bouquets. Even so the Holy Spirit of God disposes and arranges the devout teaching which He imparts through the lips and pen of His servants with such endless variety, that, although the doctrine is ever one and the same, their treatment of it is different, according to the varying minds whence that treatment flows. Assuredly I neither desire, nor ought to write in this book anything but what has been already said by others before me. I offer you the same flowers, dear reader, but the bouquet will be somewhat different from theirs, because it is differently made up.

Almost all those who have written concerning the devout life have had chiefly in view persons who have altogether quitted the world; or at any rate they have taught a manner of devotion which would lead to such total retirement. But my object is to teach those who are living in towns, at court, in their own households, and whose calling obliges them to a social life, so far as externals are concerned. Such persons are apt to reject all attempt to lead a devout life under the plea of impossibility; imagining that like as no animal presumes to eat of the plant commonly called Palma Christi, so no one who is immersed in the tide of temporal affairs ought to presume to seek the palm of Christian piety.

And so I have shown them that, like as the mother-of-pearl lives in the sea without ever absorbing one drop of salt water; and as near the Chelidonian Isles springs of sweet water start forth in the midst of the ocean; [2] and as the firemoth [3] hovers in the flames without burning her wings; even so a true stedfast soul may live in the world untainted by worldly breath, finding a well-spring of holy piety amid the bitter waves of society, and hovering amid the flames of earthly lusts without singeing the wings of its devout life. Of a truth this is not easy, and for that very reason I would have Christians bestow more care and energy than heretofore on the attempt, and thus it is that, while conscious of my own weakness, I endeavour by this book to afford some help to those who are undertaking this noble work with a generous heart.

It is not, however, my own choice or wish which brings this Introduction before the public. A certain soul, abounding in uprightness and virtue, some time since conceived a great desire, through God's Grace, to aspire more earnestly after a devout life, and craved my private help with this view. I was bound to her by various ties, and had long observed her remarkable capacity for this attainment, so I took great pains to teach her, and having led her through the various exercises suitable to her circumstances and her aim, I let her keep written records thereof, to which she might have recourse when necessary. These she communicated to a learned and devout Religious, who, believing that they might be profitable to others, urged me to publish them, in which he succeeded the more readily that his friendship exercised great influence upon my will, and his judgment great authority over my judgment.

So, in order to make the work more useful and acceptable, I have reviewed the papers and put them together, adding several matters carrying out my intentions; but all this has been done with scarce a moment's leisure. Consequently you will find very little precision in the work, but rather a collection of well-intentioned instructions, explained in clear intelligible words, at least that is what I have sought to give. But as to a polished style, I have not given that a thought, having so much else to do.

I have addressed my instructions to Philothea, [4] as adapting what was originally written for an individual to the common good of souls. I have made use of a name suitable to all who seek after the devout life, Philothea meaning one who loves God. Setting then before me a soul, who through the devout life seeks after the love of God, I have arranged this Introduction in five parts, in the first of which I seek by suggestions and exercises to turn Philothea's mere desire into a hearty resolution; which she makes after her general confession, by a deliberate protest, followed by Holy Communion, in which, giving herself to her Saviour and receiving Him, she is happily received into His Holy Love. After this, I lead her on by showing her two great means of closer union with His Divine Majesty; the Sacraments, by which that Gracious Lord comes to us, and mental prayer, by which He draws us to Him. This is the Second Part.

In the Third Part I set forth how she should practise certain virtues most suitable to her advancement, only dwelling on such special points as she might not find elsewhere, or be able to make out for herself. In the Fourth Part I bring to light the snares of some of her enemies, and show her how to pass through them safely and come forth unhurt. And finally, in the Fifth Part, I lead her apart to refresh herself and take breath, and renew her strength, so that she may go on more bravely afterwards, and make good progress in the devout life.

This is a cavilling age, and I foresee that many will say that only Religious and persons living apart are fit to undertake the guidance of souls in such special devout ways; that it requires more time than a Bishop of so important a diocese as mine can spare, and that it must take too much thought from the important duties with which I am charged.

But, dear reader, I reply with S. Denis that the task of leading souls towards perfection appertains above all others to Bishops, and that because their Order is supreme among men, as the Seraphim among Angels, and therefore their leisure cannot be better spent. The ancient Bishops and Fathers of the Primitive Church were, to say the least, as devoted to their duties as we are, yet they did not refuse to undertake the individual guidance of souls which sought their help, as we see by their epistles; thereby imitating the Apostles, who, while reaping the universal world-harvest, yet found time to gather up certain individual sheaves with special and personal affection. Who can fail to remember that Timothy, Titus, Philemon, Onesimus, Thekla, Appia, were the beloved spiritual children of S. Paul, as S. Mark and S. Petronilla were of S. Peter (for Baronius and Galonius have given learned and absolute proof that S. Petronilla was not his carnal but spiritual daughter). And is not one of S. John's Canonical Epistles addressed to the "elect lady" whom he loved in the faith?

I grant that the guidance of individual souls is a labour, but it is a labour full of consolation, even as that of harvesters and grape-gatherers, who are never so well pleased as when most heavily laden. It is a labour which refreshes and invigorates the heart by the comfort which it brings to those who bear it; as is said to be the case with those who carry bundles of cinnamon in Arabia Felix. It is said that when the tigress finds one of her young left behind by the hunter in order to delay her while he carries off the rest of her cubs, she takes it up, however big, without seeming over-weighted, and speeds only the more swiftly to her lair, maternal love lightening the load. How much more readily will the heart of a spiritual father bear the burden of a soul he finds craving after perfection-- carrying it in his bosom as a mother her babe, without feeling weary of the precious burden?

But unquestionably it must be a really paternal heart that can do this, and therefore it is that the Apostles and their apostolic followers are wont to call their disciples not merely their children, but, even more tenderly still, their "little children."

One thing more, dear reader. It is too true that I who write about the devout life am not myself devout, but most certainly I am not without the wish to become so, and it is this wish which encourages me to teach you. A notable literary man has said that a good way to learn is to study, a better to listen, and the best to teach. And S. Augustine, writing to the devout Flora, [5] says, that giving is a claim to receive, and teaching a way to learn.

Alexander caused the lovely Campaspe, [6] who was so dear to him, to be painted by the great Apelles, who, by dint of contemplating her as he drew, so graved her features in his heart and conceived so great a passion for her, that Alexander discovered it, and, pitying the artist, gave him her to wife, depriving himself for love of Apelles of the dearest thing he had in the world, in which, says Pliny, he displayed the greatness of his soul as much as in the mightiest victory. And so, friendly reader, it seems to me that as a Bishop, God wills me to frame in the hearts of His children not merely ordinary goodness, but yet more His own most precious devotion; and on my part I undertake willingly to do so, as much out of obedience to the call of duty as in the hope that, while fixing the image in others' hearts, my own may haply conceive a holy love; and that if His Divine Majesty sees me deeply in love, He may give her to me in an eternal marriage. The beautiful and chaste Rebecca, as she watered Isaac's camels, was destined to be his bride, and received his golden earrings and bracelets, and so I rely on the boundless Goodness of my God, that while I lead His beloved lambs to the wholesome fountain of devotion, He will take my soul to be His bride, giving me earrings of the golden words of love, and strengthening my arms to carry out its works, wherein lies the essence of all true devotion, the which I pray His Heavenly Majesty to grant to me and to all the children of His Church -- that Church to which I would ever submit all my writings, actions, words, will and thoughts.

ANNECY, S. Magdalene's Day, 1608.

Footnotes:

1. 1 Pausias of Sicyon (B.C. 368); see Plin. Hist. Nat. xxxv. 11-40. A portrait of Glycera, the young flower-girl whom he loved, with a garland of flowers, was one of his masterpieces. It was called the Stephane-plocos [Stephane - plokos], or garland wreather, and was purchased by L. Lucullus at Athens for two talents, or about 430 pounds.

2. These islands are in the Mediterranean Sea, in the Gulf of Lycia.

3. Puraustes

4. The address to Philothea by name has been omitted, as being somewhat stiff and stilted, and the

term child or daughter used instead, but the omission in no way alters the sense or application of any sentence.

5. This is probably the person mentioned as "our most religious daughter Flora" in S. Augustine's Treatise "On care to be had for the Dead", addressed to his fellow Bishop Paulinus. See Library of the Fathers, S. Augustine's Short Treatises, p. 517.

6. Plin. Hist. Nat. l. xxv. c. 10.

PART I - COUNSELS AND PRACTICES SUITABLE FOR THE SOUL'S GUIDANCE FROM THE FIRST ASPIRATION AFTER A DEVOUT LIFE TO THE POINT WHEN IT ATTAINS A CONFIRMED RESOLUTION TO FOLLOW THE SAME

CHAPTER I - What true Devotion is

YOU aim at a devout life, dear child, because as a Christian you know that such devotion is most acceptable to God's Divine Majesty. But seeing that the small errors people are wont to commit in the beginning of any under taking are apt to wax greater as they advance, and to become irreparable at last, it is most important that you should thoroughly understand wherein lies the grace of true devotion;--and that because while there undoubtedly is such a true devotion, there are also many spurious and idle semblances thereof; and unless you know which is real, you may mistake, and waste your energy in pursuing an empty, profitless shadow. Arelius was wont to paint all his pictures with the features and expression of the women he loved, and even so we all colour devotion according to our own likings and dispositions. One man sets great value on fasting, and believes himself to be leading a very devout life, so long as he fasts rigorously, although the while his heart is full of bitterness;--and while he will not moisten his lips with wine, perhaps not even with water, in his great abstinence, he does not scruple to steep them in his neighbour's blood, through slander and detraction. Another man reckons himself as devout because he repeats many prayers daily, although at the same time he does not refrain from all manner of angry, irritating, conceited or insulting speeches among his family and neighbours. This man freely opens his purse in almsgiving, but closes his heart to all gentle and forgiving feelings towards those who are opposed to him; while that one is ready enough to forgive his enemies, but will never pay his rightful debts save under pressure. Meanwhile all these people are conventionally called religious, but nevertheless they are in no true sense really devout. When Saul's servants sought to take David, Michal induced them to suppose that the lifeless figure lying in his bed, and covered with his garments, was the man they sought; and in like manner many people dress up an exterior with the visible acts expressive of earnest devotion, and the world supposes them to be really devout and spiritual-minded, while all the time they are mere lay figures, mere phantasms of devotion.

But, in fact, all true and living devotion presupposes the love of God;--and indeed it is neither more nor less than a very real love of God, though not always of the same kind; for that Love one while shining on the soul we call grace, which makes us acceptable to His Divine Majesty;--when it strengthens us to do well, it is called Charity;--but when it attains its fullest perfection, in which it not only leads us to do well, but to act carefully, diligently, and promptly, then it is called Devotion. The ostrich never flies,--the hen rises with difficulty, and achieves but a brief and rare flight, but the eagle, the dove, and the swallow, are continually on the wing, and soar high;--even so sinners do not rise towards God, for all their movements are earthly and earthbound. Well-meaning people, who have not as yet attained a true devotion, attempt a manner of flight by means of their good actions, but rarely, slowly and heavily; while really devout men rise up to God frequently, and with a swift and soaring wing. In short, devotion is simply a spiritual activity and liveliness by means of which Divine Love works in us, and causes us to work briskly and lovingly; and just as charity leads us to a general practice of all God's Commandments, so devotion leads us to practise them readily and diligently. And therefore we cannot call him who neglects to observe all God's Commandments either good or devout, because in order to be good, a man must be filled with love, and to be devout, he must further be very ready and apt to perform the deeds of love. And forasmuch as devotion consists in a high degree of real love, it not only makes us ready, active, and diligent in following all God's Commands, but it also excites us to be ready and loving in performing as many good works as possible, even such as are not enjoined upon us,

11

but are only matters of counsel or inspiration. Even as a man just recovering from illness, walks only so far as he is obliged to go, with a slow and weary step, so the converted sinner journeys along as far as God commands him but slowly and wearily, until he attains a true spirit of devotion, and then, like a sound man, he not only gets along, but he runs and leaps in the way of God's Commands, and hastens gladly along the paths of heavenly counsels and inspirations. The difference between love and devotion is just that which exists between fire and flame;--love being a spiritual fire which becomes devotion when it is fanned into a flame;--and what devotion adds to the fire of love is that flame which makes it eager, energetic and diligent, not merely in obeying God's Commandments, but in fulfilling His Divine Counsels and inspirations.

CHAPTER II - The Nature and Excellence of Devotion

THOSE who sought to discourage the Israelites from going up to the Promised Land, told them that it was "a land which eateth up the inhabitants thereof;" [7] that is, that the climate was so unhealthy that the inhabitants could not live long, and that the people thereof were "men of a great stature," who looked upon the new-comers as mere locusts to be devoured. It is just so, my daughter, that the world runs down true devotion, painting devout people with gloomy, melancholy aspect, and affirming that religion makes them dismal and unpleasant. But even as Joshua and Caleb protested that not only was the Promised Land a fair and pleasant country, but that the Israelites would take an easy and peaceful possession thereof, so the Holy Spirit tells us through His Saints, and our Lord has told us with His Own Lips, that a devout life is very sweet, very happy and very loveable.

The world, looking on, sees that devout persons fast, watch and pray, endure injury patiently, minister to the sick and poor, restrain their temper, check and subdue their passions, deny themselves in all sensual indulgence, and do many other things which in themselves are hard and difficult. But the world sees nothing of that inward, heartfelt devotion which makes all these actions pleasant and easy. Watch a bee hovering over the mountain thyme;--the juices it gathers are bitter, but the bee turns them all to honey,--and so tells the worldling, that though the devout soul finds bitter herbs along its path of devotion, they are all turned to sweetness and pleasantness as it treads;--and the martyrs have counted fire, sword, and rack but as perfumed flowers by reason of their devotion. And if devotion can sweeten such cruel torments, and even death itself, how much more will it give a charm to ordinary good deeds? We sweeten unripe fruit with sugar, and it is useful in correcting the crudity even of that which is good. So devotion is the real spiritual sweetness which takes away all bitterness from mortifications; and prevents consolations from disagreeing with the soul: it cures the poor of sadness, and the rich of presumption; it keeps the oppressed from feeling desolate, and the prosperous from insolence; it averts sadness from the lonely, and dissipation from social life; it is as warmth in winter and refreshing dew in summer; it knows how to abound and how to suffer want; how to profit alike by honour and contempt; it accepts gladness and sadness with an even mind, and fills men's hearts with a wondrous sweetness.

Ponder Jacob's ladder:--it is a true picture of the devout life; the two poles which support the steps are types of prayer which seeks the love of God, and the Sacraments which confer that love; while the steps themselves are simply the degrees of love by which we go on from virtue to virtue, either descending by good deeds on behalf of our neighbour or ascending by contemplation to a loving union with God. Consider, too, who they are who trod this ladder; men with angels' hearts, or angels with human forms. They are not youthful, but they seem to be so by reason of their vigour and spiritual activity. They have wings wherewith to fly, and attain to God in holy prayer, but they have likewise feet wherewith to tread in human paths by a holy gracious intercourse with men; their faces are bright and beautiful, inasmuch as they accept all things gently and sweetly; their heads and limbs are uncovered, because their thoughts, affections and actions have no motive or object save that of pleasing God; the rest of their bodies is covered with a light shining garment, because while they use the world and the things of this life, they use all such purely and honestly, and no further than is needful for their condition--such are the truly devout. Believe me, dear child, devotion is the sweetest of sweets, the queen of virtues, the perfection of love. If love is the milk of life, devotion is the cream thereof; if it is a fruitful plant, devotion is the blossom; if it is a precious stone, devotion is its brightness; if it is a precious balm, devotion is its perfume, even that sweet odour which delights men and causes the angels to rejoice.

Footnote:

7. Numb. xiii. 32.

CHAPTER III - Devotion is suitable to every Vocation and Profession

WHEN God created the world He commanded each tree to bear fruit after its kind; [8] and even so He bids Christians,--the living trees of His Church,--to bring forth fruits of devotion, each one according to his kind and vocation. A different exercise of devotion is required of each--the noble, the artisan, the servant, the prince, the maiden and the wife; and furthermore such practice must be modified according to the strength, the calling, and the duties of each individual. I ask you, my child, would it be fitting that a Bishop should seek to lead the solitary life of a Carthusian? And if the father of a family were as regardless in making provision for the future as a Capucin, if the artisan spent the day in church like a Religious, if the Religious involved himself in all manner of business on his neighbour's behalf as a Bishop is called upon to do, would not such a devotion be ridiculous, ill-regulated, and intolerable? Nevertheless such a mistake is often made, and the world, which cannot or will not discriminate between real devotion and the indiscretion of those who fancy themselves devout, grumbles and finds fault with devotion, which is really nowise concerned in these errors. No indeed, my child, the devotion which is true hinders nothing, but on the contrary it perfects everything; and that which runs counter to the rightful vocation of any one is, you may be sure, a spurious devotion. Aristotle says that the bee sucks honey from flowers without damaging them, leaving them as whole and fresh as it found them;-- but true devotion does better still, for it not only hinders no manner of vocation or duty, but, contrariwise, it adorns and beautifies all. Throw precious stones into honey, and each will grow more brilliant according to its several colour:--and in like manner everybody fulfils his special calling better when subject to the influence of devotion:--family duties are lighter, married love truer, service to our King more faithful, every kind of occupation more acceptable and better performed where that is the guide.

It is an error, nay more, a very heresy, to seek to banish the devout life from the soldier's guardroom, the mechanic's workshop, the prince's court, or the domestic hearth. Of course a purely contemplative devotion, such as is specially proper to the religious and monastic life, cannot be practised in these outer vocations, but there are various other kinds of devotion well-suited to lead those whose calling is secular, along the paths of perfection. The Old Testament furnishes us examples in Abraham, Isaac and Jacob, David, Job, Tobias, Sarah, Rebecca and Judith; and in the New Testament we read of St. Joseph, Lydia and Crispus, who led a perfectly devout life in their trades:--we have S. Anne, Martha, S. Monica, Aquila and Priscilla, as examples of household devotion, Cornelius, S. Sebastian, and S. Maurice among soldiers;--Constantine, S. Helena, S. Louis, the Blessed Amadaeus, [9] and S. Edward on the throne. And we even find instances of some who fell away in solitude,--usually so helpful to perfection,--some who had led a higher life in the world, which seems so antagonistic to it. S. Gregory dwells on how Lot, who had kept himself pure in the city, fell in his mountain solitude. Be sure that wheresoever our lot is cast we may and must aim at the perfect life.

Footnotes:

8. Gen. i. 12.

9. It is probable that S. Francis here means to indicate Amadeo IX., Duke of Savoy, who died 1472.

CHAPTER IV - The Need of a Guide for those who would enter upon and advance in the Devout Life

WHEN Tobias was bidden to go to Rages, he was willing to obey his father, but he objected that he knew not the way;--to which Tobit answered, "Seek thee a man which may go with thee:" [10] and even so, daughter, I say to you, If you would really tread the paths of the devout life, seek some holy man to guide and conduct you. This is the precept of precepts, says the devout Avila,--seek as you will you can never so surely discover God's Will as through the channel of humble obedience so universally taught and practised by all the Saints of olden time. When the blessed Teresa read of the great penances performed by Catherine of Cordova, she desired exceedingly to imitate them, contrary to the mind of her Confessor, who forbade her to do the like, and she was tempted to disobey him therein. Then God spoke to Teresa, saying, "My child, thou art on a good and safe road:--true, thou seest all this penance, but verily I esteem thy obedience as a yet greater virtue:"--and thenceforth S. Teresa so greatly loved the virtue of obedience, that in addition to that due to her superiors, she took a vow of special obedience to a pious ecclesiastic, pledging herself to follow his direction and guidance, which proved an inexpressible help to her. And even so before and after her many pious souls have subjected their will to God's ministers in order the better to submit themselves to Him, a practice much commended by S. Catherine of Sienna in her Dialogues. The devout Princess S. Elisabeth gave an unlimited obedience to the venerable Conrad; and one of the parting counsels given by S. Louis to his son ere he died was, "Confess thyself often,--choose a single-minded, worthy confessor, who is able wisely to teach thee how to do that which is needful for thee." [11] "A faithful friend," we are told in Holy Scripture, "is a strong defence, and he that hath found such an one hath found a treasure;" [12] and again: "A faithful friend is the medicine of life; and they that fear the Lord shall find him." [13] These sacred words have chiefly reference, as you see, to the immortal life, with a view to which we specially need a faithful friend, who will guide us by his counsel and advice, thereby guarding us against the deceits and snares of the Evil One:--he will be as a storehouse of wisdom to us in our sorrows, trials and falls; he will be as a healing balm to stay and soothe our heart in the time of spiritual sickness,--he will shield us from evil, and confirm that which is good in us, and when we fall through infirmity, he will avert the deadly nature of the evil, and raise us up again.

But who can find such a friend? The Wise Man answers:--"He that feareth the Lord:" [14] that is to say, the truly humble soul which earnestly desires to advance in the spiritual life. So, daughter, inasmuch as it concerns you so closely to set forth on this devout journey under good guidance, do you pray most earnestly to God to supply you with a guide after His Own Heart, and never doubt but that He will grant you one who is wise and faithful, even should He send you an angel from Heaven, as He sent to Tobias.

In truth, your spiritual guide should always be as a heaven-sent angel to you;--by which I mean that when you have found him, you are not to look upon him, or trust in him or his wisdom as an ordinary man; but you must look to God, Who will help you and speak to you through this man, putting into his heart and mouth that which is needful to you; so that you ought to hearken as though he were an angel come down from Heaven to lead you thither. Deal with him in all sincerity and faithfulness, and with open heart; manifesting alike your good and your evil, without pretence or dissimulation. Thus your good will be examined and confirmed, and your evil corrected and remedied;--you will be soothed and strengthened in trouble, moderated and regulated in prosperity. Give your guide a hearty confidence mingled with sacred reverence, so that reverence in no way shall hinder your confidence, and confidence nowise lessen your reverence: trust him with the respect of a daughter for her father; respect him with the confidence of a son in his mother. In a word, such a friendship should be strong and sweet; altogether holy, sacred, divine and spiritual. And with such an aim, choose one among a thousand, Avila says;--and I say among ten thousand, for there are fewer than one would think capable of this office. He must needs be full of love, of wisdom and of discretion; for if either of these three be wanting there is danger. But once more I say, ask such help of God, and when you have found it, bless His Holy Name; be stedfast, seek no more, but go on simply, humbly and trustfully, for you are safe to make a prosperous journey.

Footnotes:

10. Tob. v. 3.

11. "Confesse-toi souvent, eslis un confesseur idoine, qui soit prudhomme, et qui te puisse seurement enseigner a faire les choses qui te seront necessaires."

12. Ecclus. vi. 14.

13. Ecclus. v. 16.

14. Ecclus. vi. 17.

CHAPTER V - The First Step must be Purifying the Soul

"THE flowers appear on the earth," [15] says the Heavenly Bridegroom, and the time for pruning and cutting is come. And what, my child, are our hearts' flowers save our good desires? Now, so soon as these begin to appear, we need the pruning-hook to cut off all dead and superfluous works from our conscience. When the daughter of a strange land was about to espouse an Israelite, the law commanded her to put off the garment of her captivity, to pare her nails, and to shave her head; [16] even so the soul which aims at the dignity of becoming the spouse of Christ, must put off the old man, and put on the new man, forsaking sin: moreover, it must pare and shave away every impediment which can hinder the Love of God. The very first step towards spiritual health is to be purged from our sinful humours. S. Paul received perfect purification instantaneously, and the like grace was conferred on S. Magdalene, S. Catherine of Genoa, S. Pelagia, and some others, but this kind of purgation is as miraculous and extraordinary in grace as the resurrection of the dead in nature, nor dare we venture to aspire to it. The ordinary purification, whether of body or soul, is only accomplished by slow degrees, step by step, gradually and painfully.

The angels on Jacob's ladder had wings, yet nevertheless they did not fly, but went in due order up and down the steps of the ladder. The soul which rises from out of sin to a devout life has been compared to the dawn, which does not banish darkness suddenly, but by degrees. That cure which is gradually effected is always the surest; and spiritual maladies, like those of the body, are wont to come on horseback and express, while they depart slowly and on foot. So that we must needs be brave and patient, my daughter, in this undertaking. It is a woeful thing to see souls beginning to chafe and grow disheartened because they find themselves still subject to imperfection after having made some attempt at leading a devout life, and well-nigh yielding to the temptation to give up in despair and fall back; but, on the other hand, there is an extreme danger surrounding those souls who, through the opposite temptation, are disposed to imagine themselves purified from all imperfection at the very outset of their purgation; who count themselves as full-grown almost before they are born, and seek to fly before they have wings. Be sure, daughter, that these are in great danger of a relapse through having left their physician too soon. "It is but lost labour to rise up early and late take rest," unless the Lord prosper all we do.

The work of the soul's purification neither may nor can end save with life itself;--do not then let us be disheartened by our imperfections,--our very perfection lies in diligently contending against them, and it is impossible so to contend without seeing them, or to overcome without meeting them face to face. Our victory does not consist in being insensible to them, but in not consenting to them. Now to be afflicted by our imperfections is certainly not to consent thereto, and for the furtherance of humility it is needful that we sometimes find ourselves worsted in this spiritual battle, wherein, however, we shall never be conquered until we lose either life or courage. Moreover, imperfections and venial sins cannot destroy our spiritual life, which is only to be lost through mortal sin; consequently we have only need to watch well that they do not imperil our courage. David continually asks the Lord to strengthen his heart against cowardice and discouragement; and it is our privilege in this war that we are certain to vanquish so long as we are willing to fight.

Footnotes:

15. Cant. ii. 12.
16. Deut. xxi. 12.

CHAPTER VI - The First Purification, namely, from Mortal Sin

THE first purification to be made is from sin;--the means whereby to make it, the sacrament of penance. Seek the best confessor within your reach, use one of the many little books written in order to help the examination of conscience. [17] Read some such book carefully, examining point by point wherein you have sinned, from the first use of your reason to the present time. And if you mistrust your memory, write down the result of your examination. Having thus sought out the evil spots in your conscience, strive to detest them, and to reject them with the greatest abhorrence and contrition of which your heart is capable;--bearing in mind these four things:--that by sin you have lost God's Grace, rejected your share in Paradise, accepted the pains of Hell, and renounced God's Eternal Love. You see, my child, that I am now speaking of a general confession of your whole life, which, while I grant it is not always necessary, I yet believe will be found most helpful in the beginning of your pursuit after holiness, and therefore I earnestly advise you to make it. Not unfrequently the ordinary confessions of persons leading an everyday life are full of great faults, and that because they make little or no preparation, and have not the needful contrition. Owing to this deficiency such people go to confession with a tacit intention of returning to their old sins, inasmuch as they will not avoid the occasions of sin, or take the necessary measures for amendment of life, and in all such cases a general confession is required to steady and fix the soul. But, furthermore, a general confession forces us to a clearer selfknowledge, kindles a wholesome shame for our past life, and rouses gratitude for God's Mercy, Which has so long waited patiently for us;--it comforts the heart, refreshes the spirit, excites good resolutions, affords opportunity to our spiritual Father for giving the most suitable advice, and opens our hearts so as to make future confessions more effectual. Therefore I cannot enter into the subject of a general change of life and entire turning to God, by means of a devout life, without urging upon you to begin with a general confession.

Footnote:

17. S. Francis suggests Grenada, Bruno, Arias, Augez, authors little known now, though we have the substance of their teaching in numerous valuable helps for those who are preparing for confession: such as "Pardon through the Precious Blood," "Helps for Confirmation and First Communion" (Masters), "Manual for Confession," "Repentance," (Rev. T. T. Carter), "Hints to Penitents" (Palmer), Brett's "Guide to Faith and Piety," Crake's "Bread of Life" (Mowbray), "Paradise of the Christian Soul," etc.

CHAPTER VII - The Second Purification, from all Sinful Affections

ALL the children of Israel went forth from the land of Egypt, but not all went forth heartily, and so, when wandering in the desert, some of them sighed after the leeks and onions,--the fleshpots of Egypt. Even so there are penitents who forsake sin, yet without forsaking their sinful affections; that is to say, they intend to sin no more, but it goes sorely against them to abstain from the pleasures of sin;--they formally renounce and forsake sinful acts, but they turn back many a fond lingering look to what they have left, like Lot's wife as she fled from Sodom. They are like a sick man who abstains from eating melon when the doctor says it would kill him, but who all the while longs for it, talks about it, bargains when he may have it, would at least like just to sniff the perfume, and thinks those who are free to eat of it very fortunate. And so these weak cowardly penitents abstain awhile from sin, but reluctantly;--they would fain be able to sin without incurring damnation;--they talk with a lingering taste of their sinful deeds, and envy those who are yet indulging in the like. Thus a man who has meditated some revenge gives it up in confession, but soon after he is to be found talking about the quarrel, averring that but for the fear of God he would do this or that; complaining that it is hard to keep the Divine rule of forgiveness; would to God it were lawful to avenge one's self! Who can fail to see that even if this poor man is not actually committing sin, he is altogether bound with the affections thereof, and although he may have come out of Egypt, he yet hungers after it, and longs for the leeks and onions he was wont to feed upon there! It is the same with the woman who, though she has given up her life of sin, yet takes delight in being sought after and admired. Alas! of a truth, all such are in great peril.

Be sure, my daughter, that if you seek to lead a devout life, you must not merely forsake sin; but you must further cleanse your heart from all affections pertaining to sin; for, to say nothing of the danger of a relapse, these wretched affections will perpetually enfeeble your mind, and clog it, so that you will be unable to be diligent, ready and frequent in good works, wherein nevertheless lies the very essence of all true devotion. Souls which, in spite of having forsaken sin, yet retain such likings and longings, remind us of those persons who, without being actually ill, are pale and sickly, languid in all they do, eating without appetite, sleeping without refreshment, laughing without mirth, dragging themselves about rather than walking briskly. Such souls as I have described lose all the grace of their good deeds, which are probably few and feeble, through their spiritual languor.

CHAPTER VIII - How to effect this Second Purification

THE first inducement to attain this second purification is a keen and lively apprehension of the great evils resulting from sin, by means of which we acquire a deep, hearty contrition. For just as contrition, (so far as it is real,) however slight, when joined to the virtue of the Sacraments, purges away sin; so, when it becomes strong and urgent, it purges away all the affections which cling around habits of sin. A moderate, slight hatred makes men dislike its object and avoid his society; but when a violent, mortal hatred exists, they not only abhor and shun the person who excites it, but they loathe him, they cannot endure the approach of his relations or connexions, nor even his likeness or anything that concerns him. Just so when a penitent only hates sin through a weakly although real contrition, he will resolve to avoid overt acts of sin; but when his contrition is strong and hearty, he will not merely abhor sin, but every affection, every link and tendency to sin. Therefore, my daughter, it behoves us to kindle our contrition and repentance as much as we possibly can, so that it may reach even to the very smallest appearance of sin. Thus it was that the Magdalen, when converted, so entirely lost all taste for her past sin and its pleasures, that she never again cast back one thought upon them; and David declared that he hated not only sin itself, but every path and way which led thereto. This it is which is that "renewing of the soul" which the same Prophet compares to the eagle's strength. [18]

Now, in order to attain this fear and this contrition, you must use the following meditations carefully; for if you practise them stedfastly, they (by God's Grace) will root out both sin and its affections from your heart. It is to that end that I have prepared them: do you use them one after another, in the order in which they come, only taking one each day, and using that as early as possible, for the morning is the best time for all spiritual exercises;--and then you will ponder and ruminate it through the day. If you have not as yet been taught how to meditate, you will find instructions to that purpose in the Second Part.

Footnote:

18. Ps. ciii. 5, Bible version.

CHAPTER IX - FIRST MEDITATION

Of Creation.

Preparation.
    1. PLACE yourself in the Presence of God. 2. Ask Him to inspire your heart.
    Considerations.
    1. Consider that but a few years since you were not born into the world, and your soul was as yet non-existent. Where wert thou then, O my soul? the world was already old, and yet of thee there was no sign.
    2. God brought you out of this nothingness, in order to make you what you are, not because He had any need of you, but solely out of His Goodness.
    3. Consider the being which God has given you; for it is the foremost being of this visible world, adapted to live eternally, and to be perfectly united to God's Divine Majesty.
    Affections and Resolutions.
    1. Humble yourself utterly before God, saying with the Psalmist, O Lord, I am nothing in respect of Thee--what am I, that Thou shouldst remember me? O my soul, thou wert yet lost in that abyss of nothingness, if God had not called thee forth, and what of thee in such a case?
    2. Give God thanks. O Great and Good Creator, what do I not owe Thee, Who didst take me from out that nothingness, by Thy Mercy to make me what I am? How can I ever do enough worthily to praise Thy Holy Name, and render due thanks to Thy Goodness?
    3. Confess your own shame. But alas, O my Creator, so far from uniting myself to Thee by a loving service, I have rebelled against Thee through my unruly affections, departing from Thee, and giving myself up to sin, and ignoring Thy Goodness, as though Thou hadst not created me.
    4. Prostrate thyself before God. O my soul, know that the Lord He is thy God, it is He that hath made thee, and not thou thyself. O God, I am the work of Thy Hands; henceforth I will not seek to rest in myself, who am nought. Wherein hast thou to glory, who art but dust and ashes? how canst thou, a very nothing, exalt thyself? In order to my own humiliation, I will do such and such a thing,--I will endure such contempt:--I will alter my ways and henceforth follow my Creator, and realise that I am honoured by His calling me to the being He has given, I will employ it solely to obey His Will, by means of the teaching He has given me, of which I will inquire more through my spiritual Father.

Conclusion.
    1. Thank God. Bless the Lord, O my soul, and praise His Holy Name with all thy being, because His Goodness called me forth from nothingness, and His Mercy created me.
    2. Offer. O my God, I offer Thee with all my heart the being Thou hast given me, I dedicate and consecrate it to Thee.
    3. Pray. O God, strengthen me in these affections and resolutions. Dear Lord, I commend me, and all those I love, to Thy neverfailing Mercy. OUR FATHER, etc.
    At the end of your meditation linger a while, and gather, so to say, a little spiritual bouquet from the thoughts you have dwelt upon, the sweet perfume whereof may refresh you through the day.

CHAPTER X - SECOND MEDITATION

Of the End for which we were Created.

Preparation.
    1. PLACE yourself before God. 2. Ask Him to inspire your heart.

Considerations.
    1. God did not bring you into the world because He had any need of you, useless as you are; but solely that He might show forth His Goodness in you, giving you His Grace and Glory. And to this end He gave you understanding that you might know Him, memory that you might think of Him, a will that you might love Him, imagination that you might realise His mercies, sight that you might behold the marvels of His works, speech that you might praise Him, and so on with all your other faculties.
    2. Being created and placed in the world for this intent, all contrary actions should be shunned and rejected, as also you should avoid as idle and superfluous whatever does not promote it.
    2. Consider how unhappy they are who do not think of all this,--who live as though they were created only to build and plant, to heap up riches and amuse themselves with trifles.
    Affections and Resolutions.
    1. Humble yourself in that hitherto you have so little thought upon all this. Alas, my God, of what was I thinking when I did not think of Thee? what did I remember when I forgot Thee? what did I love when I loved Thee not? Alas, when I ought to have been feeding on the truth, I was but filling myself with vanity, and serving the world, which was made to serve me.
    2. Abhor your past life. I renounce ye, O vain thoughts and useless cogitations, frivolous and hateful memories: I renounce all worthless friendships, all unprofitable efforts, and miserably ungrateful self-indulgence, all pitiful compliances.
    3. Turn to God. Thou, my God and Saviour shalt henceforth be the sole object of my thoughts; no more will I give my mind to ideas which are displeasing to Thee. All the days of my life I will dwell upon the greatness of Thy Goodness, so lovingly poured out upon me. Thou shalt be henceforth the delight of my heart, the resting-place of all my affections. From this time forth I will forsake and abhor the vain pleasures and amusements, the empty pursuits which have absorbed my time;--the unprofitable ties which have bound my heart I will loosen henceforth, and to that end I will use such and such remedies.

Conclusion.
    1. Thank God, Who has made you for so gracious an end. Thou hast made me, O Lord, for Thyself, that I may eternally enjoy the immensity of Thy Glory; when shall I be worthy thereof, when shall I know how to bless Thee as I ought?
    2. Offer. O Dearest Lord, I offer Thee all my affections and resolutions, with my whole heart and soul.
    3. Pray. I entreat Thee, O God, that Thou wouldest accept my desires and longings, and give Thy Blessing to my soul, to enable me to fulfil them, through the Merits of Thy Dear Son's Precious Blood shed upon the Cross for me. OUR FATHER, etc. Gather your little spiritual bouquet.

CHAPTER XI - THIRD MEDITATION

Of the Gifts of God.

Preparation.
    1. PLACE yourself in the Presence of God. 2. Ask Him to inspire your heart.
    Considerations.
    1. Consider the material gifts God has given you--your body, and the means for its preservation; your health, and all that maintains it; your friends and many helps. Consider too how many persons more deserving than you are without these gifts; some suffering in health or limb, others exposed to injury, contempt and trouble, or sunk in poverty, while God has willed you to be better off.
    2. Consider the mental gifts He has given you. Why are you not stupid, idiotic, insane like many you wot of? Again, God has favoured you with a decent and suitable education, while many have grown up in utter ignorance.
    3. Further, consider His spiritual gifts. You are a child of His Church, God has taught you to know Himself from your youth. How often has He given you His Sacraments? what inspirations and interior light, what reproofs, He has given to lead you aright; how often He has forgiven you, how often delivered you from occasions of falling; what opportunities He has granted for your soul's progress! Dwell somewhat on the detail, see how Loving and Gracious God has been to you.

Affections and Resolutions.
    1. Marvel at God's Goodness. How good He has been to me, how abundant in mercy and plenteous in loving-kindness! O my soul, be thou ever telling of the great things the Lord has done for thee!
    2. Marvel at your own ingratitude. What am I, Lord, that Thou rememberest me? How unworthy am I! I have trodden Thy Mercies under foot, I have abused Thy Grace, turning it against Thy very Self; I have set the depth of my ingratitude against the deep of Thy Grace and Favour.
    3. Kindle your gratitude. O my soul, be no more so faithless and disloyal to thy mighty Benefactor! How should not my whole soul serve the Lord, Who has done such great things in me and for me?
    4. Go on, my daughter, to refrain from this or that material indulgence; let your body be wholly the servant of God, Who has done so much for it: set your soul to seek Him by this or that devout practice suitable thereto. Make diligent use of the means provided by the Church to help you to love God and save your soul. Resolve to be constant in prayer and seeking the Sacraments, in hearing God's Word, and in obeying His inspirations and counsels.

Conclusion.
    1. Thank God for the clearer knowledge He has given you of His benefits and your own duty.
    2. Offer your heart and all its resolutions to Him.
    3. Ask Him to strengthen you to fulfil them faithfully by the Merits of the Death of His Son. OUR FATHER, etc. Gather the little spiritual bouquet.

CHAPTER XII - FOURTH MEDITATION

On Sin.

Preparation.
1. PLACE yourself in the Presence of God. 2. Ask Him to inspire your heart.

Considerations.
1. Consider how long it is since you first began to commit sin, and how since that first beginning sin has multiplied in your heart; how every day has added to the number of your sins against God, against yourself and against your neighbour, by deed, word, thought and desire.
2. Consider your evil tendencies, and how far you have followed them. These two points will show you that your sins are more in number than the hairs of your head, or the sand on the seashore.
3. Apart from sin, consider your ingratitude towards God, which is in itself a sin enfolding all the others, and adding to their enormity: consider the gifts which God has given you, and which you have turned against the Giver; especially the inspirations you have neglected, and the promptings to good which you have frustrated. Review the many Sacraments you have received, and see where are their fruits. Where are the precious jewels wherewith your Heavenly Bridegroom decked you? with what preparation have you received them? Reflect upon the ingratitude with which, while God sought to save you, you have fled from Him and rushed upon destruction.

Affections and Resolutions.
1. Humble yourself in your wretchedness. O my God, how dare I come before Thine Eyes? I am but a corrupt being, a very sink of ingratitude and wickedness. Can it be that I have been so disloyal, that not one sense, not one faculty but has been sullied and stained;--not one day has passed but I have sinned before Thee? Was this a fitting return for all my Creator's gifts, for my Redeemer's Blood?
2. Ask pardon;--throw yourself at the Lord's Feet as the prodigal son, as the Magdalene, as the woman convicted of adultery. Have mercy, Lord, on me a sinner! O Living Fountain of Mercy, have pity on me, unworthy as I am.
3. Resolve to do better. Lord, with the help of Thy Grace I will never again give myself up to sin. I have loved it too well;--henceforth I would abhor it and cleave to Thee. Father of Mercy, I would live and die to Thee.
4. In order to put away past sin, accuse yourself bravely of it, let there not be one sinful act which you do not bring to light.
5. Resolve to make every effort to tear up the roots of sin from your heart, especially this and that individual sin which troubles you most.
6. In order to do this, resolve stedfastly to follow the advice given you, and never think that you have done enough to atone for your past sin.

Conclusion.
1. Thank God for having waited till now for you, and for rousing these good intentions in your heart. 2. Offer Him all your heart to carry them to good effect. 3. Pray that He would strengthen you.

CHAPTER XIII - FIFTH MEDITATION

Of Death.

Preparation.
    1. PLACE yourself in the Presence of God. 2. Ask His Grace. 3. Suppose yourself to be on your deathbed, in the last extremity, without the smallest hope of recovery.

Considerations.
    1. Consider the uncertainty as to the day of your death. One day your soul will quit this body--will it be in summer or winter? in town or country? by day or by night? will it be suddenly or with warning? will it be owing to sickness or an accident? will you have time to make your last confession or not? will your confessor or spiritual father be at hand or will he not? Alas, of all these things we know absolutely nothing: all that we do know is that die we shall, and for the most part sooner than we expect.
    2. Consider that then the world is at end as far as you are concerned, there will be no more of it for you, it will be altogether overthrown for you, since all pleasures, vanities, worldly joys, empty delights will be as a mere fantastic vision to you. Woe is me, for what mere trifles and unrealities I have ventured to offend my God? Then you will see that what we preferred to Him was nought. But, on the other hand, all devotion and good works will then seem so precious and so sweet:--Why did I not tread that pleasant path? Then what you thought to be little sins will look like huge mountains, and your devotion will seem but a very little thing.
    3. Consider the universal farewell which your soul will take of this world. It will say farewell to riches, pleasures, and idle companions; to amusements and pastimes, to friends and neighbours, to husband, wife and child, in short to all creation. And lastly it will say farewell to its own body, which it will leave pale and cold, to become repulsive in decay.
    4. Consider how the survivors will hasten to put that body away, and hide it beneath the earth--and then the world will scarce give you another thought, or remember you, any more than you have done to those already gone. "God rest his soul!" men will say, and that is all. O death, how pitiless, how hard thou art!
    5. Consider that when it quits the body the soul must go at once to the right hand or the left. To which will your soul go? what side will it take? none other, be sure, than that to which it had voluntarily drawn while yet in this world.

Affections and Resolutions.
    1. Pray to God, and throw yourself into His Arms. O Lord, be Thou my stay in that day of anguish! May that hour be blessed and favourable to me, if all the rest of my life be full of sadness and trial.
    2. Despise the world. Forasmuch as I know not the hour in which I must quit the world, I will not grow fond of it. O dear friends, beloved ones of my heart, be content that I cleave to you only with a holy friendship which may last for ever; why should I cling to you with a tie which must needs be broken?
    I will prepare for the hour of death and take every precaution for its peaceful arrival; I will thoroughly examine into the state of my conscience, and put in order whatever is wanting.

Conclusion.
    Thank God for inspiring you with these resolutions: offer them to His Majesty: intreat Him anew to grant you a happy death by the Merits of His Dear Son's Death. Ask the prayers of the Blessed Virgin and the Saints. OUR FATHER, etc.
    Gather a bouquet of myrrh.

CHAPTER XIV - SIXTH MEDITATION

On Judgment.

Preparation.
    1. PLACE yourself in the Presence of God. 2. Intreat Him to inspire you.

Considerations.
    1. When the time comes which God has appointed for the end of this world, and after many terrible signs and warnings, which will overwhelm men with fear,--the whole earth will be destroyed, and nothing then left.
    2. Afterwards, all men, save those already risen, shall rise from the dead, and at the voice of the Archangel appear in the valley of Jehoshaphat. But alas, with what divers aspects! for some will be glorious and shining, others horrible and ghastly.
    3. Consider the majesty with which the Sovereign Judge will appear surrounded by all His Saints and Angels; His Cross, the Sign of Grace to the good and of terror to the evil, shining brighter than the sun.
    4. This Sovereign Judge will with His awful word, instantly fulfilled, separate the evil and the good, setting the one on His Right Hand, the other on His Left--an eternal separation, for they will never meet again.
    5. This separation made, the books of conscience will be opened, and all men will behold the malice of the wicked, and how they have contemned God; as also the penitence of the good, and the results of the grace they received. Nothing will be hid. O my God, what confusion to the one, what rejoicing to the other! Consider the final sentence of the wicked. "Depart from Me, ye cursed, into everlasting fire, prepared for the devil and his angels." Dwell upon these awful words. "Go," He says-- for ever discarding these wretched sinners, banishing them for ever from His Presence. He calls them "cursed:" O my soul, what a curse: a curse involving all other maledictions, all possible evil, an irrevocable curse, including all time and eternity; condemning them to everlasting fire. Think what that eternity of suffering implies.
    6. Then consider the sentence of the good. "Come," the Judge says--O blessed loving word with which God draws us to Himself and receives us in His Bosom. "Blessed of My Father"--O blessing above all blessings! "inherit the Kingdom prepared for you from the beginning of the world." O my God, and that Kingdom will know no end!

Affections and Resolutions.
    1. Tremble, my soul, at the thought. O God, who will be my stay in that hour when the pillars of the earth are shaken?
    2. Abhor your sins, which alone can cause you to be lost when that fearful day comes. Surely I will judge myself now, that I be not judged;--I will examine my conscience, accuse, condemn, punish myself, that the Judge may not condemn me then. I will confess my faults, and follow the counsels given me.

Conclusion.
    Thank God for having given you means of safety in that terrible Day, and time for repentance. Offer Him your heart, and ask for grace to use it well. OUR FATHER, etc.
    Gather your bouquet.

CHAPTER XV - SEVENTH MEDITATION

Of Hell.

Preparation.
    1. PLACE yourself in God's Presence.2. Humble yourself, and ask His Aid.3. Picture to yourself a dark city, reeking with the flames of sulphur and brimstone, inhabited by citizens who cannot get forth.

Considerations.
    1. Even so the lost are plunged in their infernal abyss;--suffering indescribable torture in every sense and every member; and that because having used their members and senses for sin, it is just that through them they should suffer now. Those eyes which delighted in impure vicious sights, now behold devils; the ears which took pleasure in unholy words, now are deafened with yells of despair;--and so on with the other senses. 2. Beyond all these sufferings, there is one greater still, the privation and pain of loss of God's Glory, which is for ever denied to their vision. If Absalom cared not to be released from exile, if he might not see his father's face, [19] how much sorer will it be to be deprived for ever of the blessed vision of God?
    3. Consider how insupportable the pains of Hell will be by reason of their eternal duration. If the irritating bite of an insect, or the restlessness of fever, makes an ordinary night seem so long and tedious, how terrible will the endless night of eternity be, where nought will be found save despair, blasphemy and fury!

Affections and Resolutions.
    1. Read the Prophet's descriptions of the terrors of the Lord, [20] and ask your soul whether it can face them--whether you can bear to lose your God for ever?
    2. Confess that you have repeatedly deserved to do so. Resolve henceforth to act differently, and to rescue yourself from this abyss. Resolve on distinct definite acts by which you may avoid sin, and thereby eternal death.
    Give thanks, offer yourself, pray.

Footnotes:
    19. 2 Sam. xiv. 32.
    20. Isa. xxxiii. 14. "Who among us shall dwell with the devouring fire? who among us shall dwell with everlasting burnings?"

CHAPTER XVI - EIGHTH MEDITATION

On Paradise.

Preparation.
    1. PLACE yourself in the Presence of God. 2. Invoke His Aid.

Considerations.
    1. Represent to yourself a lovely calm night, when the heavens are bright with innumerable stars: add to the beauty of such a night the utmost beauty of a glorious summer's day,--the sun's brightness not hindering the clear shining of moon or stars, and then be sure that it all falls immeasurably short of the glory of Paradise. O bright and blessed country, O sweet and precious place!
    2. Consider the beauty and perfection of the countless inhabitants of that blessed country;--the millions and millions of angels, Cherubim and Seraphim; the glorious company of Apostles, martyrs, confessors, virgins, and saints. O blessed company, any one single member of which surpasses all the glory of this world, what will it be to behold them all, to sing with them the sweet Song of the Lamb? They rejoice with a perpetual joy, they share a bliss unspeakable, and unchangeable delights.
    3. Consider how they enjoy the Presence of God, Who fills them with the richness of His Vision, which is a perfect ocean of delight; the joy of being for ever united to their Head. They are like happy birds, hovering and singing for ever within the atmosphere of divinity, which fills them with inconceivable pleasures. There each one vies without jealousy in singing the praises of the Creator. "Blessed art Thou for ever, O Dear and Precious Lord and Redeemer, Who dost so freely give us of Thine Own Glory," they cry; and He in His turn pours out His ceaseless Blessing on His Saints. "Blessed are ye,--Mine own for ever, who have served Me faithfully, and with a good courage."

Affections and Resolutions.
    1. Admire and rejoice in the Heavenly Country; the glorious and blessed New Jerusalem.
    2. Reprove the coldness of your own heart for having hitherto so little sought after that glorious abode. Why have I so long lingered indifferent to the eternal happiness set before me? Woe is me that, for the sake of poor savourless earthly things, I have so often forgotten those heavenly delights. How could I neglect such real treasures for mere vain and contemptible earthly matters?
    3. Aspire earnestly after that blessed abode. Forasmuch, O Dear Lord, as Thou hast been pleased to turn my feet into Thy ways, never will I again look back. Go forth, my soul, towards thy promised rest, journey unweariedly to that hoped-for land; wherefore shouldest thou tarry in Egypt?
    4. Resolve to give up such and such things, which hinder you on the way, and to do such others as will help you thitherwards.
    Give thanks, offer, pray.

CHAPTER XVII - NINTH MEDITATION

On the Choice upon to you between Heaven and Hell.

Preparation.
    1. PLACE yourself in the Presence of God.2. Humble yourself before Him, and ask His inspiration.

Considerations.
    1. Imagine yourself alone with your good angel in an open plain, as was Tobit on his way to Rages. Suppose the Angel to set before you Paradise, full of delights and joys; and on the other hand Hell, with all its torments. Contemplate both, kneeling in imagination before your guardian Angel. Consider that you are most truly standing between Hell and Paradise, and that both the one and the other are open to receive you, according to your own choice.
    2. Consider that the choice you make in this life will last for ever in the next.
    3. Consider too, that while both are open to receive you according to your choice, yet God, Who is prepared to give the one by reason of His Justice, the other by reason of His Mercy, all the while desires unspeakably that you should select Paradise; and your good Angel is urging you with all his might to do so, offering you countless graces on God's part, countless helps to attain to it.
    4. Consider that Jesus Christ, enthroned in Heaven, looks down upon you in loving invitation: "O beloved one, come unto Me, and joy for ever in the eternal blessedness of My Love!" Behold His mother yearning over you with maternal tenderness--" Courage, my child, do not despise the Goodness of my Son, or my earnest prayers for thy salvation." Behold the Saints, who have left you their example, the millions of holy souls who long after you, desiring earnestly that you may one day be for ever joined to them in their song of praise, urging upon you that the road to Heaven is not so hard to find as the world would have you think. "Press on boldly, dear friend,"--they cry. "Whoso will ponder well the path by which we came hither, will discover that we attained to these present delights by sweeter joys than any this world can give."

The Choice.
    1. O Hell, I abhor thee now and for ever; I abhor thy griefs and torments, thine endless misery, the unceasing blasphemies and maledictions which thou pourest out upon my God;--and turning to thee, O blessed Paradise, eternal glory, unfading happiness, I choose thee for ever as my abode, thy glorious mansions, thy precious and abiding tabernacles. O my God, I bless Thy Mercy which gives me the power to choose--O Jesus, Saviour, I accept Thine Eternal Love, and praise Thee for the promise Thou hast given me of a place prepared for me in that blessed New Jerusalem, where I shall love and bless Thee for ever.
    2. Dwell lovingly upon the example set before you by the Blessed Virgin and the Saints, and strive to follow where they point you. Give yourself up to your guardian Angel, that he may be your guide, and gird up your courage anew to make this choice.

CHAPTER XVIII - TENTH MEDITATION

How the Soul chooses the Devout Life.

Preparation.
    1. PLACE yourself in the Presence of God.2. Humble yourself before Him, and ask His Aid.

Considerations.
    1. Once more imagine yourself in an open plain, alone with your guardian Angel, and represent to yourself on the left hand the Devil sitting on a high and mighty throne, surrounded by a vast troop of worldly men, who bow bareheaded before him, doing homage to him by the various sins they commit. Study the countenances of the miserable courtiers of that most abominable king;--some raging with fury, envy and passion, some murderous in their hatred;--others pale and haggard in their craving after wealth, or madly pursuing every vain and profitless pleasure;--others sunk and lost in vile, impure affections. See how all alike are hateful, restless, wild: see how they despise one another, and only pretend to an unreal self-seeking love. Such is the miserable reign of the abhorred Tyrant.
    2. On the other hand, behold Jesus Christ Crucified, calling these unhappy wretches to come to Him, and interceding for them with all the Love of His Precious Heart. Behold the company of devout souls and their guardian Angels, contemplate the beauty of this religious Kingdom. What lovelier than the troop of virgin souls, men and women, pure as lilies:--widows in their holy desolation and humility; husbands and wives living in all tender love and mutual cherishing. See how such pious souls know how to combine their exterior and interior duties;--to love the earthly spouse without diminishing their devotion to the Heavenly Bridegroom. Look around--one and all you will see them with loving, holy, gentle countenances listening to the Voice of their Lord, all seeking to enthrone Him more and more within their hearts.
    They rejoice, but it is with a peaceful, loving, sober joy; they love, but their love is altogether holy and pure. Such among these devout ones as have sorrows to bear, are not disheartened thereby, and do not grieve overmuch, for their Saviour's Eye is upon them to comfort them, and they all seek Him only.
    3. Surely you have altogether renounced Satan with his weary miserable troop, by the good resolutions you have made;--but nevertheless you have not yet wholly attained to the King Jesus, or altogether joined His blessed company of devout ones:--you have hovered betwixt the two.
    4. The Blessed Virgin, S. Joseph, S. Louis, S. Monica, and hundreds of thousands more who were once like you, living in the world, call upon you and encourage you.
    5. The Crucified King Himself calls you by your own name: "Come, O my beloved, come, and let Me crown thee!"

The Choice.
    1. O world, O vile company, never will I enlist beneath thy banner; for ever I have forsaken thy flatteries and deceptions. O proud king, monarch of evil, infernal spirit, I renounce thee and all thy hollow pomp, I detest thee and all thy works.
    2. And turning to Thee, O Sweet Jesus, King of blessedness and of eternal glory, I cleave to Thee with all the powers of my soul, I adore Thee with all my heart, I choose Thee now and ever for my King, and with inviolable fidelity I would offer my irrevocable service, and submit myself to Thy holy laws and ordinances.
    3. O Blessed Virgin Mother of God, you shall be my example, I will follow you with all reverence and respect.
    O my good Angel, bring me to this heavenly company, leave me not until I have reached them, with whom I will sing for ever, in testimony of my choice, "Glory be to Jesus, my Lord!"

CHAPTER XIX - How to make a General Confession

SUCH meditations as these, my daughter, will help you, and having made them, go on bravely in the spirit of humility to make your general confession;--but I entreat you, be not troubled by any sort of fearfulness. The scorpion who stings us is venomous, but when his oil has been distilled, it is the best remedy for his bite;--even so sin is shameful when we commit it, but when reduced to repentance and confession, it becomes salutary and honourable. Contrition and confession are in themselves so lovely and sweet-savoured, that they efface the ugliness and disperse the ill savour of sin. Simon the leper called Magdalene a sinner, [21] but our Lord turned the discourse to the perfume of her ointment and the greatness of her love. If we are really humble, my daughter, our sins will be infinitely displeasing to us, because they offend God;--but it will be welcome and sweet to accuse ourselves thereof because in so doing we honour God; and there is always somewhat soothing in fully telling the physician all details of our pain.

When you come to your spiritual father, imagine yourself to be on Mount Calvary, at the Feet of the Crucified Saviour, Whose Precious Blood is dropping freely to cleanse you from all your sin. Though it is not his actual Blood, yet it is the merit of that outpoured Blood which is sprinkled over His penitents as they kneel in Confession. Be sure then that you open your heart fully, and put away your sins by confessing them, for in proportion as they are put out, so will the Precious Merits of the Passion of Christ come in and fill you with blessings.

Tell everything simply and with straightforwardness, and thoroughly satisfy your conscience in doing so. Then listen to the admonitions and counsels of God's Minister, saying in your heart, "Speak, Lord, for Thy servant heareth." It is truly God to Whom you hearken, forasmuch as He has said to His representatives, "Whoso heareth you, heareth Me." [22] Then take the following protest, as a summary of your contrition, having carefully studied and meditated upon it beforehand: read it through with as earnest an intention as you can make.

Footnotes:

21. S. Mark xiv. and S. Luke vii. 39.
22. S. Luke x. 16.

CHAPTER XX - A hearty Protest made with the object of confirming the Soul's resolution to serve God, as a conclusion to its acts of Penitence

I, THE undersigned,--in the Presence of God and of all the company of Heaven, having considered the Infinite Mercy of His Heavenly Goodness towards me, a most miserable, unworthy creature, whom He has created, preserved, sustained, delivered from so many dangers, and filled with so many blessings: having above all considered the incomprehensible mercy and loving-kindness with which this most Good God has borne with me in my sinfulness, leading me so tenderly to repentance, and waiting so patiently for me till this--(present) year of my life, notwithstanding all my ingratitude, disloyalty and faithlessness, by which I have delayed turning to Him, and despising His Grace, have offended Him anew: and further, remembering that in my Baptism I was solemnly and happily dedicated to God as His child, and that in defiance of the profession then made in my name, I have so often miserably profaned my gifts, turning them against God's Divine Majesty:--I, now coming to myself prostrate in heart and soul before the Throne of His Justice, acknowledge and confess that I am duly accused and convicted of treason against His Majesty, and guilty of the Death and Passion of Jesus Christ, by reason of the sins I have committed, for which He died, bearing the reproach of the Cross; so that I deserve nothing else save eternal damnation.

But turning to the Throne of Infinite Mercy of this Eternal God, detesting the sins of my past life with all my heart and all my strength, I humbly desire and ask grace, pardon, and mercy, with entire absolution from my sin, in virtue of the Death and Passion of that same Lord and Redeemer, on Whom I lean as the only ground of my hope. I renew the sacred promise of faithfulness to God made in my name at my Baptism; renouncing the devil, the world, and the flesh, abhorring their accursed suggestions, vanities and lusts, now and for all eternity. And turning to a Loving and Pitiful God, I desire, intend, and deliberately resolve to serve and love Him now and eternally, devoting my mind and all its faculties, my soul and all its powers, my heart and all its affections, my body and all its senses, to His Will. I resolve never to misuse any part of my being by opposing His Divine Will and Sovereign Majesty, to which I wholly immolate myself in intention, vowing ever to be His loyal, obedient and faithful servant without any change or recall. But if unhappily, through the promptings of the enemy, or human infirmity, I should in anywise fail in this my resolution and dedication, I do most earnestly resolve by the grace of the Holy Spirit to rise up again so soon as I shall perceive my fall, and turn anew, without any delay, to seek His Divine Mercy. This is my firm will and intention,--my inviolable, irrevocable resolution, which I make and confirm without any reserve, in the Holy Presence of God, in the sight of the Church triumphant, and before the Church militant, which is my mother, who accepts this my declaration, in the person of him who, as her representative, hears me make it. Be pleased, O Eternal, All-Powerful, and All-Loving God,--Father, Son, and Holy Spirit, to confirm me in this my resolution, and accept my hearty and willing offering. And inasmuch as Thou hast been pleased to inspire me with the will to make it, give me also the needful strength and grace to keep it. O God, Thou art my God, the God of my heart, my soul, and spirit, and as such I acknowledge and adore Thee, now and for all eternity. Glory be to Jesus. Amen.

CHAPTER XXI - Conclusion of this First Purification

HAVING made this resolution, wait attentively, and open the ears of your heart, that you may in spirit hear the absolution which the Lord of your soul, sitting on the throne of His Mercy, will speak in Heaven before the Saints and Angels when His Priest absolves you here below in His Name. Be sure that all that company of blessed ones rejoice in your joy, and sing a song of untold gladness, embracing you and accepting you as cleansed and sanctified. Of a truth, my daughter, this is a marvellous deed, and a most blessed bargain for you, inasmuch as giving yourself to His Divine Majesty, you gain Him, and save yourself for eternal life. No more remains to do, save to take the pen and heartily sign your protest, and then hasten to the Altar, where God on His side will sign and seal your absolution, and His promise of Paradise, giving Himself to you in His Sacrament, as a sacred seal placed upon your renewed heart. And thus, dear child, your soul will be cleansed from sin, and from all its affections. But forasmuch as these affections are easily rekindled, thanks to our infirmity and concupiscence (which maybe mortified, but which can never be altogether extinguished while we live), I will give you certain counsels by the practice of which you may henceforth avoid mortal sin, and the affections pertaining thereto. And as these counsels will also help you to attain a yet more perfect purification, before giving them, I would say somewhat concerning that absolute perfection to which I seek to lead you.

CHAPTER XXII - The Necessity of Purging away all tendency to Venial Sins

AS daylight waxes, we, gazing into a mirror, see more plainly the soils and stains upon our face; and even so as the interior light of the Holy Spirit enlightens our conscience, we see more distinctly the sins, inclinations and imperfections which hinder our progress towards real devotion. And the selfsame light which shows us these blots and stains, kindles in us the desire to be cleansed and purged therefrom. You will find then, my child, that besides the mortal sins and their affections from which your soul has already been purged, you are beset by sundry inclinations and tendencies to venial sin; mind, I do not say you will find venial sins, but the inclination and tendency to them. Now, one is quite different from the other. We can never be altogether free from venial sin,--at least not until after a very long persistence in this purity; but we can be without any affection for venial sin. It is altogether one thing to have said something unimportant not strictly true, out of carelessness or liveliness, and quite a different matter to take pleasure in lying, and in the habitual practice thereof. But I tell you that you must purify your soul from all inclination to venial sin;--that is to say, you must not voluntarily retain any deliberate intention of permitting yourself to commit any venial sin whatever. It would be most unworthy consciously to admit anything so displeasing to God, as the will to offend Him in anywise. Venial sin, however small, is displeasing to God, although it be not so displeasing as the greater sins which involve eternal condemnation; and if venial sin is displeasing to Him, any clinging which we tolerate to mortal sin is nothing less than a resolution to offend His Divine Majesty. Is it really possible that a rightly disposed soul can not only offend God, but take pleasure therein?

These inclinations, my daughter, are in direct opposition to devotion, as inclinations to mortal sin are to love:--they weaken the mental power, hinder Divine consolations, and open the door to temptations;--and although they may not destroy the soul, at least they bring on very serious disease. "Dead flies cause the ointment to send forth a stinking savour," says the Wise Man. [23] He means that the flies which settle upon and taste of the ointment only damage it temporarily, leaving the mass intact, but if they fall into it, and die there, they spoil and corrupt it. Even so venial sins which pass over a devout soul without being harboured, do not permanently injure it, but if such sins are fostered and cherished, they destroy the sweet savour of that soul--that is to say, its devotion. The spider cannot kill bees, but it can spoil their honey, and so encumber their combs with its webs in course of time, as to hinder the bees materially. Just so, though venial sins may not lose the soul, they will spoil its devotion, and so cumber its faculties with bad habits and evil inclinations, as to deprive it of all that cheerful readiness which is the very essence of true devotion; that is to say, if they are harboured in the conscience by delight taken therein. A trifling inaccuracy, a little hastiness in word or action, some small excess in mirth, in dress, in gaiety, may not be very important, if these are forthwith heeded and swept out as spiritual cobwebs;-- but if they are permitted to linger in the heart, or, worse still, if we take pleasure in them and indulge them, our honey will soon be spoilt, and the hive of our conscience will be cumbered and damaged. But I ask again, how can a generous heart take delight in anything it knows to be displeasing to its God, or wish to do what offends Him?

Footnote:

23. Eccles. x. 1.

CHAPTER XXIII - It is needful to put away all Inclination for Useless and Dangerous Things

SPORTS, balls, plays, festivities, pomps, are not in themselves evil, but rather indifferent matters, capable of being used for good or ill; but nevertheless they are dangerous, and it is still more dangerous to take great delight in them. Therefore, my daughter, I say that although it is lawful to amuse yourself, to dance, dress, feast, and see seemly plays,--at the same time, if you are much addicted to these things, they will hinder your devotion, and become extremely hurtful and dangerous to you. The harm lies, not in doing them, but in the degree to which you care for them. It is a pity to sow the seed of vain and foolish tastes in the soil of your heart, taking up the place of better things, and hindering the soul from cultivating good dispositions. It was thus that the Nazarites of old abstained not merely from all intoxicating liquors, but from grapes fresh or dried, and from vinegar, not because these were intoxicating, but because they might excite the desire for fermented liquors. Just so, while I do not forbid the use of these dangerous pleasures, I say that you cannot take an excessive delight in them without their telling upon your devotion. When the stag has waxed fat he hides himself amid the thicket, conscious that his fleetness is impaired should he be in need to fly: and so the human heart which is cumbered with useless, superfluous, dangerous clingings becomes incapacitated for that earnest following after God which is the true life of devotion. No one blames children for running after butterflies, because they are children, but is it not ridiculous and pitiful to see full-grown men eager about such worthless trifles as the worldly amusements before named, which are likely to throw them off their balance and disturb their spiritual life? Therefore, dear child, I would have you cleanse your heart from all such tastes, remembering that while the acts themselves are not necessarily incompatible with a devout life, all delight in them must be harmful.

CHAPTER XXIV - All Evil Inclinations must be purged away

FURTHERMORE, my daughter, we have certain natural inclinations, which are not strictly speaking either mortal or venial sins, but rather imperfections; and the acts in which they take shape, failings and deficiencies. Thus S. Jerome says that S. Paula had so strong a tendency to excessive sorrow, that when she lost her husband and children she nearly died of grief: that was not a sin, but an imperfection, since it did not depend upon her wish and will. Some people are naturally easy, some oppositions; some are indisposed to accept other men's opinions, some naturally disposed to be cross, some to be affectionate--in short, there is hardly any one in whom some such imperfections do not exist. Now, although they be natural and instinctive in each person, they may be remedied and corrected, or even eradicated, by cultivating the reverse disposition. And this, my child, must be done. Gardeners have found how to make the bitter almond tree bear sweet fruit, by grafting the juice of the latter upon it, why should we not purge out our perverse dispositions and infuse such as are good? There is no disposition so good but it may be made bad by dint of vicious habits, and neither is there any natural disposition so perverse but that it may be conquered and overcome by God's Grace primarily, and then by our earnest diligent endeavour. I shall therefore now proceed to give you counsels and suggest practices by which you may purify your soul from all dangerous affections and imperfections, and from all tendencies to venial sin, thereby strengthening yourself more and more against mortal sin. May God give you grace to use them.

PART II - CONTAINING SUNDRY COUNSELS AS TO UPLIFTING THE SOUL TO GOD IN PRAYER AND THE USE OF THE SACRAMENTS

CHAPTER I - The Necessity of Prayer

1. PRAYER opens the understanding to the brightness of Divine Light, and the will to the warmth of Heavenly Love--nothing can so effectually purify the mind from its many ignorances, or the will from its perverse affections. It is as a healing water which causes the roots of our good desires to send forth fresh shoots, which washes away the soul's imperfections, and allays the thirst of passion.

2. But especially I commend earnest mental prayer to you, more particularly such as bears upon the Life and Passion of our Lord. If you contemplate Him frequently in meditation, your whole soul will be filled with Him, you will grow in His Likeness, and your actions will be moulded on His. He is the Light of the world; therefore in Him, by Him, and for Him we shall be enlightened and illuminated; He is the Tree of Life, beneath the shadow of which we must find rest;--He is the Living Fountain of Jacob's well, wherein we may wash away every stain. Children learn to speak by hearing their mother talk, and stammering forth their childish sounds in imitation; and so if we cleave to the Savior in meditation, listening to His words, watching His actions and intentions, we shall learn in time, through His Grace, to speak, act and will like Himself. Believe me, my daughter, there is no way to God save through this door. Just as the glass of a mirror would give no reflection save for the metal behind it, so neither could we here below contemplate the Godhead, were it not united to the Sacred Humanity of our Saviour, Whose Life and Death are the best, sweetest and most profitable subjects that we can possibly select for meditation. It is not without meaning that the Saviour calls Himself the Bread come down from Heaven;--just as we eat bread with all manner of other food, so we need to meditate and feed upon our Dear Lord in every prayer and action. His Life has been meditated and written about by various authors. I should specially commend to you the writings of S. Bonaventura, Bellintani, Bruno, Capilla, Grenada and Da Ponte. [24]

3. Give an hour every day to meditation before dinner;--if you can, let it be early in the morning, when your mind will be less cumbered, and fresh after the night's rest. Do not spend more than an hour thus, unless specially advised to do so by your spiritual father.

4. If you can make your meditation quietly in church, it will be well, and no one, father or mother, husband or wife, can object to an hour spent there, and very probably you could not secure a time so free from interruption at home.

5. Begin all prayer, whether mental or vocal, by an act of the Presence of God. If you observe this rule strictly, you will soon see how useful it is.

6. It may help you to say the Creed, Lord's Prayer, etc., in Latin, but you should also study them diligently in your own language, so as thoroughly to gather up the meaning of these holy words, which must be used fixing your thoughts steadily on their purport, not striving to say many words so much as seeking to say a few with your whole heart. One Our Father said devoutly is worth more than many prayers hurried over.

7. The Rosary is a useful devotion when rightly used, and there are various little books to teach this. It is well, too, to say pious Litanies, and the other vocal prayers appointed for the Hours and found in Manuals of devotion,--but if you have a gift for mental prayer, let that always take the chief place, so that if, having made that, you are hindered by business or any other cause from saying your wonted vocal prayers, do not be disturbed, but rest satisfied with saying the Lord's Prayer, the Angelic Salutation, and the Creed after your meditation.

8. If, while saying vocal prayers, your heart feels drawn to mental prayer, do not resist it, but calmly let your mind fall into that channel, without troubling because you have not finished your appointed vocal prayers. The mental prayer you have substituted for them is more acceptable to God, and more profitable to your soul. I should make an exception of the Church's Offices, if you are bound to say those by your vocation--in such a case these are your duty.

9. If it should happen that your morning goes by without the usual meditation, either owing to a pressure of business, or from any other cause, (which interruptions you should try to prevent as far as possible,) try to repair the loss in the afternoon, but not immediately after a meal, or you will perhaps be drowsy, which is bad both for your meditation and your health. But if you are unable all day to make up for the omission, you must remedy it as far as may be by ejaculatory prayer, and by reading some spiritual book, together with an act of penitence for the neglect, together with a stedfast resolution to do better the next day.

Footnote:

24. S. Bonaventura, Louis of Grenada, and Da Ponte's works are still available and are admirable helps to meditation. Among more modern works might be suggested Isaac Williams on the Passion, Avrillon's Lent Guide, &c. &c.

CHAPTER II - A short Method of Meditation. And first, the Presence of God, the First Point of Preparation

IT may be, my daughter, that you do not know how to practise mental prayer, for unfortunately it is a thing much neglected now-adays. I will therefore give you a short and easy method for using it, until such time as you may read sundry books written on the subject, and above all till practice teaches you how to use it more perfectly. And first of all, the Preparation, which consists of two points: first, placing yourself in the Presence of God; and second, asking His Aid. And in order to place your self in the Presence of God, I will suggest four chief considerations which you can use at first.

First, a lively earnest realisation that His Presence is universal; that is to say, that He is everywhere, and in all, and that there is no place, nothing in the world, devoid of His Most Holy Presence, so that, even as birds on the wing meet the air continually, we, let us go where we will, meet with that Presence always and everywhere. It is a truth which all are ready to grant, but all are not equally alive to its importance. A blind man when in the presence of his prince will preserve a reverential demeanour if told that the king is there, although unable to see him; but practically, what men do not see they easily forget, and so readily lapse into carelessness and irreverence. Just so, my child, we do not see our God, and although faith warns us that He is present, not beholding Him with our mortal eyes, we are too apt to forget Him, and act as though He were afar: for, while knowing perfectly that He is everywhere, if we do not think about it, it is much as though we knew it not. And therefore, before beginning to pray, it is needful always to rouse the soul to a stedfast remembrance and thought of the Presence of God. This is what David meant when he exclaimed, "If I climb up to Heaven, Thou art there, and if I go down to hell, Thou art there also!" [25] And in like manner Jacob, who, beholding the ladder which went up to Heaven, cried out, "Surely the Lord is in this place and I knew it not" [26] meaning thereby that he had not thought of it; for assuredly he could not fail to know that God was everywhere and in all things. Therefore, when you make ready to pray, you must say with your whole heart, "God is indeed here."

The second way of placing yourself in this Sacred Presence is to call to mind that God is not only present in the place where you are, but that He is very specially present in your heart and mind, which He kindles and inspires with His Holy Presence, abiding there as Heart of your heart, Spirit of your spirit. Just as the soul animates the whole body, and every member thereof, but abides especially in the heart, so God, while present everywhere, yet makes His special abode with our spirit. Therefore David calls Him "the Strength of my heart;" [27] and S. Paul said that in Him "we live and move and have our being." [28] Dwell upon this thought until you have kindled a great reverence within your heart for God Who is so closely present to you.

The third way is to dwell upon the thought of our Lord, Who in His Ascended Humanity looks down upon all men, but most particularly on all Christians, because they are His children; above all, on those who pray, over whose doings He keeps watch. Nor is this any mere imagination, it is very truth, and although we see Him not, He is looking down upon us. It was given to S. Stephen in the hour of martyrdom thus to behold Him, and we may well say with the Bride of the Canticles, "He looketh forth at the windows, shewing Himself through the lattice." [29]

The fourth way is simply to exercise your ordinary imagination, picturing the Saviour to yourself in His Sacred Humanity as if He were beside you just as we are wont to think of our friends, and fancy that we see or hear them at our side. But when the Blessed Sacrament of the Altar is there, then this Presence is no longer imaginary, but most real; and the sacred species are but as a veil from behind which the Present Saviour beholds and considers us, although we cannot see Him as He is.

Make use of one or other of these methods for placing yourself in the Presence of God before you begin to pray;--do not try to use them all at once, but take one at a time, and that briefly and simply.

Footnotes:

25. Ps. cxxxix. 7.
26. Gen. xxviii. 16.
27. Ps. lxxiii. 26.
28. Acts xvii. 28.
29. Cant. ii. 9.

CHAPTER III - Invocation, the Second Point of Preparation

INVOCATION is made as follows: your soul, having realised God's Presence, will prostrate itself with the utmost reverence, acknowledging its unworthiness to abide before His Sovereign Majesty; and yet knowing that He of His Goodness would have you come to Him, you must ask of Him grace to serve and worship Him in this your meditation. You may use some such brief and earnest words as those of David: "Cast me not away from Thy Presence, and take not Thy Holy Spirit from me." [30] "Shew me Thy Ways, O Lord, and teach me Thy paths." [31] "Give me understanding, and I shall keep Thy Law: yea, I shall keep it with my whole heart." [32] "I am Thy servant, O grant me understanding."[33] Dwell too upon the thought of your guardian Angel, and of the Saints connected with the special mystery you are considering, as the Blessed Virgin, S. John, the Magdalene, the good thief, etc., if you are meditating in the Passion, so that you may share in their devout feelings and intention,--and in the same way with other subjects.

Footnotes:

30. Ps. li. 11.
31. Ps. xxv. 4.
32. Ps. cxix. 34.
33. Ps. cxix. 125.

CHAPTER IV - The Third Point of Preparation, representing the Mystery to be meditated to Your Imagination

FOLLOWING upon these two ordinary points, there ere is a third, which is not necessary to all meditation, called by some the local representation, and by others the interior picture. It is simply kindling a vivid picture of the mystery to be meditated within your imagination, even as though you were actually beholding it. For instance, if you wish to meditate upon our Lord on His Cross, you will place yourself in imagination on Mount Calvary, as though you saw and heard all that occurred there during the Passion; or you can imagine to yourself all that the Evangelists describe as taking place where you are. In the same way, when you meditate upon death, bring the circumstances that will attend your own vividly to mind, and so of hell, or any subjects which involve visible, tangible circumstances. When it is a question of such mysteries as God's Greatness, His Attributes, the end of our creation, or other invisible things, you cannot make this use of your imagination. At most you may employ certain comparisons and similitudes, but these are not always opportune, and I would have you follow a very simple method, and not weary your mind with striving after new inventions. Still, often this use of the imagination tends to concentrate the mind on the mystery we wish to meditate, and to prevent our thoughts from wandering hither and thither, just as when you shut a bird within a cage, or fasten a hawk by its lures. Some people will tell you that it is better to confine yourself to mere abstract thought, and a simple mental and spiritual consideration of these mysteries, but this is too difficult for beginners; and until God calls you up higher, I would advise you, my daughter, to abide contentedly in the lowly valley I have pointed out.

CHAPTER V - Considerations, the Second Part of Meditation

AFTER this exercise of the imagination, we come to that of the understanding: for meditations, properly so called, are certain considerations by which we raise the affections to God and heavenly things. Now meditation differs therein from study and ordinary methods of thought which have not the Love of God or growth in holiness for their object, but some other end, such as the acquisition of learning or power of argument. So, when you have, as I said, limited the efforts of your mind within due bounds,--whether by the imagination, if the subject be material, or by propositions, if it be a spiritual subject,--you will begin to form reflections or considerations after the pattern of the meditations I have already sketched for you. And if your mind finds sufficient matter, light and fruit wherein to rest in any one consideration, dwell upon it, even as the bee, which hovers over one flower so long as it affords honey. But if you do not find wherewith to feed your mind, after a certain reasonable effort, then go on to another consideration,--only be quiet and simple, and do not be eager or hurried.

CHAPTER VI - The Third Part of Meditation, Affections and Resolutions

MEDITATION excites good desires in the will, or sensitive part of the soul,--such as love of God and of our neighbour, a craving for the glory of Paradise, zeal for the salvation of others, imitation of our Lord's Example, compassion, thanksgiving, fear of God's wrath and of judgment, hatred of sin, trust in God's Goodness and Mercy, shame for our past life; and in all such affections you should pour out your soul as much as possible. If you want help in this, turn to some simple book of devotions, the Imitation of Christ, the Spiritual Combat, or whatever you find most helpful to your individual wants.

But, my daughter, you must not stop short in general affections, without turning them into special resolutions for your own correction and amendment. For instance, meditating on Our Dear Lord's First Word from the Cross, you will no doubt be roused to the desire of imitating Him in forgiving and loving your enemies. But that is not enough, unless you bring it to some practical resolution, such as, "I will not be angered any more by the annoying things said of me by such or such a neighbour, nor by the slights offered me by such an one; but rather I will do such and such things in order to soften and conciliate them." In this way, my daughter, you will soon correct your faults, whereas mere general resolutions would take but a slow and uncertain effect.

CHAPTER VII - The Conclusion and Spiritual Bouquet

THE meditation should be concluded by three acts, made with the utmost humility. First, an act of thanksgiving;--thanking God for the affections and resolutions with which He has inspired you, and for the Mercy and Goodness He has made known to you in the mystery you have been meditating. Secondly, an act of oblation, by which you offer your affections and resolutions to God, in union with His Own Goodness and Mercy, and the Death and Merits of His Son. The third act is one of petition, in which you ask God to give you a share in the Merits of His Dear Son, and a blessing on your affections and resolutions, to the end that you may be able to put them in practice. You will further pray for the Church, and all her Ministers, your relations, friends, and all others, using the Our Father as the most comprehensive and necessary of prayers.

Besides all this, I bade you gather a little bouquet of devotion, and what I mean is this. When walking in a beautiful garden most people are wont to gather a few flowers as they go, which they keep, and enjoy their scent during the day. So, when the mind explores some mystery in meditation, it is well to pick out one or more points that have specially arrested the attention, and are most likely to be helpful to you through the day, and this should be done at once before quitting the subject of your meditation.

CHAPTER VIII - Some Useful Hints as to Meditation

ABOVE all things, my daughter, strive when your meditation is ended to retain the thoughts and resolutions you have made as your earnest practice throughout the day. This is the real fruit of meditation, without which it is apt to be unprofitable, if not actually harmful--inasmuch as to dwell upon virtues without practising them lends to puff us up with unrealities, until we begin to fancy ourselves all that we have meditated upon and resolved to be; which is all very well if our resolutions are earnest and substantial, but on the contrary hollow and dangerous if they are not put in practice. You must then diligently endeavour to carry out your resolutions, and seek for all opportunities, great or small. For instance, if your resolution was to win over those who oppose you by gentleness, seek through the day any occasion of meeting such persons kindly, and if none offers, strive to speak well of them, and pray for them.

When you leave off this interior prayer, you must be careful to keep your heart in an even balance, lest the balm it has received in meditation be scattered. I mean, try to maintain silence for some brief space, and let your thoughts be transferred gradually from devotion to business, keeping alive the feelings and affections aroused in meditation as long as possible. Supposing some one to have received a precious porcelain vessel, filled with a most costly liquid, which he is going to carry home; how carefully he would go, not looking about, but watching stedfastly lest he trip or stumble, or lest he spill any of the contents of his vessel. Just so, after meditation, do not allow yourself forthwith to be distracted, but look straight before you. Of course, if you meet any one to whom you are bound to attend, you must act according to the circumstances in which you find yourself, but even thus give heed to your heart, so as to lose as little as possible of the precious fruits of your meditation. You should strive, too, to accustom yourself to go easily from prayer to all such occupations as your calling or position lawfully require of you, even although such occupations may seem uncongenial to the affections and thoughts just before forming part of your prayer. Thus the lawyer should be able to go from meditation to his pleading, the tradesman to his business, the mistress of a family to the cares of her household and her wifely duties, so calmly and gently as not to be in any way disturbed by so doing. In both you are fulfilling God's Will, and you should be able to turn from one to the other in a devout and humble spirit.

It may be that sometimes, immediately after your preparation, your affections will be wholly drawn to God, and then, my child, you must let go the reins, and not attempt to follow any given method; since, although as a general rule your considerations should precede your affections and resolutions, when the Holy Spirit gives you those affections at once, it is unnecessary to use the machinery which was intended to bring about the same result. In short, whenever such affections are kindled in your heart, accept them, and give them place in preference to all other considerations. The only object in placing the affections after the points of consideration in meditation, is to make the different parts of meditation clearer, for it is a general rule that when affections arise they are never to be checked, but always encouraged to flow freely. And this applies also to the acts of thanksgiving, of oblation and petition, which must not be restrained either, although it is well to repeat or renew them at the close of your meditation. But your resolutions must be made after the affections, and quite at the end of your meditation, and that all the more because in these you must enter upon ordinary familiar subjects and things which would be liable to cause distractions if they were intruded among your spiritual affections.

Amid your affections and resolutions it is well occasionally to make use of colloquies, and to speak sometimes to your Lord, sometimes to your guardian Angel, or to those persons who are concerned in the mystery you are meditating, to the Saints, to yourself, your own heart, to sinners, and even to the inanimate creation around, as David so often does in the Psalms, as well as other Saints in their meditations and prayers.

CHAPTER IX - *Concerning Dryness in Meditation*

SHOULD it happen sometimes, my daughter, that you have no taste for or consolation in your meditation, I entreat you not to be troubled, but seek relief in vocal prayer, bemoan yourself to our Lord, confess your unworthiness, implore His Aid, kiss His Image, if it be beside you, and say in the words of Jacob, "I will not let Thee go, except Thou bless me;" or with the Canaanitish woman, "Yes, Lord, I am as a dog before Thee, but the dogs eat of the crumbs which fall from their master's table."

Or you can take a book, and read attentively till such time as your mind is calmed and quickened; or sometimes you may find help from external actions, such as prostrating yourself folding your hands upon your breast, kissing your Crucifix,--that is, supposing you are alone. But if, after all this, you are still unrelieved, do not be disturbed at your dryness, however great it be, but continue striving after a devout attitude in God's Sight. What numbers of courtiers appear a hundred times at court without any hope of a word from their king, but merely to pay their homage and be seen of him. Just so, my daughter, we ought to enter upon mental prayer purely to fulfil our duty and testify our loyalty. If it pleases God's Divine Majesty to speak to us, and discourse in our hearts by His Holy Inspirations and inward consolations, it is doubtless a great honour, and very sweet to our soul; but if He does not vouchsafe such favours, but makes as though He saw us not,--as though we were not in His Presence,-- nevertheless we must not quit it, but on the contrary we must remain calmly and devoutly before Him, and He is certain to accept our patient waiting, and give heed to our assiduity and perseverance; so that another time He will impart to us His consolations, and let us taste all the sweetness of holy meditation. But even were it not so, let us, my child, be satisfied with the privilege of being in His Presence and seen of Him.

CHAPTER X - *Morning Prayer*

BESIDES your systematic meditation and your other vocal prayers, there are five shorter kinds of prayer, which are as aids and assistants to the great devotion, and foremost among these is your morning prayer, as a general preparation for all the day's work. It should be made in this wise.

1. Thank God, and adore Him for His Grace which has kept you safely through the night, and if in anything you have offended against Him, ask forgiveness.

2. Call to mind that the day now beginning is given you in order that you may work for Eternity, and make a stedfast resolution to use this day for that end.

3. Consider beforehand what occupations, duties and occasions are likely this day to enable you to serve God; what temptations to offend Him, either by vanity, anger, etc., may arise; and make a fervent resolution to use all means of serving Him and confirming your own piety; as also to avoid and resist whatever might hinder your salvation and God's Glory. Nor is it enough to make such a resolution,--you must also prepare to carry it into effect. Thus, if you foresee having to meet some one who is hottempered and irritable, you must not merely resolve to guard your own temper, but you must consider by what gentle words to conciliate him. If you know you will see some sick person, consider how best to minister comfort to him, and so on.

4. Next, humble yourself before God, confessing that of yourself you could carry out nothing that you have planned, either in avoiding evil or seeking good. Then, so to say, take your heart in your hands, and offer it and all your good intentions to God's Gracious Majesty, entreating Him to accept them, and strengthen you in His Service, which you may do in some such words as these: "Lord, I lay before Thee my weak heart, which Thou dost fill with good desires. Thou knowest that I am unable to bring the same to good effect, unless Thou dost bless and prosper them, and therefore, O Loving Father, I entreat of Thee to help me by the Merits and Passion of Thy Dear Son, to Whose Honour I would devote this day and my whole life."

All these acts should be made briefly and heartily, before you leave your room if possible, so that all the coming work of the day may be prospered with God's blessing; but anyhow, my daughter, I entreat you never to omit them.

CHAPTER XI - Evening Prayer and Examination of Conscience

AS I have counselled you before your material dinner to make a spiritual repast in meditation, so before your evening meal you should make at least a devout spiritual collation. Make sure of some brief leisure before suppertime, and then prostrating yourself before God, and recollecting yourself in the Presence of Christ Crucified, setting Him before your mind with a stedfast inward glance, renew the warmth of your morning's meditation by some hearty aspirations and humble upliftings of your soul to your Blessed Saviour, either repeating those points of your meditation which helped you most, or kindling your heart with anything else you will.

As to the examination of conscience, which we all should make before going to bed, you know the rules:

1. Thank God for having preserved you through the day past.

2. Examine how you have conducted yourself through the day, in order to which recall where and with whom you have been, and what you have done.

3. If you have done anything good, offer thanks to God; if you have done amiss in thought, word, or deed, ask forgiveness of His Divine Majesty, resolving to confess the fault when opportunity offers, and to be diligent in doing better.

4. Then commend your body and soul, the Church, your relations and friends, to God. Ask that the Saints and Angels may keep watch over you, and with God's Blessing go to the rest He has appointed for you. Neither this practice nor that of the morning should ever be omitted; by your morning prayer you open your soul's windows to the sunshine of Righteousness, and by your evening devotions you close them against the shades of hell.

CHAPTER XII - On Spiritual Retirement

THIS is a matter, dear daughter, to which I am very anxious to win your attention, for in it lies one of the surest means of spiritual progress. Strive as often as possible through the day to place yourself in God's Presence by some one of the methods already suggested. Consider what God does, and what you are doing;--you will see His Eyes ever fixed upon you in Love incomparable. "O my God," you will cry out, "why cannot I always be looking upon Thee, even as Thou lookest on me? why do I think so little about Thee? O my soul, thy only resting-place is God, and yet how often dost thou wander?" The birds have nests in lofty trees, and the stag his refuge in the thick coverts, where he can shelter from the sun's burning heat; and just so, my daughter, our hearts ought daily to choose some resting-place, either Mount Calvary, or the Sacred Wounds, or some other spot close to Christ, where they can retire at will to seek rest and refreshment amid toil, and to be as in a fortress, protected from temptation. Blessed indeed is the soul which can truly say, "Thou, Lord, art my Refuge, my Castle, my Stay, my Shelter in the storm and in the heat of the day."

Be sure then, my child, that while externally occupied with business and social duties, you frequently retire within the solitude of your own heart. That solitude need not be in any way hindered by the crowds which surround you--they surround your body, not your soul, and your heart remains alone in the Sole Presence of God. This is what David sought after amid his manifold labours;--the Psalms are full of such expressions as "Lord, I am ever with Thee. The Lord is always at my right hand. I lift up mine eyes to Thee, O Thou Who dwellest in the heavens. Mine eyes look unto God."

There are few social duties of sufficient importance to prevent an occasional retirement of the heart into this sacred solitude. When S. Catherine of Sienna was deprived by her parents of any place or time for prayer and meditation, Our Lord inspired her with the thought of making a little interior oratory in her mind, into which she could retire in heart, and so enjoy a holy solitude amid her outward duties. And henceforward, when the world assaulted her, she was able to be indifferent, because, so she said, she could retire within her secret oratory, and find comfort with her Heavenly Bridegroom. So she counselled her spiritual daughters to make a retirement within their heart, in which to dwell. Do you in like manner let your heart withdraw to such an inward retirement, where, apart from all men, you can lay it bare, and treat face to face with God, even as David says that he watched like a "pelican in the wilderness, or an owl in the desert, or a sparrow sitting alone upon the housetop." [34] These words have a sense beyond their literal meaning, or King David's habit of retirement for contemplation;--and we may find in them three excellent kinds of retreats in which to seek solitude after the Saviour's Example, Who is symbolised as He hung upon Mount Calvary by the pelican of the wilderness, feeding her young ones with her blood. [35] So again His Nativity in a lonely stable might find a foreshadowing in the owl of the desert, bemoaning and lamenting: and in His Ascension He was like the sparrow rising high above the dwellings of men. Thus in each of these ways we can make a retreat amid the daily cares of life and its business.

When the blessed Elzear, Count of Arian-enProvence, had been long separated from his pious and beloved wife Delphine, she sent a messenger to inquire after him, and he returned answer, "I am well, dear wife, and if you would see me, seek me in the Wounded Side of our Dear Lord Jesus; that is my sure dwelling-place, and elsewhere you will seek me in vain." Surely he was a true Christian knight who spoke thus.

Footnotes:

34. Ps. cii. 6, 7.

35. The Egyptians used the pelican as a symbol of parental devotion; and among the early Christians, as may be seen in the Catacombs, it was employed to shadow forth the deep mysteries of Christ's love. On many a monumental brass, church window, or chalice of old time, occurs this device, with the motto, "Sic Christus dilexit nos." "Thus hath Christ loved us." And so Saint Thomas in his Eucharistic Hymn "Adoro Te devote,"--"Pie Pelicane, Jesu Domine, Me immundum munda, Tuo sausguine!"

CHAPTER XIII - *Aspirations, Ejaculatory Prayer and Holy Thoughts*

WE retire with God, because we aspire to Him, and we aspire in order to retire with Him; so that aspiration after God and spiritual retreat excite one another, while both spring from the one Source of all holy thoughts. Do you then, my daughter, aspire continually to God, by brief, ardent upliftings of heart; praise His Excellence, invoke His Aid, cast yourself in spirit at the Foot of His Cross, adore His Goodness, offer your whole soul a thousand times a day to Him, fix your inward gaze upon Him, stretch out your hands to be led by Him, as a little child to its father, clasp Him to your breast as a fragrant nosegay, upraise Him in your soul as a standard. In short, kindle by every possible act your love for God, your tender, passionate desire for the Heavenly Bridegroom of souls. Such is ejaculatory prayer, as it was so earnestly inculcated by S. Augustine upon the devout Proba; and be sure, my daughter, that if you seek such nearness and intimacy with God your whole soul will imbibe the perfume of His Perfections. Neither is this a difficult practice,--it may be interwoven with all our duties and occupations, without hindering any; for neither the spiritual retreat of which I have spoken, nor these inward upliftings of the heart, cause more than a very brief distraction, which, so far from being any hindrance, will rather promote whatever you have in hand. When a pilgrim pauses an instant to take a draught of wine, which refreshes his lips and revives his heart, his onward journey is nowise hindered by the brief delay, but rather it is shortened and lightened, and he brings it all the sooner to a happy end, pausing but to advance the better.

Sundry collections of ejaculatory prayer have been put forth, which are doubtless very useful, but I should advise you not to tie yourself to any formal words, but rather to speak with heart or mouth whatever springs forth from the love within you, which is sure to supply you with all abundance. There are certain utterances which have special force, such as the ejaculatory prayers of which the Psalms are so full, and the numerous loving invocations of Jesus which we find in the Song of Songs. Many hymns too may be used with the like intention, provided they are sung attentively. In short, just as those who are full of some earthly, natural love are ever turning in thought to the beloved one, their hearts overflowing with tenderness, and their lips ever ready to praise that beloved object; comforting themselves in absence by letters, carving the treasured name on every tree;--so those who love God cannot cease thinking of Him, living for Him, longing after Him, speaking of Him, and fain would they grave the Holy Name of Jesus in the hearts of every living creature they behold. And to such an outpour of love all creation bids us--nothing that He has made but is filled with the praise of God, and, as says S. Augustine, everything in the world speaks silently but clearly to the lovers of God of their love, exciting them to holy desires, whence gush forth aspirations and loving cries to God. St. Gregory Nazianzen tells his flock, how, walking along the seashore, he watched the waves as they washed up shells and sea weeds, and all manner of small substances, which seemed, as it were, rejected by the sea, until a return wave would often wash part thereof back again; while the rocks remained firm and immoveable, let the waves beat against them never so fiercely. And then the Saint went on to reflect that feeble hearts let themselves be carried hither and thither by the varying waves of sorrow or consolation, as the case might be, like the shells upon the seashore, while those of a nobler mould abide firm and immoveable amid every storm;--whence he breaks out into David's cry, "Lord, save me, for the waters are gone over my soul; deliver me from the great deep, all Thy waves and storms are gone over me;" for he was himself then in trouble by reason of the ungodly usurpation of his See by Maximus.

When S. Fulgentius, Bishop of Ruspe, heard Theodoric, King of the Goths, harangue a general assembly of Roman nobles, and beheld their splendour, he exclaimed, "O God, how glorious must Thy Heavenly Jerusalem be, if even earthly Rome be thus!" [36] And if this world can afford so much gratification to mere earthly lovers of vanity, what must there be in store hereafter for those who love the truth?

"If thus Thy lower works are fair,--If thus Thy glories gild the spanOf ruined earth and guilty man,--How glorious must the mansions beWhere Thy redeemed dwell with Thee!"

We are told that S. Anselm of Canterbury, (our mountains may glory in being his birthplace [37]) was much given to such thoughts. On one occasion a hunted hare took refuge from imminent death beneath the Bishop's horse, the hounds clamouring round, but not daring to drag it from its asylum, whereat his attendants began to laugh; but the great Anselm wept, saying, "You may laugh forsooth, but to the poor hunted beast it is no laughing matter; even so the soul which has been led astray in all manner of sin finds a host of enemies waiting at its last hour to devour it, and terrified, knows not where to seek a refuge, and if it can find none, its enemies laugh and rejoice." And so he went on his way, sighing.

Constantine the Great wrote with great respect to S. Anthony, at which his religious expressed their surprise. "Do you marvel," he said, "that a king should write to an ordinary man? Marvel rather that God should have written His Law for men, and yet more that He should have spoken with them Face to face through His Son." When S. Francis saw a solitary sheep amid a flock of goats; "See," said he to his companion, "how gentle the poor sheep is among the goats, even as was Our Lord among the Pharisees;" and seeing a boar devour a little lamb, "Poor little one," he exclaimed, weeping, "how vividly is my Saviour's Death set forth in thee!"

A great man of our own day, Francis Borgia, then Duke of Candia, was wont to indulge in many devout imaginations as he was hunting. "I used to ponder," he said, "how the falcon returns to one's wrist, and lets one hood its eyes or chain it to the perch, and yet men are so perverse in refusing to turn at God's call." St. Basil the Great says that the rose amid its thorns preaches a lesson to men. "All that is pleasant in this life" (so it tells us mortals) "is mingled with sadness--no joy is altogether pure--all enjoyment is liable to be marred by regrets, marriage is saddened by widowhood, children bring anxiety, glory often turns to shame, neglect follows upon honour, weariness on pleasure, sickness on health. Truly the rose is a lovely flower," the Saint goes on to say, "but it moves me to sadness, reminding me as it does that for my sin the earth was condemned to bring forth thorns."

Another devout soul, gazing upon a brook wherein the starlit sky of a calm summer's night was reflected, exclaims, "O my God, when Thou callest me to dwell in Thy heavenly tabernacles, these stars will be beneath my feet; and even as those stars are now reflected here below, so are we Thy creatures reflected above in the living waters of Thy Divine Love." So another cried out, beholding a rapid river as it flowed, "Even thus my soul will know no rest until it plunge into that Divine Sea whence it came forth!" S. Frances, as she knelt to pray beside the banks of a pleasant streamlet, cried out in ecstasy, "The Grace of my Dear Lord flows softly and sweetly even as these refreshing waters" And another saintly soul, looking upon the blooming orchards, cried out, "Why am I alone barren in the Church's garden!" So S. Francis of Assisi, beholding a hen gathering her chickens beneath her wings, exclaimed, "Keep me, O Lord, under the shadow of Thy Wings" And looking upon the sunflower, he ejaculated, "When, O Lord, will my soul follow the attractions of Thy Love?" [38] And gathering pansies in a garden which are fair to see, but scentless, [39] "Ah," he cried out, "even so are the thoughts of my heart, fair to behold, but without savour or fruit!"

Thus it is, my daughter, that good thoughts and holy aspirations may be drawn from all that surrounds us in our ordinary life. Woe to them that turn aside the creature from the Creator, and thrice blessed are they who turn all creation to their Creator's Glory, and make human vanities subservient to the truth. "Verily," says Saint Gregory Nazianzen, "I am wont to turn all things to my spiritual profit."

Read the pious epitaph written for S. Paula by S. Jerome; it is marvellous therein to see how she conceived spiritual thoughts and aspirations at every turn.

Now, in the practice of this spiritual retreat and of these ejaculatory prayers the great work of devotion lies: it can supply all other deficiencies, but there is hardly any means of making up where this is lacking. Without it no one can lead a true contemplative life, and the active life will be but imperfect where it is omitted: without it rest is but indolence, labour but weariness,--therefore I beseech you to adopt it heartily, and never let it go.

Footnotes:

36. Was it in imitation of this that the hymn was written?

37. S. Anselm was born at Aosta in Piedmont, A.D. 1033.

38. Moore has preserved the graceful imagery of the sunflower, anciently called "tourne-soleil" (as by S. Francis here). "Oh the heart that once truly loved, never forgets, But as truly loves on to the close, As the sunflower turns to her God when he sets The same look which she turned when he rose."

39. "Pensees." This play on words is common--as Ophelia says in Hamlet, Act iv. sc. 5: "There is pansies--that's for thoughts." But the name of this pretty viola is really derived from panacea, signifying all-heal, just as Tansy is derived from Athanasia, i.e. immortelle or everlasting. Its other name of heart's-ease also refers to the potent virtues ascribed to it of old. Cawdray, in his Treasurie of Similies, London, 1609, says: "As the herb Panax or Panace hath in it a remedy against all diseases, so is the Death of Christ against all sin sufficient and effectual." In the preface to our English Bible of 1611, the translators speak of "Panaces, the herb that is good for all diseases."

CHAPTER XIV - Of Holy Communion, and how to join in it

1. SO far I have said nothing concerning the Sun of all spiritual exercises, even the most holy, sacred and Sovereign Sacrifice and Sacrament of the Eucharist,--the very centre point of our Christian religion, the heart of all devotion, the soul of piety;--that Ineffable Mystery which embraces the whole depth of Divine Love, by which God, giving Himself really to us, conveys all His Graces and favours to men with royal magnificence.

2. Prayer made in union with this Divine Sacrifice has untold power; through which, indeed, the soul overflows with heavenly grace, and leaning on her Beloved, becomes so filled with spiritual sweetness and perfume, that we may ask in the words of the Canticles: "Who is this that cometh out of the wilderness like pillars of smoke, perfumed with myrrh and frankincense, with all powders of the merchant? " [40]

3. Strive then to your utmost to be present every day at this holy Celebration, in order that with the priest you may offer the Sacrifice of your Redeemer on behalf of yourself and the whole Church to God the Father. Saint Chrysostom says that the Angels crowd around it in adoration, and if we are found together with them, united in one intention, we cannot but be most favourably influenced by such society. Moreover, all the heavenly choirs of the Church triumphant, as well as those of the Church militant, are joined to our Dear Lord in this divine act, so that with Him, in Him, and by Him, they may win the favour of God the Father, and obtain His Mercy for us. How great the blessing to my soul to contribute its share towards the attainment of so gracious a gift!

4. If any imperative hindrance prevents your presence at this sovereign sacrifice of Christ's most true Presence, at least be sure to take part in it spiritually. If you cannot go to Church, choose some morning hour in which to unite your intention to that of the whole Christian world, and make the same interior acts of devotion wherever you are that you would make if you were really present at the Celebration of the Holy Eucharist in Church.

5. In order to join in this rightly, whether actually or mentally, you must give heed to several things: (1) In the beginning, and before the priest goes up to the Altar, make your preparation with his--placing yourself in God's Presence, confessing your unworthiness, and asking forgiveness. (2) Until the Gospel, dwell simply and generally upon the Coming and the Life of our Lord in this world. (3) From the Gospel to the end of the Creed, dwell upon our Dear Lord's teaching, and renew your resolution to live and die in the faith of the Holy Catholic Church. (4) From thence, fix your heart on the mysteries of the Word, and unite yourself to the Death and Passion of our Redeemer, now actually and essentially set forth in this holy Sacrifice, which, together with the priest and all the congregation, you offer to God the Father, to His Glory and your own salvation. (5) Up to the moment of communicating, offer all the longings and desires of your heart, above all desiring most earnestly to be united for ever to our Saviour by His Eternal Love. (6) From the time of Communion to the end, thank His Gracious Majesty for His Incarnation, His Life, Death, Passion, and the Love which He sets forth in this holy Sacrifice, intreating through it His favour for yourself, your relations and friends, and the whole Church; and humbling yourself sincerely, devoutly receive the blessing which our Dear Lord gives you through the channel of His minister. If, however, you wish to follow your daily course of meditation on special mysteries during the Sacrifice, it is not necessary that you should interrupt yourself by making these several acts but it will suffice that at the beginning you dispose your intention to worship and to offer the holy Sacrifice in your meditation and prayer; since every meditation includes all the abovenamed acts either explicitly or implicitly.

Footnote:

40. Cant. iii. 6.

CHAPTER XV - Of the other Public Offices of the Church

FURTHERMORE, my daughter, you should endeavour to assist at the Offices, Hours, Vespers, etc., as far as you are able, especially on Sundays and Festivals, days which are dedicated to God, wherein we ought to strive to do more for His Honour and Glory than on others. You will greatly increase the fervour of your devotion by so doing, even as did S. Augustine, who tells us in his Confessions, that in the early days of his conversion he was touched to the quick, and his heart overflowed in happy tears, when he took part in the Offices of the Church. [41] Moreover (let me say it here once for all), there is always more profit and more consolation in the public Offices of the Church than in private acts of devotion, God having willed to give the preference to communion in prayer over all individual action. Be ready to take part in any confraternities and associations you may find in the place where you are called to dwell, especially such as are most fruitful and edifying. This will be pleasing to God; for although confraternities are not ordained, they are recommended by the Church, which grants various privileges to those who are united thereby. And it is always a work of love to join with others and take part in their good works. And although it may be possible that you can use equally profitable devotions by yourself as in common with others,--perhaps even you may like doing so best,-- nevertheless God is more glorified when we unite with our brethren and neighbours and join our offerings to theirs.

I say the same concerning all public services and prayers, in which, as far as possible, each one of us is bound to contribute the best example we can for our neighbour's edification, and our hearty desire for God's Glory and the general good of all men.

Footnote:

41. "Nor was I sated in those days with the wondrous sweetness of considering the depth of Thy counsels concerning the salvation of mankind. How did I weep, in Thy hymns and canticles, touched to the quick by the voices of Thy sweet-attuned church The voices flowed into mine ears, and the truth distilled into my heart, whence the affections of my devotion overflowed, and tears ran down, and happy was I therein."--conf. bk. ix. 14.

CHAPTER XVI - *How the Saints are united to us*

INASMUCH as God continually sends us inspirations by means of His Angels, we may fitly send back our aspirations through the same channel. The souls of the holy dead, resting in Paradise, who are, as our Lord Himself has told us, "as the Angels in Heaven," [42] are also united to us in their prayers. My child, let us gladly join our hearts with these heavenly blessed ones; for even as the newly-fledged nightingale learns to sing from the elder birds, so by our sacred communing with the Saints we shall learn better to pray and sing the praises of the Lord. David is continually uniting his prayers with those of all the Saints and Angels.

Honour, revere and respect the Blessed Virgin Mary with a very special love; she is the Mother of our Sovereign Lord, and so we are her children. Let us think of her with all the love and confidence of affectionate children; let us desire her love, and strive with true filial hearts to imitate her graces.

Seek to be familiar with the Angels; learn to realise that they are continually present, although invisible. Specially love and revere the Guardian Angel of the Diocese in which you live, those of the friends who surround you, and your own. Commune with them frequently, join in their songs of praise, and seek their protection and help in all you do, spiritual or temporal.

That pious man Peter Faber, the first companion of Saint Ignatius, and the first priest, first preacher and first theological teacher of the Company of the Jesuits, who was a native of our Diocese, [43] once passing through this country on his way from Germany, (where he had been labouring for God's Glory,) told how great comfort he had found as he went among places infested with heresy in communing with the guardian Angels thereof, whose help had often preserved him from danger, and softened hearts to receive the faith. He spoke with such earnestness, that a lady who, when quite young, heard him, was so impressed, that she repeated his words to me only four years ago, sixty years after their utterance, with the utmost feeling. I had the happiness only last year of consecrating an altar in the place where it pleased God to give that blessed man birth, the little village of Villaret, amid the wildest of our mountains.

You will do well to choose out for yourself some individual Saint, whose life specially to study and imitate, and whose prayers may be more particularly offered on your behalf. The Saint bearing your own baptismal name would seem to be naturally assigned to you.

Footnotes:

42. S. Mark xii. 25.
43. Faber was a Savoyard.

CHAPTER XVII - How to Hear and Read God's Word

CULTIVATE a special devotion to God's Word, whether studied privately or in public; always listen to it with attention and reverence, strive to profit by it, and do not let it fall to the ground, but receive it within your heart as a precious balm, thereby imitating the Blessed Virgin, who "kept all these sayings in her heart." [44] Remember that our Lord receives our words of prayer according to the way in which we receive His words in teaching.

You should always have some good devout book at hand, such as the writings of S. Bonaventura, Gerson, Denis the Carthusian, Blosius, Grenada, Stella, Arias, Pinella, Da Ponte, Avila, the Spiritual Combat, the Confessions of S. Augustine, S. Jerome's Epistles, or the like; and daily read some small portion attentively, as though you were reading letters sent by the Saints from Paradise to teach you the way thither, and encourage you to follow them. Read the Lives of the Saints too, which are as a mirror to you of Christian life, and try to imitate their actions according to your circumstances; for although many things which the Saints did may not be practicable for those who live in the world, they may be followed more or less. Thus, in our spiritual retreats we imitate the solitude of the first hermit, S. Paul; in the practice of poverty we imitate S. Francis, and so on. Of course some Lives throw much more light upon our daily course than others, such as the Life of Saint Theresa, which is most admirable, the first Jesuits, Saint Charles Borromeo, Archbishop of Milan, S. Louis, S. Bernard, S. Francis, and such like. Others are more the subjects of our admiring wonder than of imitation, such as S. Mary of Egypt, S. Simeon Stylites, S. Catherine of Genoa, and S. Catherine of Sienna, S. Angela, etc., although these should tend to kindle a great love of God in our hearts.

Footnote:

44. S. Luke ii. 51.

CHAPTER XVIII - *How to receive Inspirations*

BY inspirations I mean all drawings, feelings, interior reproaches, lights and intuitions, with which God moves us, preventing our hearts by His Fatherly love and care, and awakening, exciting, urging, and attracting them to goodness, to Heavenly love, to good resolutions, in short, to whatever tends to our eternal welfare. This it is of which we read in the Canticles, when the Bridegroom knocks at the door, awakens His beloved, calls upon her, seeks her, bids her eat of His honey, gather the fruit and flowers of His garden, and let Him hear her voice, which is sweet to Him. [45]

Let me make use of an illustration of my meaning. In contracting a marriage, the bride must be a party to three separate acts: first, the bridegroom is proposed to her; secondly, she entertains the proposal; and thirdly, she gives her consent. Just so when God intends to perform some act of love in us, by us, and with us; He first suggests it by His inspiration; secondly, we receive that inspiration; and thirdly, we consent to it: for, like as we fall into sin by three steps, temptation, delectation, and consent, so there are three steps whereby we ascend to virtue; inspiration, as opposed to temptation; delectation in God's inspiration, as opposed to that of temptation; and consent to the one instead of to the other. Were God's inspirations to last all our lives, we should be nowise more acceptable to Him, unless we took pleasure therein; on the contrary, we should rather offend Him as did the Israelites, of whom He says that they "grieved Him for forty years long, refusing to hear His pleadings, so that at last" I "sware in My wrath that they should not enter into My rest." [46] And (to recur to my first illustration) one who has long been devoted to his lady-love, would feel greatly injured if, after all, she would not consent to the alliance he seeks.

The delight we take in God's inspirations is an important step gained towards His Glory, and we begin at once to please Him thereby; for although such delectation is not the same thing as a full consent, it shows a strong tendency thereto; and if it is a good and profitable sign when we take pleasure in hearing God's Word, which is, so to say, an external inspiration, still more is it good and acceptable in His Sight when we take delight in His interior inspirations. Such is the delight of which the Bride says, "My soul melted within me when my Beloved spake." [47] And so, too, the earthly lover is well satisfied when he sees that his lady-love finds pleasure in his attentions.

But, after all, consent only perfects the good action; for if we are inspired of God, and take pleasure in that inspiration, and yet, nevertheless, refuse our consent to His inspiration, we are acting a very contemptuous, offensive part towards Him. We read of the Bride, that although the voice of her Beloved touched her heart, she made trivial excuses, and delayed opening the door to Him, and so He withdrew Himself and "was gone." [48] And the earthly lover, who had long sought a lady, and seemed acceptable to her, would have the more ground for complaint if at last he was spurned and dismissed, than if he had never been favourably received.

Do you, my daughter, resolve to accept whatever inspirations God may vouchsafe you, heartily; and when they offer themselves, receive them as the ambassadors of your Heavenly King, seeking alliance with you. Hearken gently to their propositions, foster the love with which you are inspired, and cherish the holy Guest. Give your consent, and let it be a full, loving, stedfast consent to His holy inspirations; for, so doing, God will reckon your affection as a favour, although truly we can confer none upon Him. But, before consenting to inspirations which have respect to important or extraordinary things, guard against self-deception, by consulting your spiritual guide, and let him examine whether the inspiration be real or no; and that the rather, because when the enemy sees a soul ready to hearken to inspirations, he is wont to set false delusions in the way to deceive it,--a snare you will not fall into so long as you humbly obey your guide.

Consent once given, you must carefully seek to produce the intended results, and carry out the inspiration, the crown of true virtue; for to give consent, without producing the result thereof, were like planting a vine without meaning it to bear fruit. All this will be greatly promoted by careful attention to your morning exercises, and the spiritual retirement already mentioned, because therein you learn to carry general principles to a special application.

Footnotes:

45. Cant. v. vii. ii.

46. Ps. xcv. 10, 11.

47. In the English version this passage is, "My soul failed when he spake." (Cant. V. 6.) But in the Vulgate it is in the far more expressive form quoted by S. Francis de Sales, "Anima mea liquefacta est, ut locutus est."

48. Cant. v. 6.

CHAPTER XIX - On Confession

OUR Saviour has bequeathed the Sacrament of Penitence and Confession to His Church, [49] in order that therein we may be cleansed from all our sins, however and whenever we may have been soiled thereby. Therefore, my child, never allow your heart to abide heavy with sin, seeing that there is so sure and safe a remedy at hand. If the lioness has been in the neighbourhood of other beasts she hastens to wash away their scent, lest it should be displeasing to her lord; and so the soul which has ever so little consented to sin, ought to abhor itself and make haste to seek purification, out of respect to His Divine Gaze Who beholds it always. Why should we die a spiritual death when there is a sovereign remedy available?

Make your confession humbly and devoutly every week, and always, if you can, before communicating, even although your conscience is not burdened with mortal sin; for in confession you do not only receive absolution for your venial sins, but you also receive great strength to help you in avoiding them henceforth, clearer light to discover your failings, and abundant grace to make up whatever loss you have incurred through those faults. You exercise the graces of humility, obedience, simplicity and love, and by this one act of confession you practise more virtue than in any other.

Be sure always to entertain a hearty sorrow for the sins you confess, however small they are; as also a stedfast resolution to correct them in future. Some people go on confessing venial sins out of mere habit, and conventionally, without making any effort to correct them, thereby losing a great deal of spiritual good. Supposing that you confess having said something untrue, although without evil consequences, or some careless words, or excessive amusement;--repent, and make a firm resolution of amendment: it is a mere abuse to confess any sin whatever, be it mortal or venial, without intending to put it altogether away, that being the express object of confession.

Beware of unmeaning self-accusations, made out of a mere routine, such as, "I have not loved God as much as I ought; I have not prayed with as much devotion as I ought; I have not loved my neighbour as I ought; I have not received the Sacraments with sufficient reverence;" and the like. Such things as these are altogether useless in setting the state of your conscience before your Confessor, inasmuch as all the Saints in Paradise and all men living would say the same. But examine closely what special reason you have for accusing yourself thus, and when you have discovered it, accuse yourself simply and plainly of your fault. For instance, when confessing that you have not loved your neighbour as you ought, it may be that what you mean is, that having seen some one in great want whom you could have succoured, you have failed to do so. Well then, accuse yourself of that special omission: say, "Having come across a person in need, I did not help him as I might have done," either through negligence, or hardness, or indifference, according as the case may be. So again, do not accuse yourself of not having prayed to God with sufficient devotion; but if you have given way to voluntary distractions, or if you have neglected the proper circumstances of devout prayer--whether place, time, or attitude--say so plainly, just as it is, and do not deal in generalities, which, so to say, blow neither hot nor cold.

Again, do not be satisfied with mentioning the bare fact of your venial sins, but accuse yourself of the motive cause which led to them. For instance, do not be content with saying that you told an untruth which injured no one; but say whether it was out of vanity, in order to win praise or avoid blame, out of heedlessness, or from obstinacy. If you have exceeded in society, say whether it was from the love of talking, or gambling for the sake of money, and so on. Say whether you continued long to commit the fault in question, as the importance of a fault depends greatly upon its continuance: e.g., there is a wide difference between a passing act of vanity which is over in a quarter of an hour, and one which fills the heart for one or more days. So you must mention the fact, the motive and the duration of your faults. It is true that we are not bound to be so precise in confessing venial sins, or even, technically speaking, to confess them at all; but all who aim at purifying their souls in order to attain a really devout life, will be careful to show all their spiritual maladies, however slight, to their spiritual physician, in order to be healed.

Do not spare yourself in telling whatever is necessary to explain the nature of your fault, as, for instance, the reason why you lost your temper, or why you encouraged another in wrong-doing. Thus, some one whom I dislike says a chance word in joke, I take it ill, and put myself in a passion. If one I like had said a stronger thing I should not have taken it amiss; so in confession, I ought to say that I lost my temper with a person, not because of the words spoken so much as because I disliked the speaker;

and if in order to explain yourself clearly it is necessary to particularize the words, it is well to do so; because accusing one's self thus simply one discovers not merely one's actual sins, but one's bad habits, inclinations and ways, and the other roots of sin, by which means one's spiritual Father acquires a fuller knowledge of the heart he is dealing with, and knows better what remedies to apply. But you must always avoid exposing any one who has borne any part in your sin as far as possible. Keep watch over a variety of sins, which are apt to spring up and flourish, often insensibly, in the conscience, so that you may confess them and put them away; and with this view read Chapters VI., XXVII., XXVIII., XXIX., XXXV. and XXXVI. of Part III., and Chapter VII. of Part IV., attentively.

Do not lightly change your Confessor, but having chosen him, be regular in giving account of your conscience to him at the appointed seasons, telling him your faults simply and frankly, and from time to time--say every month or every two months, show him the general state of your inclinations, although there be nothing wrong in them; as, for instance, whether you are depressed and anxious, or cheerful, desirous of advancement, or money, and the like.

Footnote:

49. S. Matt. xvi. 19, xviii. 18; S. John xx. 23.

CHAPTER XX - Of Frequent Communion

IT is said that Mithridates, King of Pontus, who invented the poison called after him, mithridate, so thoroughly impregnated his system with it, that when eventually he tried to poison himself to avoid becoming the Romans' slave, he never could succeed. The Saviour instituted the most holy Sacrament of the Eucharist, really containing His Body and His Blood, in order that they who eat it might live for ever. And therefore whosoever receives it frequently and devoutly, so strengthens the health and life of his soul, that it is hardly possible for him to be poisoned by any evil desires. We cannot be fed by that Living Flesh and hold to the affections of death; and just as our first parents could not die in Paradise, because of the Tree of Life which God had placed therein, so this Sacrament of Life makes spiritual death impossible. The most fragile, easily spoilt fruits, such as cherries, apricots, and strawberries, can be kept all the year by being preserved in sugar or honey; so what wonder if our hearts, frail and weakly as they are, are kept from the corruption of sin when they are preserved in the sweetness ("sweeter than honey and the honeycomb") of the Incorruptible Body and Blood of the Son of God. O my daughter, those Christians who are lost will indeed have no answer to give when the Just Judge sets before them that they have voluntarily died the spiritual death, since it was so easy for them to have preserved life and health, by eating His Body which He gave them for that very end. "Miserable men!" He will say, "wherefore would ye die, with the Bread of Life itself in your hands?"

As to daily Communion, I neither commend nor condemn it; but with respect to communicating every Sunday, I counsel and exhort every one to do so, providing the mind has no attachment to sin. So says S. Augustine, and with him I neither find fault nor unconditionally commend daily Communion, leaving that matter to the discretion of every person's own spiritual Guide; as the requisite dispositions for such frequent Communion are too delicate for one to advise it indiscriminately. On the other hand, these very special dispositions may be found in sundry devout souls, and therefore it would not be well to discourage everybody. It is a subject which must be dealt with according to each individual mind; it were imprudent to advise such frequent Communion to all, while, on the other hand, it would be presumptuous to blame any one for it, especially if he therein follows the advice of some wise director. Saint Catherine of Sienna, when blamed for her frequent Communions, under the plea that Saint Augustine neither commended nor condemned daily Communion, replied gently, "Well, then, since Saint Augustine does not condemn it, neither, I pray you, do you condemn it, and I shall be content." But Saint Augustine earnestly exhorts all to communicate every Sunday. And as I presume, my daughter, that you have no attachment either to mortal or venial sins, you are in the condition which Saint Augustine requires; and if your spiritual Father approves, you may profitably communicate more frequently. Nevertheless, there are various hindrances which may arise, not so much from yourself, as from those among whom you live, which may lead a wise director to tell you not to communicate so often. For instance, if you are in a position of subjection, and those whom you are bound to obey should be so ignorant or so prejudiced, as to be uneasy at your frequent Communions, all things considered, it may be well to show consideration for their weakness, and to make your Communion fortnightly; only, of course, where there is no possible way of overcoming the difficulty otherwise. But one cannot give any general rule on such a point, each person must follow the advice of their own spiritual Guide; only this much I will say, that monthly Communions are the very fewest which any one seeking to serve God devoutly can make.

If you are discreet, neither father nor mother, husband nor wife, will ever hinder you from communicating frequently, and that because on the day of your Communion you will give good heed always to be more than usually gentle and amiable towards them, doing all you can to please them, so that they are not likely to prevent your doing a thing which in nowise inconveniences themselves, unless they were most particularly unreasonable and perverse, in which case, as I have said, your Director might advise you to yield. There is nothing in the married life to hinder frequent Communion. Most certainly the Christians of the Primitive Church communicated daily, whether married or single. Neither is any malady a necessary impediment, except, indeed, anything producing constant sickness.

Those who communicate weekly must be free from mortal sin, and also from any attachment to venial sin, and they should feel a great desire for Communion; but for daily Communion people should furthermore have conquered most of their inclinations to evil, and no one should practise it without the advice of their spiritual Guide.

CHAPTER XXI - How to Communicate

BEGIN your preparation over-night, by sundry aspirations and loving ejaculations. Go to bed somewhat earlier than usual, so that you may get up earlier the next morning; and if you should wake during the night, fill your heart and lips at once with sacred words wherewith to make your soul ready to receive the Bridegroom, Who watches while you sleep, and Who intends to give you countless gifts and graces, if you on your part are prepared to accept them. In the morning rise with joyful expectation of the Blessing you hope for, and (having made your Confession) go with the fullest trust, but at the same time with the fullest humility, to receive that Heavenly Food which will sustain your immortal life. And after having said the sacred words, "Lord, I am not worthy," do not make any further movement whatever, either in prayer or otherwise, but gently opening your mouth, in the fulness of faith, hope, and love, receive Him in Whom, by Whom, and through Whom, you believe, hope, and love. O my child, bethink you that just as the bee, having gathered heaven's dew and earth's sweetest juices from amid the flowers, carries it to her hive; so the Priest, having taken the Saviour, God's Own Son, Who came down from Heaven, the Son of Mary, Who sprang up as earth's choicest flower, from the Altar, feeds you with that Bread of Sweetness and of all delight. When you have received it kindle your heart to adore the King of our Salvation, tell Him of all your own personal matters, and realise that He is within you, seeking your best happiness. In short, give Him the very best reception you possibly can, and act so that in all you do it may be evident that God is with you. When you cannot have the blessing of actual Communion, at least communicate in heart and mind, uniting yourself by ardent desire to the Life-giving Body of the Saviour.

Your main intention in Communion should be to grow, strengthen, and abound in the Love of God; for Love's Sake receive that which Love Alone gives you. Of a truth there is no more loving or tender aspect in which to gaze upon the Saviour than this act, in which He, so to say, annihilates Himself, and gives Himself to us as food, in order to fill our souls, and to unite Himself more closely to the heart and flesh of His faithful ones.

If men of the world ask why you communicate so often, tell them that it is that you may learn to love God; that you may be cleansed from imperfections, set free from trouble, comforted in affliction, strengthened in weakness. Tell them that there are two manner of men who need frequent Communion--those who are perfect, since being ready they were much to blame did they not come to the Source and Fountain of all perfection; and the imperfect, that they may learn how to become perfect; the strong, lest they become weak, and the weak, that they may become strong; the sick that they may be healed, and the sound lest they sicken. Tell them that you, imperfect, weak and ailing, need frequently to communicate with your Perfection, your Strength, your Physician. Tell them that those who are but little engaged in worldly affairs should communicate often, because they have leisure; and those who are heavily pressed with business, because they stand so much in need of help; and he who is hard worked needs frequent and substantial food. Tell them that you receive the Blessed Sacrament that you may learn to receive it better; one rarely does that well which one seldom does. Therefore, my child, communicate frequently,--as often as you can, subject to the advice of your spiritual Father. Our mountain hares turn white in winter, because they live in, and feed upon, the snow, and by dint of adoring and feeding upon Beauty, Goodness, and Purity itself in this most Divine Sacrament you too will become lovely, holy, pure.

PART III - CONTAINING COUNSELS CONCERNING THE PRACTICE OF VIRTUE

CHAPTER I - *How to select that which we should chiefly Practise*

THE queen bee never takes wing without being surrounded by all her Subjects; even so Love never enters the heart but it is sure to bring all other virtues in its train; marshalling and employing them as a captain his soldiers; yet, nevertheless, Love does not set them all to work suddenly, or equally, at all times and everywhere. The righteous man is "like a tree planted by the water side, that will bring forth his fruit in due season;" [50] inasmuch as Love, watering and refreshing the soul, causes it to bring forth good works, each in season as required. There is an old proverb to the effect that the sweetest music is unwelcome at a time of mourning; and certain persons have made a great mistake when, seeking to cultivate some special virtue, they attempt to obtrude it on all occasions, like the ancient philosophers we read of, who were always laughing or weeping. Worse still if they take upon themselves to censure those who do not make a continual study of this their pet virtue. S. Paul tells us to "rejoice with them that do rejoice, and weep with them that weep;" [51] and Charity is patient, kind, liberal, prudent, indulgent.

At the same time, there are virtues of universal account, which must not only be called into occasional action, but ought to spread their influence over everything. We do not very often come across opportunities for exercising strength, magnanimity, or magnificence; but gentleness, temperance, modesty, and humility, are graces which ought to colour everything we do. There may be virtues of a more exalted mould, but at all events these are the most continually called for in daily life. Sugar is better than salt, but we use salt more generally and oftener. Consequently, it is well to have a good and ready stock in hand of those general virtues of which we stand in so perpetual a need.

In practising any virtue, it is well to choose that which is most according to our duty, rather than most according to our taste. It was Saint Paula's liking to practise bodily mortifications with a view to the keener enjoyment of spiritual sweetness, but obedience to her superiors was a higher duty; and therefore Saint Jerome acknowledges that she was wrong in practising excessive abstinence contrary to the advice of her Bishop. And the Apostles, whose mission it was to preach the Gospel, and feed souls with the Bread of Life, judged well that it was not right for them to hinder this holy work in order to minister to the material wants of the poor, weighty as that work was also. [52] Every calling stands in special need of some special virtue; those required of a prelate, a prince, or a soldier, are quite different; so are those beseeming a wife or a widow, and although all should possess every virtue, yet all are not called upon to exercise them equally, but each should cultivate chiefly those which are important to the manner of life to which he is called.

Among such virtues as have no special adaptation to our own calling, choose the most excellent, not the most showy. A comet generally looks larger than the stars, and fills the eye more; but all the while comets are not nearly so important as the stars, and only seem so large to us because they are nearer to us than stars, and are of a grosser kind. So there are certain virtues which touch us very sensibly and are very material, so to say, and therefore ordinary people give them the preference. Thus the common run of men ordinarily value temporal almsgiving more than spiritual; and think more of fasting, exterior discipline and bodily mortification than of meekness, cheerfulness, modesty, and other interior mortifications, which nevertheless are far better. Do you then, my daughter, choose the best virtues, not those which are most highly esteemed; the most excellent, not the most visible; the truest, not the most conspicuous.

It is well for everybody to select some special virtue at which to aim, not as neglecting any others, but as an object and pursuit to the mind. Saint John, Bishop of Alexandria, saw a vision of a lovely maiden, brighter than the sun, in shining garments, and wearing an olive crown, who said to him, "I am the King's eldest daughter, and if thou wilt have me for thy friend, I will bring thee to see His Face." Then he knew that it was pity for the poor which God thus commended to him, and from that time he gave himself so heartily to practise it, that he is universally known as Saint John the Almoner. Eulogius Alexandrinus desired to devote himself wholly to God, but he had not courage either to adopt the solitary life, or to put himself under obedience, and therefore he took a miserable beggar, seething in dirt and leprosy, to live with him; and to do this more thoroughly, he vowed to honour and serve him as a servant does his lord and master. After a while, both feeling greatly tempted to part company, they referred to the great Saint Anthony, who said, "Beware of separating, my sons, for you are both near your end, and if the Angel find you not together, you will be in danger of losing your crowns."

Saint Louis counted it a privilege to visit the hospitals, where he used to tend the sick with his own royal hands. Saint Francis loved poverty above all things, and called her his lady-love. Saint Dominic gave himself up to preaching, whence his Order takes its name. [53] Saint Gregory the Great specially delighted to receive pilgrims after the manner of faithful Abraham, and like him entertained the King of Glory under a pilgrim's garb. Tobit devoted himself to the charitable work of burying the dead. Saint Elizabeth, albeit a mighty princess, loved above all things to humble herself. When Saint Catherine of Genoa became a widow, she gave herself up to work in an hospital. Cassian relates how a certain devout maiden once besought Saint Athanasius to help her in cultivating the grace of patience; and he gave her a poor widow as companion, who was cross, irritable, and altogether intolerable, and whose perpetual fretfulness gave the pious lady abundant opportunity of practising gentleness and patience. And so some of God's servants devote themselves to nursing the sick, helping the poor, teaching little children in the faith, reclaiming the fallen, building churches, and adorning the altar, making peace among men. Therein they resemble embroidresses who work all manner of silks, gold and silver on various grounds, so producing beautiful flowers. Just so the pious souls who undertake some special devout practice use it as the ground of their spiritual embroidery, and frame all manner of other graces upon it, ordering their actions and affections better by means of this their chief thread which runs through all.

"Upon Thy Right Hand did stand the Queen in a vesture of gold wrought about with divers colours." [54]

When we are beset by any particular vice, it is well as far as possible to make the opposite virtue our special aim, and turn everything to that account; so doing, we shall overcome our enemy, and meanwhile make progress in all virtue. Thus, if I am beset with pride or anger, I must above all else strive to cultivate humility and gentleness, and I must turn all my religious exercises,--prayer, sacraments, prudence, constancy, moderation, to the same object. The wild boar sharpens its tusks by grinding them against its other teeth, which by the same process are sharpened and pointed; and so when a good man endeavours to perfect himself in some virtue which he is conscious of specially needing, he ought to give it edge and point by the aid of other virtues, which will themselves be confirmed and strengthened as he uses them with that object. It was so with Job, who, while specially exercising the virtue of patience amid the numberless temptations which beset him, was confirmed in all manner of holiness and godly virtues. And Saint Gregory Nazianzen says, that sometimes a person has attained the height of goodness by one single act of virtue, performed with the greatest perfection; instancing Rahab as an example, who, having practised the virtue of hospitality very excellently, reached a high point of glory. [55] Of course, any such action must needs be performed with a very exceeding degree of fervour and charity.

Footnotes:

50. Ps. i. 3.
51. Rom. xii. 15.
52. Acts vi. 2.
53. The Preaching Friars.
54. Psalm 5. 13, 14. "En son beau vestement de drap d'or recame, Et d'ouvrages divers a l'aiguile seme."
55. S. Francis evidently alludes here to the mention made of Rahab by S. Paul. Heb. xi. 31.

CHAPTER II - The same Subject continued

SAINT AUGUSTINE says very admirably, that beginners in devotion are wont to commit certain faults which, while they are blameable according to the strict laws of perfection, are yet praiseworthy by reason of the promise they hold forth of a future excellent goodness, to which they actually tend. For instance, that common shrinking fear which gives rise to an excessive scrupulosity in the souls of some who are but just set free from a course of sin, is commendable at that early stage, and is the almost certain forerunner of future purity of conscience. But this same fear would be blameable in those who are farther advanced, because love should reign in their hearts, and love is sure to drive away all such servile fear by degrees.

In his early days, Saint Bernard was very severe and harsh towards those whom he directed, telling them, to begin with, that they must put aside the body, and come to him with their minds only. In confession, he treated all faults, however small, with extreme severity, and his poor apprentices in the study of perfection were so urged onwards, that by dint of pressing he kept them back, for they lost heart and breath when they found themselves thus driven up so steep and high an ascent. Therein, my daughter, you can see that, although it was his ardent zeal for the most perfect purity which led that great Saint so to act, and although such zeal is a great virtue, still it was a virtue which required checking. And so God Himself checked it in a vision, by which He filled S. Bernard with so gentle, tender, and loving a spirit, that he was altogether changed, blaming himself heavily for having been so strict and so severe, and becoming so kindly and indulgent, that he made himself all things to all men in order to win all.

S. Jerome tells us that his beloved daughter, S. Paula, was not only extreme, but obstinate in practising bodily mortifications, and refusing to yield to the advice given her upon that head by her Bishop, S. Epiphanius; and furthermore, she gave way so excessively to her grief at the death of those she loved as to peril her own life. Whereupon S. Jerome says: "It will be said that I am accusing this saintly woman rather than praising her, but I affirm before Jesus, Whom she served, and Whom I seek to serve, that I am not saying what is untrue on one side or the other, but simply describing her as one Christian another; that is to say, I am writing her history, not her panegyric, and her faults are the virtues of others." He means to say that the defects and faults of S. Paula would have been looked upon as virtues in a less perfect soul; and indeed there are actions which we must count as imperfections in the perfect, which yet would be highly esteemed in the imperfect. When at the end of a sickness the invalid's legs swell, it is a good sign, indicating that natural strength is returning, and throwing off foul humours; but it would be a bad sign in one not avowedly sick, as showing that nature was too feeble to disperse or absorb those humours.

So, my child, we must think well of those whom we see practising virtues, although imperfectly, since the Saints have done the like; but as to ourselves we must give heed to practise them, not only diligently, but discreetly, and to this end we shall do well strictly to follow the Wise Man's counsel, [56] and not trust in our own wisdom, but lean on those whom God has given as our guides. And here I must say a few words concerning certain things which some reckon as virtues, although they are nothing of the sort--I mean ecstasies, trances, rhapsodies, extraordinary transformations, and the like, which are dwelt on in some books, and which promise to raise the soul to a purely intellectual contemplation, an altogether supernatural mental altitude, and a life of pre-eminent excellence. But I would have you see, my child, that these perfections are not virtues, they are rather rewards which God gives to virtues, or perhaps, more correctly speaking, tokens of the joys of everlasting life, occasionally granted to men in order to kindle in them a desire for the fulness of joy which is only to be found in Paradise. But we must not aspire to such graces, which are in nowise necessary to us in order to love and serve God, our only lawful ambition. Indeed, for the most part, these graces are not to be acquired by labour or industry, and that because they are rather passions than actions, which we may receive, but cannot create. Moreover, our business only is to become good, devout people, pious men and women; and all our efforts must be to that end. If it should please God further to endow us with angelic perfection, we should then be prepared to become good angels; but meanwhile let us practise, in all simplicity, humility and devotion, those lowly virtues to the attainment of which our Lord has bidden us labour,--I mean patience, cheerfulness, self-mortification, humility, obedience, poverty, chastity, kindness to our neighbour, forbearance towards his failings, diligence, and a holy fervour. Let us willingly resign the higher eminences to lofty souls. We are not worthy to take so high a rank in God's service; let us be content to be as scullions, porters, insignificant attendants in His household, leaving it to Him if He should hereafter see fit to call us to His own council chamber. Of a truth, my child, the King of Glory does not reward His servants according to the dignity of their office, but according to the humility and love with which they have exercised it. While Saul was seeking his father's asses, he found the kingdom of Israel: [57] Rebecca watering Abraham's camels, became his son's wife: [58] Ruth gleaning after Boaz' reapers, and lying down at his feet, was raised up to become his bride. [59] Those who pretend to such great and extraordinary graces are very liable to delusions and mistakes, so that sometimes it turns out that people who aspire to be angels are not ordinarily good men, and that their goodness lies more in high-flown words than in heart and deed. But we must beware of despising or presumptuously condemning anything. Only, while thanking God for the pre-eminence of others, let us abide contentedly in our own lower but safer path,--a path of less distinction, but more suitable to our lowliness, resting satisfied that if we walk steadily and faithfully therein, God will lift us up to greater things.

Footnotes:

56. Ecclus. vi. 2, 32, 36.
57. 1 Sam. ix.
58. Gen. xxiv.
59. Ruth ii. iii.

CHAPTER III - On Patience

"YE have need of patience, that, after ye have done the Will of God, ye might receive the promise," says Saint Paul; [60] and the Saviour said, "In your patience possess ye your souls." [61] The greatest happiness of any one is "to possess his soul;" and the more perfect our patience, the more fully we do so possess our souls. Call often to mind that our Saviour redeemed us by bearing and suffering, and in like manner we must seek our own salvation amid sufferings and afflictions; bearing insults, contradictions and troubles with all the gentleness we can possibly command. Do not limit your patience to this or that kind of trial, but extend it universally to whatever God may send, or allow to befall you. Some people will only bear patiently with trials which carry their own salve of dignity,--such as being wounded in battle, becoming a prisoner of war, being ill-used for the sake of their religion, being impoverished by some strife out of which they came triumphant. Now these persons do not love tribulation, but only the honour which attends it. A really patient servant of God is as ready to bear inglorious troubles as those which are honourable. A brave man can easily bear with contempt, slander and false accusation from an evil world; but to bear such injustice at the hands of good men, of friends and relations, is a great test of patience. I have a greater respect for the gentleness with which the great S. Charles Borromeo long endured the public reproaches which a celebrated preacher of a reformed Order used to pour out upon him, than for all the other attacks he bore with. For, just as the sting of a bee hurts far more than that of a fly, so the injuries or contradictions we endure from good people are much harder to bear than any others. But it is a thing which very often happens, and sometimes two worthy men, who are both highly well-intentioned after their own fashion, annoy and even persecute one another grievously.

Be patient, not only with respect to the main trials which beset you, but also under the accidental and accessory annoyances which arise out of them. We often find people who imagine themselves ready to accept a trial in itself who are impatient of its consequences. We hear one man say, "I should not mind poverty, were it not that I am unable to bring up my children and receive my friends as handsomely as I desire." And another says, "I should not mind, were it not that the world will suppose it is my own fault;" while another would patiently bear to be the subject of slander provided nobody believed it. Others, again, accept one side of a trouble but fret against the rest--as, for instance, believing themselves to be patient under sickness, only fretting against their inability to obtain the best advice, or at the inconvenience they are to their friends. But, dear child, be sure that we must patiently accept, not sickness only, but such sickness as God chooses to send, in the place, among the people, and subject to the circumstances which He ordains;--and so with all other troubles. If any trouble comes upon you, use the remedies with which God supplies you. Not to do this is to tempt Him; but having done so, wait whatever result He wills with perfect resignation. If He pleases to let the evil be remedied, thank Him humbly; but if it be His will that the evil grow greater than the remedies, patiently bless His Holy Name.

Follow Saint Gregory's advice: When you are justly blamed for some fault you have committed, humble yourself deeply, and confess that you deserve the blame. If the accusation be false, defend yourself quietly, denying the fact; this is but due respect for truth and your neighbour's edification. But if after you have made your true and legitimate defence you are still accused, do not be troubled, and do not try to press your defence--you have had due respect for truth, have the same now for humility. By acting thus you will not infringe either a due care for your good name, or the affection you are bound to entertain for peace, humility and gentleness of heart.

Complain as little as possible of your wrongs, for as a general rule you may be sure that complaining is sin; [62] the rather that self-love always magnifies our injuries: above all, do not complain to people who are easily angered and excited. If it is needful to complain to some one, either as seeking a remedy for your injury, or in order to soothe your mind, let it be to some calm, gentle spirit, greatly filled with the Love of God; for otherwise, instead of relieving your heart, your confidants will only provoke it to still greater disturbance; instead of taking out the thorn which pricks you, they will drive it further into your foot.

Some people when they are ill, or in trouble, or injured by any one, restrain their complaints, because they think (and that rightly) that to murmur betokens great weakness or a narrow mind; but nevertheless, they exceedingly desire and maneuvre to make others pity them, desiring to be considered as suffering with patience and courage. Now this is a kind of patience certainly, but it is a spurious patience, which in reality is neither more nor less than a very refined, very subtle form of ambition and vanity. To them we may apply the Apostle's words, "He hath whereof to glory, but not before God." [63] A really patient man neither complains nor seeks to be pitied; he will speak simply and truly of his trouble, without exaggerating its weight or bemoaning himself; if others pity him, he will accept their compassion patiently, unless they pity him for some ill he is not enduring, in which case he will say so with meekness, and abide in patience and truthfulness, combating his grief and not complaining of it.

As to the trials which you will encounter in devotion (and they are certain to arise), bear in mind our dear Lord's words: "A woman, when she is in travail, hath sorrow, because her hour is come; but as soon as she is delivered of the child, she remembereth no more the anguish, for joy that a child is born into the world." [64] You, too, have conceived in your soul the most gracious of children, even Jesus Christ, and before He can be brought forth you must inevitably travail with pain; but be of good cheer, for when these pangs are over, you will possess an abiding joy, having brought such a man into the world. And He will be really born for you, when He is perfected in your heart by love, and in your actions by imitating His life.

When you are sick, offer all your pains and weakness to our Dear Lord, and ask Him to unite them to the sufferings which He bore for you. Obey your physician, and take all medicines, remedies and nourishment, for the Love of God, remembering the vinegar and gall He tasted for love of us; desire your recovery that you may serve Him; do not shrink from languor and weakness out of obedience to Him, and be ready to die if He wills it, to His Glory, and that you may enter into His Presence.

Bear in mind that the bee while making its honey lives upon a bitter food: and in like manner we can never make acts of gentleness and patience, or gather the honey of the truest virtues, better than while eating the bread of bitterness, and enduring hardness. And just as the best honey is that made from thyme, a small and bitter herb, so that virtue which is practised amid bitterness and lowly sorrow is the best of all virtues.

Gaze often inwardly upon Jesus Christ crucified, naked, blasphemed, falsely accused, forsaken, overwhelmed with every possible grief and sorrow, and remember that none of your sufferings can ever be compared to His, either in kind or degree, and that you can never suffer anything for Him worthy to be weighed against what He has borne for you.

Consider the pains which martyrs have endured, and think how even now many people are bearing afflictions beyond all measure greater than yours, and say, "Of a truth my trouble is comfort, my torments are but roses as compared to those whose life is a continual death, without solace, or aid or consolation, borne down with a weight of grief tenfold greater than mine."

Footnotes:

60. Heb. x. 36.
61. S. Luke xxi. 19.
62. "Qui se plaint, peche."
63. Rom. iv. 2.
64. S. John xvi. 21.

CHAPTER IV - On Greater Humility

ELISHA bade the poor widow "borrow vessels, even empty vessels not a few, and pour oil into all those vessels;" [65] and so in order to receive God's Grace in our hearts, they must be as empty vessels-- not filled with self-esteem. The swallow with its sharp cry and keen glance has the power of frightening away birds of prey, and for that reason the dove prefers it to all other birds, and lives surely beside it;-- even so humility drives Satan away, and cherishes the gifts and graces of the Holy Spirit within us, and for that reason all the Saints--and especially the King of Saints and His Blessed Mother--have always esteemed the grace of humility above all other virtues.

We call that vainglory which men take to themselves, either for what is not in them, or which being in them is not their own, or which being in them and their own yet is not worthy of their self-satisfaction. For instance, noble birth, favour of great men, popular applause, all these are things nowise belonging to ourselves, but coming from our forefathers, or the opinion of others. Some people are proud and conceited because they ride a fine horse, wear a feather in their hat, and are expensively dressed, but who can fail to see their folly, or that if any one has reason to be proud over such things, it would be the horse, the bird, and the tailor! Or what can be more contemptible than to found one's credit on a horse, a plume, or a ruff? Others again pride themselves upon their dainty moustaches, their well-trimmed beard or curled hair, their white hands, or their dancing, singing and the like: but is it not a petty vanity which can seek to be esteemed for any such trivial and frivolous matters? Then again, some look for the world's respect and honour because they have acquired some smatterings of science, expecting all their neighbours to listen and yield to them, and such men we call pedants. Others make great capital of their personal beauty, and imagine that every one is lost in admiration of it; but all this is utterly vain, foolish and impertinent, and the glory men take to themselves for such matters must be called vain, childish and frivolous.

You may test real worth as we test balm, which is tried by being distilled in water, and if it is precipitated to the bottom, it is known to be pure and precious. So if you want to know whether a man is really wise, learned, generous or noble, see if his life is moulded by humility, modesty and submission. If so, his gifts are genuine; but if they are only surface and showy, you may be sure that in proportion to their demonstrativeness so is their unreality. Those pearls which are formed amid tempest and storm have only an outward shell, and are hollow within; and so when a man's good qualities are fed by pride, vanity and boasting, they will soon have nothing save empty show, without sap, marrow or substance.

Honour, rank and dignity are like the saffron, which never thrives so well as when trodden under foot. Beauty only attracts when it is free from any such aim. Self-conscious beauty loses its charm, and learning becomes a discredit and degenerates into pedantry, when we are puffed up by it.

Those who are punctilious about rank, title or precedence, both lay themselves open to criticism and degradation, and also throw contempt on all such things; because an honour which is valuable when freely paid, is worthless when sought for or exacted. When the peacock opens his showy tail, he exhibits the ugliness of his body beneath; and many flowers which are beautiful while growing, wither directly we gather them. And just as men who inhale mandragora from afar as they pass, find it sweet, while those who breathe it closely are made faint and ill by the same, so honour may be pleasant to those who merely taste it as they pass, without seeking or craving for it, but it will become very dangerous and hurtful to such as take delight in and feed upon it.

An active effort to acquire virtue is the first step towards goodness; but an active effort to acquire honour is the first step towards contempt and shame. A well-conditioned mind will not throw away its powers upon such sorry trifles as rank, position or outward forms--it has other things to do, and will leave all that to meaner minds. He who can find pearls will not stop to pick up shells; and so a man who aims at real goodness will not be keen about outward tokens of honour. Undoubtedly every one is justified in keeping his own place, and there is no want of humility in that so long as it is done simply and without contention. Just as our merchant-ships coming from Peru with gold and silver often bring apes and parrots likewise, because these cost but little and do not add to the weight of a cargo, so good men seeking to grow in grace can take their natural rank and position, so long as they are not engrossed by such things, and do not involve themselves in anxiety, contention or ill-will on their account. I am not speaking here of those whose position is public, or even of certain special private persons whose dignity may be important. In all such cases each man must move in his own sphere, with prudence and discretion, together with charity and courtesy.

Footnote:

65. 2 Kings iv. 3, 4.

CHAPTER V - On Interior Humility

TO you however, my daughter, I would teach a deeper humility, for that of which I have been speaking is almost more truly to be called worldly wisdom than humility. There are some persons who dare not or will not think about the graces with which God has endowed them, fearing lest they should become self-complacent and vain-glorious; but they are quite wrong. For if, as the Angelic Doctor says, the real way of attaining to the Love of God is by a careful consideration of all His benefits given to us, then the better we realise these the more we shall love Him; and inasmuch as individual gifts are more acceptable than general gifts, so they ought to be more specially dwelt upon. Of a truth, nothing so tends to humble us before the Mercy of God as the multitude of His gifts to us; just as nothing so tends to humble us before His Justice as the multitude of our misdeeds. Let us consider what He has done for us, and what we have done contrary to His Will, and as we review our sins in detail, so let us review His Grace in the same. There is no fear that a perception of what He has given you will puff you up, so long as you keep steadily in mind that whatever is good in you is not of yourself. Do mules cease to be clumsy, stinking beasts because they are used to carry the dainty treasures and perfumes of a prince? "What hast thou that thou didst not receive? Now, if thou didst receive it, why dost thou glory as if thou hadst not received it?" [66] On the contrary, a lively appreciation of the grace given to you should make you humble, for appreciation begets gratitude. But if, when realising the gifts God has given you, any vanity should beset you, the infallible remedy is to turn to the thought of all our ingratitude, imperfection, and weakness. Any one who will calmly consider what he has done without God, cannot fail to realise that what he does with God is no merit of his own; and so we may rejoice in that which is good in us, and take pleasure in the fact, but we shall give all the glory to God Alone, Who Alone is its Author.

It was in this spirit that the Blessed Virgin confessed that God had done "great things" to her; [67] only that she might humble herself and exalt Him. "My soul doth magnify the Lord," she said, by reason of the gifts He had given her.

We are very apt to speak of ourselves as nought, as weakness itself, as the offscouring of the earth; but we should be very much vexed to be taken at our word and generally considered what we call ourselves. On the contrary, we often make-believe to run away and hide ourselves, merely to be followed and sought out; we pretend to take the lowest place, with the full intention of being honourably called to come up higher. But true humility does not affect to be humble, and is not given to make a display in lowly words. It seeks not only to conceal other virtues, but above all it seeks and desires to conceal itself; and if it were lawful to tell lies, or feign or give scandal, humility would perhaps sometimes affect a cloak of pride in order to hide itself utterly. Take my advice, my daughter, and either use no professions of humility, or else use them with a real mind corresponding to your outward expressions; never cast down your eyes without humbling your heart; and do not pretend to wish to be last and least, unless you really and sincerely mean it. I would make this so general a rule as to have no exception; only courtesy sometimes requires us to put forward those who obviously would not put themselves forward, but this is not deceitful or mock humility; and so with respect to certain expressions of regard which do not seem strictly true, but which are not dishonest, because the speaker really intends to give honour and respect to him to whom they are addressed; and even though the actual words may be somewhat excessive, there is no harm in them if they are the ordinary forms of society, though truly I wish that all our expressions were as nearly as possible regulated by real heart feeling in all truthfulness and simplicity. A really humble man would rather that some one else called him worthless and good-for-nothing, than say so of himself; at all events, if such things are said, he does not contradict them, but acquiesces contentedly, for it is his own opinion. We meet people who tell us that they leave mental prayer to those who are more perfect, not feeling themselves worthy of it; that they dare not communicate frequently, because they do not feel fit to do so; that they fear to bring discredit on religion if they profess it, through their weakness and frailty; while others decline to use their talents in the service of God and their neighbour, because, forsooth, they know their weakness, and are afraid of becoming proud if they do any good thing,--lest while helping others they might destroy themselves. But all this is unreal, and not merely a spurious but a vicious humility, which tacitly and secretly condemns God's gifts, and makes a pretext of lowliness while really exalting self-love, self-sufficiency, indolence, and evil tempers. "Ask thee a sign of the Lord thy God; ask it either in the depth or in the height above." [68] So spake the prophet to King Ahaz; but he answered, "I will not ask, neither will I tempt the Lord." Unhappy man! he affects to show exceeding reverence to God, and under a pretence of humility refuses to seek the grace offered by the Divine Goodness. Could he not see that when God wills to grant us a favour, it is mere pride to reject it, that God's gifts must needs be accepted, and that true humility lies in obedience and the most literal compliance with His Will! Well then, God's Will is that we should be perfect, uniting ourselves to Him, and imitating Him to the utmost of our powers. The proud man who trusts in himself may well undertake nothing, but the humble man is all the braver that he knows his own helplessness, and his courage waxes in proportion to his low opinion of himself, because all his trust is in God, Who delights to show forth His Power in our weakness, His Mercy in our misery. The safest course is humbly and piously to venture upon whatever may be considered profitable for us by those who undertake our spiritual guidance.

Nothing can be more foolish than to fancy we know that of which we are really ignorant; to affect knowledge while conscious that we are ignorant is intolerable vanity. For my part, I would rather not put forward that which I really do know, while on the other hand neither would I affect ignorance. When Charity requires it, you should readily and kindly impart to your neighbour not only that which is necessary for his instruction, but also what is profitable for his consolation. The same humility which conceals graces with a view to their preservation is ready to bring them forth at the bidding of Charity, with a view to their increase and perfection; therein reminding me of that tree in the Isles of Tylos, [69] which closes its beautiful carnation blossoms at night, only opening them to the rising sun, so that the natives say they go to sleep. Just so humility hides our earthly virtues and perfections, only expanding them at the call of Charity, which is not an earthly, but a heavenly, not a mere moral, but a divine virtue; the true sun of all virtues, which should all be ruled by it, so that any humility which controverts charity is unquestionably false.

I would not affect either folly or wisdom; for just as humility deters me from pretending to be wise, so simplicity and straightforwardness deter me from pretending to be foolish; and just as vanity is opposed to humility, so all affectation and pretence are opposed to honesty and simplicity. If certain eminent servants of God have feigned folly in order to be despised by the world, we may marvel, but not imitate them; for they had special and extraordinary reasons for doing extraordinary things, and cannot be used as a rule for such as we are. When David [70] danced more than was customary before the Ark of the Covenant, it was not with the intention of affecting folly, but simply as expressing the unbounded and extraordinary gladness of his heart. Michal his wife reproached him with his actions as folly, but he did not mind being "vile and base in his own sight," but declared himself willing to be despised for God's Sake. And so, if you should be despised for acts of genuine devotion, humility will enable you to rejoice in so blessed a contempt, the cause of which does not lie with you.

Footnotes:

66. 1 Cor. iv. 7.
67. S. Luke i. 46-49.
68. Isa. vii. 11, 12.
69. Islands in the Persian Gulf.
70. 2 Sam. vi. 14.

CHAPTER VI - Humility makes us rejoice in our own Abjection

BUT, my daughter, I am going a step further, and I bid you everywhere and in everything to rejoice in your own abjection. Perhaps you will ask in reply what I mean by that. In Latin abjection means humility, and humility means abjection, so that when Our Lady says in the Magnificat that all generations shall call her blessed, because God hath regarded the low estate of His handmaiden, [71] she means that He has accepted her abjection and lowliness in order to fill her with graces and favours. Nevertheless, there is a difference between humility and abjection; for abjection is the poverty, vileness and littleness which exist in us, without our taking heed to them; but humility implies a real knowledge and voluntary recognition of that abjection. And the highest point of humility consists in not merely acknowledging one's abjection, but in taking pleasure therein, not from any want of breadth or courage, but to give the more glory to God's Divine Majesty, and to esteem one's neighbour more highly than one's self. This is what I would have you do; and to explain myself more clearly, let me tell you that the trials which afflict us are sometimes abject, sometimes honourable. NOW many people will accept the latter, but very few are willing to accept the former. Everybody respects and pities a pious hermit shivering in his worn-out garb; but let a poor gentleman or lady be in like case, and they are despised for it,--and so their poverty is abject. A religious receives a sharp rebuke from his superior meekly, or a child from his parent, and every one will call it obedience, mortification, wisdom; but let a knight or a lady accept the like from some one, albeit for the Love of God, and they will forthwith be accused of cowardice. This again is abject suffering. One person has a cancer in the arm, another in the face; the former only has the pain to bear, but the latter has also to endure all the disgust and repulsion caused by his disease; and this is abjection. And what I want to teach you is, that we should not merely rejoice in our trouble, which we do by means of patience, but we should also cherish the abjection, which is done by means of humility. Again, there are abject and honourable virtues; for the world generally despises patience, gentleness, simplicity, and even humility itself, while, on the contrary, it highly esteems prudence, valour, and liberality. Sometimes even there may be a like distinction drawn between acts of one and the same virtue--one being despised and the other respected. Thus almsgiving and forgiveness of injuries are both acts of charity, but while every one esteems the first, the world looks down upon the last. A young man or a girl who refuses to join in the excesses of dress, amusement, or gossip of their circle, is laughed at and criticised, and their self-restraint is called affectation or bigotry. Well, to rejoice in that is to rejoice in abjection. Or, to take another shape of the same thing. We are employed in visiting the sick--if I am sent to the most wretched cases, it is an abjection in the world's sight, and consequently I like it. If I am sent to those of a better class, it is an interior abjection, for there is less grace and merit in the work, and so I can accept that abjection. If one has a fall in the street, there is the ridiculous part of it to be borne, as well as the possible pain; and this is an abjection we must accept. There are even some faults, in which there is no harm beyond their abjection, and although humility does not require us to commit them intentionally, it does require of us not to be disturbed at having committed them. I mean certain foolish acts, incivilities, and inadvertencies, which we ought to avoid as far as may be out of civility and decorum, but of which, if accidentally committed, we ought to accept the abjection heartily, out of humility. To go further still,--if in anger or excitement I have been led to use unseemly words, offending God and my neighbour thereby, I will repent heartily, and be very grieved for the offence, which I must try to repair to the utmost; but meanwhile I will accept the abjection and disgrace which will ensue, and were it possible to separate the two things, I ought earnestly to reject the sin, while I retained the abjection readily.

But while we rejoice in the abjection, we must nevertheless use all due and lawful means to remedy the evil whence it springs, especially when that evil is serious. Thus, if I have an abject disease in my face, I should endeavour to get it cured, although I do not wish to obliterate the abjection it has caused me. If I have done something awkward which hurts no one, I will not make excuses, because, although it was a failing, my own abjection is the only result; but if I have given offence or scandal through my carelessness or folly, I am bound to try and remedy it by a sincere apology. There are occasions when charity requires us not to acquiesce in abjection, but in such a case one ought the more to take it inwardly to heart for one's private edification.

Perhaps you will ask what are the most profitable forms of abjection. Unquestionably, those most helpful to our own souls, and most acceptable to God, are such as come accidentally, or in the natural course of events, because we have not chosen them ourselves, but simply accepted God's choice, which is always to be preferred to ours. But if we are constrained to choose, the greatest abjections are best; and the greatest is whatever is most contrary to one's individual inclination, so long as it is in conformity with one's vocation; for of a truth our self-will and self-pleasing mars many graces. Who can teach any of us truly to say with David, "I had rather be a doorkeeper in the house of my God, than to dwell in the tents of ungodliness"? [72] None, dear child, save He Who lived and died the scorn of men, and the outcast of the people, in order that we might be raised up. I have said things here which must seem very hard to contemplate, but, believe me, they will become sweet as honey when you try to put them in practice.

Footnotes:

71. S. Luke i. 48.
72. Ps. lxxxiv. 10.

CHAPTER VII - How to combine due care for a Good Reputation with Humility

PRAISE, honour, and glory are not bestowed on men for ordinary, but for extraordinary virtue. By praise we intend to lead men to appreciate the excellence of certain individuals; giving them honour is the expression of our own esteem for them; and I should say that glory is the combination of praise and honour from many persons. If praise and honour are like precious stones, glory is as an enamel thereof. Now, as humility forbids us to aim at excelling or being preferred to others, it likewise forbids us to aim at praise, honour, and glory; but it allows us to give heed, as the Wise Man says, to our good name, and that because a good name does not imply any one particular excellence, but a general straightforward integrity of purpose, which we may recognise in ourselves, and desire to be known as possessing, without any breach of humility. Humility might make us indifferent even to a good reputation, were it not for charity's sake; but seeing that it is a groundwork of society, and without it we are not merely useless but positively harmful to the world, because of the scandal given by such a deficiency, therefore charity requires, and humility allows, us to desire and to maintain a good reputation with care.

Moreover, just as the leaves of a tree are valuable, not merely for beauty's sake, but also as a shelter to the tender fruit, so a good reputation, if not in itself very important, is still very useful, not only as an embellishment of life, but as a protection to our virtues, especially to those which are weakly. The necessity for acting up to our reputation, and being what we are thought to be, brings a strong though kindly motive power to bear upon a generous disposition. Let us foster all our virtues, my daughter, because they are pleasing to God, the Chief Aim of all we do. But just as when men preserve fruits, they do not only conserve them, but put them into suitable vessels, so while Divine Love is the main thing which keeps us in the ways of holiness, we may also find help from the effects of a good reputation. But it will not do to be over-eager or fanciful about it. Those who are so very sensitive about their reputation are like people who are perpetually physicking themselves for every carnal ailment; they mean to preserve their health, but practically they destroy it; and those who are so very fastidious over their good name are apt to lose it entirely, for they become fanciful, fretful, and disagreeable, provoking ill-natured remarks.

As a rule, indifference to insult and slander is a much more effectual remedy than resentment, wrath, and vengeance. Slander melts away beneath contempt, but indignation seems a sort of acknowledgment of its truth. Crocodiles never meddle with any but those who are afraid of them, and slander only persists in attacking people who are disturbed by it.

An excessive fear of losing reputation indicates mistrust as to its foundations, which are to be found in a good and true life. Those towns where the bridges are built of wood are very uneasy whenever a sign of flood appears, but they who possess stone bridges are not anxious unless some very unusual storm appears. And so a soul built up on solid Christian foundations can afford to despise the outpour of slanderous tongues, but those who know themselves to be weak are for ever disturbed and uneasy. Be sure, my daughter, that he who seeks to be well thought of by everybody will be esteemed by nobody, and those people deserve to be despised who are anxious to be highly esteemed by ungodly, unworthy men.

Reputation, after all, is but a signboard giving notice where virtue dwells, and virtue itself is always and everywhere preferable. Therefore, if it is said that you are a hypocrite because you are professedly devout, or if you are called a coward because you have forgiven an insult, despise all such accusations. Such judgments are the utterances of foolish men, and you must not give up what is right, even though your reputation suffer, for fruit is better than foliage, that is to say, an inward and spiritual gain is worth all external gains. We may take a jealous care of our reputation, but not idolise it; and while we desire not to displease good men, neither should we seek to please those that are evil. A man's natural adornment is his beard, and a woman's her hair; if either be torn out they may never grow again, but if only shaven or shorn, they will grow all the thicker; and in like manner, if our reputation be shorn or even shaven by slanderous tongues (of which David says, that "with lies they cut like a sharp razor"[73]), there is no need to be disturbed, it will soon spring again, if not brighter, at all events more substantial. But if it be lost through our own vices or meanness or evil living, it will not be easily restored, because its roots are plucked up. And the root of a good name is to be found in virtue and honesty, which will always cause it to spring up afresh, however it may be assaulted. If your good name suffers from some empty pursuit, some useless habit, some unworthy friendship, they must be renounced, for a good name is worth more than any such idle indulgence; but if you are blamed or slandered for pious practices, earnestness in devotion, or whatever tends to win eternal life, then let your slanderers have their way, like dogs that bay at the moon! Be sure that, if they should succeed in rousing any evil impression against you (clipping the beard of your reputation, as it were), your good name will soon revive, and the razor of slander will strengthen your honour, just as the pruning-knife strengthens the vine and causes it to bring forth more abundant fruit. Let us keep Jesus Christ Crucified always before our eyes; let us go on trustfully and simply, but with discretion and wisdom, in His Service, and He will take care of our reputation; if He permits us to lose it, it will only be to give us better things, and to train us in a holy humility, one ounce of which is worth more than a thousand pounds of honour. If we are unjustly blamed, let us quietly meet calumny with truth; if calumny perseveres, let us persevere in humility; there is no surer shelter for our reputation or our soul than the Hand of God. Let us serve Him in good report or evil report alike, with S. Paul; [74] so that we may cry out with David, "For Thy Sake have I suffered reproof, shame hath covered my face." [75]

Of course certain crimes, so grievous that no one who can justify himself should remain silent, must be excepted; as, too, certain persons whose reputation closely affects the edification of others. In this case all theologians say that it is right quietly to seek reparation.

Footnotes:

73. Ps. lii. 2.
74. 2 Cor. vi. 8.
75. Ps. lxix. 7.

CHAPTER VIII - Gentleness towards others and Remedies against Anger

THE holy Chrism, used by the Church according to apostolic tradition, is made of olive oil mingled with balm, which, among other things, are emblematic of two virtues very specially conspicuous in our Dear Lord Himself, and which He has specially commended to us, as though they, above all things, drew us to Him and taught us to imitate Him: "Take My yoke upon you, and learn of Me, for I am meek and lowly in heart." [76] Humility makes our lives acceptable to God, meekness makes us acceptable to men. Balm, as I said before, sinking to the bottom of all liquids, is a figure of humility; and oil, floating as it does to the top, is a figure of gentleness and cheerfulness, rising above all things, and excelling all things, the very flower of Love, which, so says S. Bernard, comes to perfection when it is not merely patient, but gentle and cheerful. Give heed, then, daughter, that you keep this mystic chrism of gentleness and humility in your heart, for it is a favourite device of the Enemy to make people content with a fair outside semblance of these graces, not examining their inner hearts, and so fancying themselves to be gentle and humble while they are far otherwise. And this is easily perceived, because, in spite of their ostentatious gentleness and humility, they are stirred up with pride and anger by the smallest wrong or contradiction. There is a popular belief that those who take the antidote commonly called "Saint Paul's gift," [77] do not suffer from the viper's bite, provided, that is, that the remedy be pure; and even so true gentleness and humility will avert the burning and swelling which contradiction is apt to excite in our hearts. If, when stung by slander or ill-nature, we wax proud and swell with anger, it is a proof that our gentleness and humility are unreal, and mere artificial show. When the Patriarch Joseph sent his brethren back from Egypt to his father's house, he only gave them one counsel, "See that ye fall not out by the way." [78] And so, my child, say I to you. This miserable life is but the road to a blessed life; do not let us fall out by the way one with another; let us go on with the company of our brethren gently, peacefully, and kindly. Most emphatically I say it, If possible, fall out with no one, and on no pretext whatever suffer your heart to admit anger and passion. S. James says, plainly and unreservedly, that "the wrath of man worketh not the righteousness of God." [79] Of course it is a duty to resist evil and to repress the faults of those for whom we are responsible, steadily and firmly, but gently and quietly. Nothing so stills the elephant when enraged as the sight of a lamb; nor does anything break the force of a cannon ball so well as wool. Correction given in anger, however tempered by reason, never has so much effect as that which is given altogether without anger; for the reasonable soul being naturally subject to reason, it is a mere tyranny which subjects it to passion, and whereinsoever reason is led by passion it becomes odious, and its just rule obnoxious. When a monarch visits a country peaceably the people are gratified and flattered; but if the king has to take his armies through the land, even on behalf of the public welfare, his visit is sure to be unwelcome and harmful, because, however strictly military discipline may be enforced, there will always be some mischief done to the people. Just so when reason prevails, and administers reproof, correction, and punishment in a calm spirit, although it be strict, every one approves and is content; but if reason be hindered by anger and vexation (which Saint Augustine calls her soldiers) there will be more fear than love, and reason itself will be despised and resisted. The same Saint Augustine, writing to Profuturus, says that it is better to refuse entrance to any even the least semblance of anger, however just; and that because once entered in, it is hard to be got rid of, and what was but a little mote soon waxes into a great beam. For if anger tarries till night, and the sun goes down upon our wrath (a thing expressly forbidden by the Apostle[80]), there is no longer any way of getting rid of it; it feeds upon endless false fancies; for no angry man ever yet but thought his anger just.

Depend upon it, it is better to learn how to live without being angry than to imagine one can moderate and control anger lawfully; and if through weakness and frailty one is overtaken by it, it is far better to put it away forcibly than to parley with it; for give anger ever so little way, and it will become master, like the serpent, who easily works in its body wherever it can once introduce its head. You will ask how to put away anger. My child, when you feel its first movements, collect yourself gently and seriously, not hastily or with impetuosity. Sometimes in a law court the officials who enforce quiet make more noise than those they affect to hush; and so, if you are impetuous in restraining your temper, you will throw your heart into worse confusion than before, and, amid the excitement, it will lose all self-control.

Having thus gently exerted yourself, follow the advice which the aged S. Augustine gave to a younger Bishop, Auxilius. "Do," said he, "what a man should do." If you are like the Psalmist, ready to cry out, "Mine eye is consumed for very anger," [81] go on to say, "Have mercy upon me, O Lord;" so that God may stretch forth His Right Hand and control your wrath. I mean, that when we feel stirred with anger, we ought to call upon God for help, like the Apostles, when they were tossed about with wind and storm, and He is sure to say, "Peace, be still." But even here I would again warn you, that your very prayers against the angry feelings which urge you should be gentle, calm, and without vehemence. Remember this rule in whatever remedies against anger you may seek. Further, directly you are conscious of an angry act, atone for the fault by some speedy act of meekness towards the person who excited your anger. It is a sovereign cure for untruthfulness to unsay what you have falsely said at once on detecting yourself in falsehood; and so, too, it is a good remedy for anger to make immediate amends by some opposite act of meekness. There is an old saying, that fresh wounds are soonest closed.

Moreover, when there is nothing to stir your wrath, lay up a store of meekness and kindliness, speaking and acting in things great and small as gently as possible. Remember that the Bride of the Canticles is described as not merely dropping honey, and milk also, from her lips, but as having it "under her tongue;" [82] that is to say, in her heart. So we must not only speak gently to our neighbour, but we must be filled, heart and soul, with gentleness; and we must not merely seek the sweetness of aromatic honey in courtesy and suavity with strangers, but also the sweetness of milk among those of our own household and our neighbours; a sweetness terribly lacking to some who are as angels abroad and devils at home!

Footnotes:

76. S. Matt. xi. 29.

77. "La grace de Saint Paul," in one old edition: in another, "la graisse de Saint Paull;" the latter probably is the true reading, as there was a quack salve formerly in use for the bites of snakes, partly compounded of adders' fat. The name is obviously derived from S. Paul's adventure with the viper in the Island of Melita. (Acts xxviii.)

78. Gen. xlv. 24.

79. S. James i. 20.

80. Eph. iv. 26.

81. In the English version it is, "Mine eye is consumed for very heaviness" (Ps. xxxi. 9), but in the Vulgate we find, "Conturbatus est in ira oculus meus." (Vulg. Ps. xxx. 10.)

82. Cant. iv. 11.

CHAPTER IX - On Gentleness towards Ourselves

ONE important direction in which to exercise gentleness, is with respect to ourselves, never growing irritated with one's self or one's imperfections; for although it is but reasonable that we should be displeased and grieved at our own faults, yet ought we to guard against a bitter, angry, or peevish feeling about them. Many people fall into the error of being angry because they have been angry, vexed because they have given way to vexation, thus keeping up a chronic state of irritation, which adds to the evil of what is past, and prepares the way for a fresh fall on the first occasion. Moreover, all this anger and irritation against one's self fosters pride, and springs entirely from self-love, which is disturbed and fretted by its own imperfection. What we want is a quiet, steady, firm displeasure at our own faults. A judge gives sentence more effectually speaking deliberately and calmly than if he be impetuous and passionate (for in the latter case he punishes not so much the actual faults before him, but what they appear to him to be); and so we can chasten ourselves far better by a quiet stedfast repentance, than by eager hasty ways of penitence, which, in fact, are proportioned not by the weight of our faults, but according to our feelings and inclinations. Thus one man who specially aims at purity will be intensely vexed with himself at some very trifling fault against it, while he looks upon some gross slander of which he has been guilty as a mere laughing matter. On the other hand, another will torment himself painfully over some slight exaggeration, while he altogether overlooks some serious offence against purity; and so on with other things. All this arises solely because men do not judge themselves by the light of reason, but under the influence of passion.

Believe me, my daughter, as a parent's tender affectionate remonstrance has far more weight with his child than anger and sternness, so, when we judge our own heart guilty, if we treat it gently, rather in a spirit of pity than anger, encouraging it to amendment, its repentance will be much deeper and more lasting than if stirred up in vehemence and wrath.

For instance:--Let me suppose that I am specially seeking to conquer vanity, and yet that I have fallen conspicuously into that sin;--instead of taking myself to task as abominable and wretched, for breaking so many resolutions, calling myself unfit to lift up my eyes to Heaven, as disloyal, faithless, and the like, I would deal pitifully and quietly with myself. "Poor heart! so soon fallen again into the snare! Well now, rise up again bravely and fall no more. Seek God's Mercy, hope in Him, ask Him to keep you from falling again, and begin to tread the pathway of humility afresh. We must be more on our guard henceforth." Such a course will be the surest way to making a stedfast substantial resolution against the special fault, to which should be added any external means suitable, and the advice of one's director. If any one does not find this gentle dealing sufficient, let him use sterner self-rebuke and admonition, provided only, that whatever indignation he may rouse against himself, he finally works it all up to a tender loving trust in God, treading in the footsteps of that great penitent who cried out to his troubled soul: "Why art thou so vexed, O my soul, and why art thou so disquieted within me? O put thy trust in God, for I will yet thank Him, Which is the help of my countenance, and my God." [83]

So then, when you have fallen, lift up your heart in quietness, humbling yourself deeply before God by reason of your frailty, without marvelling that you fell;--there is no cause to marvel because weakness is weak, or infirmity infirm. Heartily lament that you should have offended God, and begin anew to cultivate the lacking grace, with a very deep trust in His Mercy, and with a bold, brave heart.

Footnote:

83. Ps. xlii. 11, 15.

CHAPTER X - We must attend to the Business of Life carefully, but without Eagerness or Over-anxiety

THE care and diligence due to our ordinary business are very different from solicitude, anxiety and restlessness. The Angels care for our salvation and seek it diligently, but they are wholly free from anxiety and solicitude, for, whereas care and diligence naturally appertain to their love, anxiety would be wholly inconsistent with their happiness; for although care and diligence can go hand in hand with calmness and peace, those angelic properties could not unite with solicitude or anxiety, much less with over-eagerness.

Therefore, my daughter, be careful and diligent in all your affairs; God, Who commits them to you, wills you to give them your best attention; but strive not to be anxious and solicitous, that is to say, do not set about your work with restlessness and excitement, and do not give way to bustle and eagerness in what you do;--every form of excitement affects both judgment and reason, and hinders a right performance of the very thing which excites us.

Our Lord, rebuking Martha, said, "Thou art careful and troubled about many things." [84] If she had been simply careful, she would not have been troubled, but giving way to disquiet and anxiety, she grew eager and troubled, and for that our Lord reproved her. The rivers which flow gently through our plains bear barges of rich merchandise, and the gracious rains which fall softly on the land fertilise it to bear the fruits of the earth;--but when the rivers swell into torrents, they hinder commerce and devastate the country, and violent storms and tempests do the like. No work done with impetuosity and excitement was ever well done, and the old proverb, "Make haste slowly," is a good one, [85] Solomon says, "There is one that laboureth and taketh pains, and maketh haste, and is so much the more behind;"[86] we are always soon enough when we do well. The bumble bee makes far more noise and is more bustling than the honey bee, but it makes nought save wax--no honey; just so those who are restless and eager, or full of noisy solicitude, never do much or well. Flies harass us less by what they do than by reason of their multitude, and so great matters give us less disturbance than a multitude of small affairs. Accept the duties which come upon you quietly, and try to fulfil them methodically, one after another. If you attempt to do everything at once, or with confusion, you will only cumber yourself with your own exertions, and by dint of perplexing your mind you will probably be overwhelmed and accomplish nothing.

In all your affairs lean solely on God's Providence, by means of which alone your plans can succeed. Meanwhile, on your part work on in quiet co-operation with Him, and then rest satisfied that if you have trusted entirely to Him you will always obtain such a measure of success as is most profitable for you, whether it seems so or not to your own individual judgment.

Imitate a little child, whom one sees holding tight with one hand to its father, while with the other it gathers strawberries or blackberries from the wayside hedge. Even so, while you gather and use this world's goods with one hand, always let the other be fast in your Heavenly Father's Hand, and look round from time to time to make sure that He is satisfied with what you are doing, at home or abroad. Beware of letting go, under the idea of making or receiving more--if He forsakes you, you will fall to the ground at the first step. When your ordinary work or business is not specially engrossing, let your heart be fixed more on God than on it; and if the work be such as to require your undivided attention, then pause from time to time and look to God, even as navigators who make for the haven they would attain, by looking up at the heavens rather than down upon the deeps on which they sail. So doing, God will work with you, in you, and for you, and your work will be blessed.

Footnote:

84. S. Luke x. 41.
85. "Festina lente." "Il faut depescher tout bellement."
86. Ecclus. xi. 11.

CHAPTER XI - On Obedience

LOVE alone leads to perfection, but the three chief means for acquiring it are obedience, chastity, and poverty. Obedience is a consecration of the heart, chastity of the body, and poverty of all worldly goods to the Love and Service of God. These are the three members of the Spiritual Cross, and all three must be raised upon the fourth, which is humility. I am not going here to speak of these three virtues as solemn vows, which only concern religious, nor even as ordinary vows, although when sought under the shelter of a vow all virtues receive an enhanced grace and merit; but it is not necessary for perfection that they should be undertaken as vows, so long as they are practised diligently. The three vows solemnly taken put a man into the state of perfection, whereas a diligent observance thereof brings him to perfection. For, observe, there is a great difference between the state of perfection and perfection itself, inasmuch as all prelates and religious are in the former, although unfortunately it is too obvious that by no means all attain to the latter. Let us then endeavour to practise these three virtues, according to our several vocations, for although we are not thereby called to a state of perfection, we may attain through them to perfection itself, and of a truth we are all bound to practise them, although not all after the same manner.

There are two kinds of obedience, one necessary, the other voluntary. The first includes a humble obedience to your ecclesiastical superiors, whether Pope, Bishop, Curate, or those commissioned by them. You are likewise bound to obey your civil superiors, king and magistrates; as also your domestic superiors, father, mother, master or mistress. Such obedience is called necessary, because no one can free himself from the duty of obeying these superiors, God having appointed them severally to bear rule over us. Therefore do you obey their commands as of right, but if you would be perfect, follow their counsels, and even their wishes as far as charity and prudence will allow: obey as to things acceptable; as when they bid you eat, or take recreation, for although there may be no great virtue in obedience in such a case, there is great harm in disobedience. Obey in things indifferent, as concerning questions of dress, coming and going, singing or keeping silence, for herein is a very laudable obedience. Obey in things hard, disagreeable and inconvenient, and therein lies a very perfect obedience. Moreover, obey quietly, without answering again, promptly, without delay, cheerfully, without reluctance; and, above all, render a loving obedience for His Sake Who became obedient even to the death of the Cross for our sake; Who, as Saint Bernard says, chose rather to resign His Life than His Obedience.

If you would acquire a ready obedience to superiors, accustom yourself to yield to your equals, giving way to their opinions where nothing wrong is involved, without arguing or peevishness; and adapt yourself easily to the wishes of your inferiors as far as you reasonably can, and forbear the exercise of stern authority so long as they do well.

It is a mistake for those who find it hard to pay a willing obedience to their natural superiors to suppose that if they were professed religious they would find it easy to obey.

Voluntary obedience is such as we undertake by our own choice, and which is not imposed by others. Persons do not choose their own King or Bishop, or parents--often not even their husband; but most people choose their confessor or director. And whether a person takes a vow of obedience to him (as Saint Theresa, beyond her formal vow to the Superior of her Order, bound herself by a simple vow to obey Father Gratian), or without any vow they resolve to obey their chosen spiritual guide, all such obedience is voluntary, because it depends upon our own will.

Obedience to lawful superiors is regulated by their official claims. Thus, in all public and legal matters, we are bound to obey our King; in ecclesiastical matters, our Bishop; in domestic matters, our father, master or husband; and in personal matters which concern the soul, our confessor or spiritual guide.

Seek to be directed in your religious exercises by your spiritual father, because thereby they will have double grace and virtue;--that which is inherent in that they are devout, and that which comes by reason of the spirit of obedience in which they are performed. Blessed indeed are the obedient, for God will never permit them to go astray.

CHAPTER XII - On Purity

PURITY is the lily among virtues--by it men approach to the Angels. There is no beauty without purity, and human purity is chastity. We speak of the chaste as honest, and of the loss of purity as dishonour; purity is an intact thing, its converse is corruption. In a word, its special glory is in the spotless whiteness of soul and body.

No unlawful pleasures are compatible with chastity; the pure heart is like the mother of pearl which admits no drop of water save that which comes from Heaven,--it is closed to every attraction save such as are sanctified by holy matrimony. Close your heart to every questionable tenderness or delight, guard against all that is unprofitable though it may be lawful, and strive to avoid unduly fixing your heart even on that which in itself is right and good.

Every one has great need of this virtue: those living in widowhood need a brave chastity not only to forego present and future delights, but to resist the memories of the past, with which a happy married life naturally fills the imagination, softening and weakening the will. Saint Augustine lauds the purity of his beloved Alipius, who had altogether forgotten and despised the carnal pleasures in which his youth was passed. While fruits are whole, you may store them up securely, some in straw, some in sand or amid their own foliage, but once bruised there is no means of preserving them save with sugar or honey. Even so the purity which has never been tampered with may well be preserved to the end, but when once that has ceased to exist nothing can ensure its existence but the genuine devotion, which, as I have often said, is the very honey and sugar of the mind.

The unmarried need a very simple sensitive purity, which will drive away all over-curious thoughts, and teach them to despise all merely sensual satisfactions. The young are apt to imagine that of which they are ignorant to be wondrous sweet, and as the foolish moth hovers around a light, and, persisting in coming too near, perishes in its inquisitive folly, so they perish through their unwise approach to forbidden pleasures. And married people need a watchful purity whereby to keep God ever before them, and to seek all earthly happiness and delight through Him Alone, ever remembering that He has sanctified the state of holy matrimony by making it the type of His own union with the Church.

The Apostle says, "Follow peace with all men, and holiness, without which no man shall see the Lord:" [87] by which holiness he means purity. Of a truth, my daughter, without purity no one can ever see God; [88] nor can any hope to dwell in His tabernacle except he lead an uncorrupt life; [89] and our Blessed Lord Himself has promised the special blessing of beholding Him to those that are pure in heart.

Footnotes:

87. Heb. xii. 14.
88. S. Matt. v. 8.
89. Ps. xv. 2.

CHAPTER XIII - How to maintain Purity

BE exceedingly quick in turning aside from the slightest thing leading to impurity, for it is an evil which approaches stealthily, and in which the very smallest beginnings are apt to grow rapidly. It is always easier to fly from such evils than to cure them.

Human bodies are like glasses, which cannot come into collision without risk of breaking; or to fruits, which, however fresh and ripe, are damaged by pressure. Never permit any one to take any manner of foolish liberty with you, since, although there may be no evil intention, the perfectness of purity is injured thereby.

Purity has its source in the heart, but it is in the body that its material results take shape, and therefore it may be forfeited both by the exterior senses and by the thoughts and desires of the heart. All lack of modesty in seeing, hearing, speaking, smelling, or touching, is impurity, especially when the heart takes pleasure therein. S. Paul says without any hesitation that impurity and uncleanness, or foolish and unseemly talking, are not to be "so much as named" [90] among Christians. The bee not only shuns all carrion, but abhors and flies far from the faintest smell proceeding therefrom. The Bride of the Canticles is represented with "hands dropping with myrrh." [91] a preservative against all corruption; her "lips are like a thread of scarlet," the type of modest words; [92] her eyes are "dove's eyes," [93] clear and soft; her "nose is as the tower of Lebanon which looketh towards Damascus" [94] an incorruptible wood; her ears are hung with earrings of pure gold; [95] and even so the devout soul should be pure, honest and transparent in hand, lip, eye, ear, and the whole body.

Remember that there are things which blemish perfect purity, without being in themselves downright acts of impurity. Anything which tends to lessen its intense sensitiveness, or to cast the slightest shadow over it, is of this nature; and all evil thoughts or foolish acts of levity or heedlessness are as steps towards the most direct breaches of the law of chastity. Avoid the society of persons who are wanting in purity, especially if they are bold, as indeed impure people always are. If a foul animal licks the sweet almond tree its fruit becomes bitter; and so a corrupt pestilential man can scarcely hold communication with others, whether men or women, without damaging their perfect purity--their very glance is venomous, and their breath blighting like the basilisk. On the other hand, seek out good and pure men, read and ponder holy things; for the Word of God is pure, and it will make those pure who study it: wherefore David likens it to gold and precious stones. [96] Always abide close to Jesus Christ Crucified, both spiritually in meditation and actually in Holy Communion; for as all those who sleep upon the plant called Agnus castus become pure and chaste, so, if you rest your heart upon Our Dear Lord, the Very Lamb, Pure and Immaculate, you will find that soon both heart and soul will be purified of all spot or stain.

Footnotes:

90. Eph. v. 4.
91. Cant. v. 5.
92. iv. 3.
93. i. 15.
94. vii. 4.
95. There is no mention of earrings in the Canticles, but S. Francis probably was writing from memory, and had in mind "Thy cheeks are comely with rows of jewels, thy neck with chains of gold." (i. 10.)
96. Ps. cxix. 127.

CHAPTER XIV - On Poverty of Spirit amid Riches

"BLESSED are the poor in spirit, for theirs is the Kingdom of God;" [97] and if so, woe be to the rich in spirit, for theirs must be the bitterness of hell. By rich in spirit I mean him whose riches engross his mind, or whose mind is buried in his riches. He is poor in spirit whose heart is not filled with the love of riches, whose mind is not set upon them. The halcyon builds its nest like a ball, and leaving but one little aperture in the upper part, launches it on the sea, so secure and impenetrable, that the waves carry it along without any water getting in, and it floats on the sea, superior, so to say, to the waves. And this, my child, is what your heart should be--open only to heaven, impenetrable to riches and earthly treasures. If you have them, keep your heart from attaching itself to them; let it maintain a higher level, and amidst riches be as though you had none,--superior to them. Do not let that mind which is the likeness of God cleave to mere earthly goods; let it always be raised above them, not sunk in them.

There is a wide difference between having poison and being poisoned. All apothecaries have poisons ready for special uses, but they are not consequently poisoned, because the poison is only in their shop, not in themselves; and so you may possess riches without being poisoned by them, so long as they are in your house or purse only, and not in your heart. It is the Christian's privilege to be rich in material things, and poor in attachment to them, thereby having the use of riches in this world and the merit of poverty in the next.

Of a truth, my daughter, no one will ever own themselves to be avaricious;--every one denies this contemptible vice:--men excuse themselves on the plea of providing for their children, or plead the duty of prudent forethought:--they never have too much, there is always some good reason for accumulating more; and even the most avaricious of men not only do not own to being such, but sincerely believe that they are not; and that because avarice is as a strong fever which is all the less felt as it rages most fiercely. Moses saw that sacred fire which burnt the bush without consuming it, [98] but the profane fire of avarice acts precisely the other way,--it consumes the miser, but without burning, for, amid its most intense heat, he believes himself to be deliciously cool, and imagines his insatiable thirst to be merely natural and right.

If you long earnestly, anxiously, and persistently after what you do not possess, it is all very well to say that you do not wish to get it unfairly, but you are all the time guilty of avarice. He who longs eagerly and anxiously to drink, though it may be water only, thereby indicates that he is feverish. I hardly think we can say that it is lawful to wish lawfully to possess that which is another's:--so doing we surely wish our own gain at the expense of that other? and he who possesses anything lawfully, surely has more right to possess it, than we to obtain it? Why should we desire that which is his? Even were the wish lawful, it is not charitable, for we should not like other men to desire what we possess, however lawfully. This was Ahab's sin when he sought to acquire Naboth's vineyard by lawful purchase, when Naboth lawfully desired to keep it himself;--he coveted it eagerly, continually, and anxiously, and so doing he displeased God. [99]

Do not allow yourself to wish for that which is your neighbour's until he wishes to part with it,-- then his wish will altogether justify yours,--and I am quite willing that you should add to your means and possessions, provided it be not merely with strict justice, but kindly and charitably done. If you cleave closely to your possessions, and are cumbered with them, setting your heart and thoughts upon them, and restlessly anxious lest you should suffer loss, then, believe me, you are still somewhat feverish;--for fever patients drink the water we give them with an eagerness and satisfaction not common to those who are well.

It is not possible to take great pleasure in anything without becoming attached to it. If you lose property, and find yourself grievously afflicted at the loss, you may be sure that you were warmly attached to it;--there is no surer proof of affection for the thing lost than our sorrow at its loss.

Therefore, do not fix your longings on anything which you do not possess; do not let your heart rest in that which you have; do not grieve overmuch at the losses which may happen to you;--and then you may reasonably believe that although rich in fact, you are not so in affection, but that you are poor in spirit, and therefore blessed, for the Kingdom of Heaven is yours.

Footnotes:

97. S. Matt. v. 3.
98. Exod. iii. 2.
99. I Kings xxi.

CHAPTER XV - How to exercise real Poverty, although actually Rich

THE painter Parrhasius drew an ingenious and imaginative representation of the Athenians, ascribing sundry opposite qualities to them, calling them at once capricious, irascible, unjust, inconstant, courteous, merciful, compassionate, haughty, vain-glorious, humble, boastful, and cowardly;--and for my part, dear daughter, I would fain see united in your heart both riches and poverty, a great care and a great contempt for temporal things.

Do you take much greater pains than is the wont of worldly men to make your riches useful and fruitful? Are not the gardeners of a prince more diligent in cultivating and beautifying the royal gardens than if they were their own? Wherefore? Surely because these gardens are the king's, to whom his gardeners would fain render an acceptable service. My child, our possessions are not ours,--God has given them to us to cultivate, that we may make them fruitful and profitable in His Service, and so doing we shall please Him. And this we must do more earnestly than worldly men, for they look carefully after their property out of self-love, and we must work for the love of God. Now self-love is a restless, anxious, over-eager love, and so the work done on its behalf is troubled, vexatious, and unsatisfactory;--whereas the love of God is calm, peaceful, and tranquil, and so the work done for its sake, even in worldly things, is gentle, trustful, and quiet. Let us take such a quiet care to preserve, and even when practicable to increase, our temporal goods, according to the duties of our position,--this is acceptable to God for His Love's Sake.

But beware that you be not deceived by self-love, for sometimes it counterfeits the Love of God so cleverly that you may mistake one for the other. To avoid this, and to prevent a due care for your temporal interests from degenerating into avarice, it is needful often to practise a real poverty amid the riches with which God has endowed you.

To this end always dispose of a part of your means by giving them heartily to the poor; you impoverish yourself by whatever you give away. It is true that God will restore it to you, not only in the next world, but in this, for nothing brings so much temporal prosperity as free almsgiving, but meanwhile, you are sensibly poorer for what you give. Truly that is a holy and rich poverty which results from almsgiving.

Love the poor and poverty,--this love will make you truly poor, since, as Holy Scripture says, we become like to that we love. [100] Love makes lovers equal. "Who is weak and I am not weak?" [101] says St. Paul? He might have said, Who is poor and I am not poor? for it was love which made him like to those he loved; and so, if you love the poor, you will indeed share their poverty, and be poor like them.

And if you love the poor, seek them out, take pleasure in bringing them to your home, and in going to theirs, talk freely with them, and be ready to meet them, whether in Church or elsewhere. Let your tongue be poor with them in converse, but let your hands be rich to distribute out of your abundance. Are you prepared to go yet further, my child? not to stop at being poor like the poor, but even poorer still? The servant is not so great as his lord; do you be the servant of the poor, tend their sickbed with your own hands, be their cook, their needlewoman. O my daughter, such servitude is more glorious than royalty! How touchingly S. Louis, one of the greatest of kings, fulfilled this duty; serving the poor in their own houses, and daily causing three to eat at his own table, often himself eating the remains of their food in his loving humility. In his frequent visits to the hospitals he would select those afflicted with the most loathsome diseases, ulcers, cancer, and the like; and these he would tend, kneeling down and bare-headed, beholding the Saviour of the world in them, and cherishing them with all the tenderness of a mother's love. Saint Elizabeth of Hungary used to mix freely with the poor, and liked to dress in their homely garments amid her gay ladies. Surely these royal personages were poor amid their riches and rich in poverty.

Blessed are the poor in spirit, for theirs is the Kingdom of Heaven. In the Day of Judgment the King of prince and peasant will say to them, "I was an hungred, and ye gave Me meat, I was naked, and ye clothed Me; come, inherit the Kingdom prepared for you from the foundation of the world." [102]

Everybody finds themselves sometimes deficient in what they need, and put to inconvenience. A guest whom we would fain receive honorably arrives, and we cannot entertain him as we would; we want our costly apparel in one place, and it all happens to be somewhere else: all the wine in our cellar suddenly turns sour: we find ourselves accidentally in some country place where everything is wanting, room, bed, food, attendance: in short, the richest people may easily be without something they want, and that is practically to suffer poverty. Accept such occurrences cheerfully, rejoice in them, bear them willingly.

Again, if you are impoverished much or little by unforeseen events, such as storm, flood, fire, drought, theft, or lawsuit; then is the real time to practise poverty, accepting the loss quietly, and adapting yourself patiently to your altered circumstances. Esau and Jacob both came to their father with hairy hands, [103] but the hair on Jacob's hands did not grow from his skin, and could be torn off without pain; while that on Esau's hands being the natural growth of his skin, he would have cried out and resisted if any one had torn it off. So if our possessions are very close to our heart, and storm or thief tear them away, we shall break forth in impatient murmurs and lamentations. But if we only cleave to them with that solicitude which God wills us to have, and not with our whole heart, we shall see them rent away without losing our sense of calmness. This is just the difference between the clothing of men and beasts; the beast's clothing grows on its flesh, and man's is only laid on so that it may be laid aside at will.

Footnotes:

100. "Their abominations were according as they loved." Hosea ix. 10.
101. 2 Cor. xi. 29.
102. S. Matt. xxv. 34-36.
103. Gen. xxvii.

CHAPTER XVI - How to possess a rich Spirit amid real Poverty

BUT if you are really poor, my daughter, for God's Sake be so in spirit; make a virtue of necessity, and turn that precious stone poverty to its true value. The brilliancy thereof is not perceived in this world, but nevertheless it is very great.

Patience then! you are in good company. Our Dear Lord, Our Lady, the Apostles, numberless Saints, both men and women, were poor, and although they might have been rich, disdained to be so. How many great ones of this world have gone through many difficulties to seek holy poverty amid hospitals and cloisters! What pains they took to find it, let S. Alexis, S. Paula, S. Paulinus, S. Angela, and many another witness; whereas to you, my child, it has come unasked--you have met poverty without seeking it--do you then embrace it as the beloved friend of Jesus Christ, Who was born, lived and died in poverty, and cherished it all His Life.

There are two great privileges connected with your poverty, through which you may acquire great merit. First, it is not your own choice, but God's Will alone, which has made you poor. Now, whatever we accept simply because it is God's Will is acceptable in His Sight, so long as we accept it heartily and out of love:--the less of self the more of God,--and a singlehearted acceptance of God's Will purifies any suffering very greatly.

The second privilege is, that this poverty is so very poor. There is a be-praised, caressed poverty, so petted and cared for, that it can hardly be called poor like the despised, contemned, neglected poverty which also exists. Now, most secular poverty is of this last kind, for those who are involuntarily poor, and cannot help themselves, are not much thought of, and for that very reason their poverty is poorer than that of religious, although religious poverty has a very special and excellent grace, through the intention and the vow by which it is accepted.

Do not complain then of your poverty, my daughter,--we only complain of that which is unwelcome, and if poverty is unwelcome to you, you are no longer poor in spirit. Do not fret under such assistance as is needful; therein lies one great grace of poverty. It were overambitious to aim at being poor without suffering any inconvenience, in other words, to have the credit of poverty and the convenience of riches.

Do not be ashamed of being poor, or of asking alms. Receive what is given you with humility, and accept a refusal meekly. Frequently call to mind Our Lady's journey into Egypt with her Holy Child, and of all the poverty, contempt and suffering they endured. If you follow their example you will indeed be rich amid your poverty.

CHAPTER XVII - On Friendship: Evil and Frivolous Friendship

FOREMOST among the soul's affections is love. Love is the ruler of every motion of the heart; drawing all to itself, and making us like to that we love. Beware, then, my daughter, of harbouring any evil affection, or you too will become evil. And friendship is the most dangerous of all affections, because any other love may exist without much mental communication, but as friendship is founded thereon, it is hardly possible to be closely bound by its ties to any one without sharing in his qualities.

All love is not friendship, for one may love without any return, and friendship implies mutual love. Further, those who are bound by such affection must be conscious that it is reciprocal,--otherwise there may be love but not friendship; and moreover, there must be something communicated between the friends as a solid foundation of friendship.

Friendship varies according to these communications, and they vary according to that which people have to communicate. If men share false and vain things, their friendship will be false and vain; if that which is good and true, their friendship will be good and true, and the better that which is the staple of the bond, so much the better will the friendship be. That honey is best which is culled from the choicest flowers, and so friendship built upon the highest and purest intercommunion is the best. And just as a certain kind of honey brought from Pontus is poisonous, being made from aconite, so that those who eat it lose their senses, so the friendship which is based on unreal or evil grounds will itself be hollow and worthless.

Mere sensual intercourse is not worthy of the name of friendship; and were there nothing more in married love it would not deserve to bear the name; but inasmuch as that involves the participation of life, industry, possessions, affections, and an unalterable fidelity, marriage, when rightly understood, is a very real and holy friendship.

Whatever is founded on mere sensuality, vanity, or frivolity, is unworthy to be called friendship. I mean such attractions as are purely external; a sweet voice, personal beauty, and the cleverness or outward show which have great weight with some. You will often hear women and young people unhesitatingly decide that such an one is very delightful, very admirable, because he is good-looking, well-dressed, sings, or dances, or talks well. Even charlatans esteem the wittiest clown amongst them as their best man. But all these things are purely sensual, and the connections built on such foundation must be vain and frivolous, more fitly to be called trifling than friendship. They spring up chiefly among young people, who are easily fascinated by personal attractions, dress, and gossip--friendships in which the tailor and hairdresser have the chief part. How can such friendships be other than shortlived, melting away like snow wreaths in the sun!

CHAPTER XVIII - On Frivolous Attachments

SUCH foolish attachments between man and woman without any matrimonial intentions as are called amourettes,--mere abortions, or rather phantoms of friendship,--must not, idle and empty as they are, profane the name of friendship or love. Yet such frivolous, contemptible attractions often snare the hearts of both men and women, and although they may end in downright sin, there is no such intention on the part of their victims, who consciously do but yield to foolish trifling and toying. Some such have no object beyond the actual indulgence of a passing inclination; others are excited by vanity, which takes pleasure in captivating hearts; some are stimulated by a combination of both these motives. But all such friendships are evil, hollow, and vain; evil, in that they often lead to sinful deeds, and draw the heart from God, and from the husband or wife who is its lawful owner; hollow, in that they are baseless and without root; vain, in that neither gain, honour, nor satisfaction can come from such. On the contrary, nothing comes of them but a loss of time and credit, and unreasoning excitement, mistrust, jealousy, and perturbation.

S. Gregory Nazianzen speaks very wisely on this subject, admonishing vain women, and his words are equally applicable to men:--"Your natural beauty will suffice your husband, but if it is exhibited to all, like a net spread before birds, what will be the end? You will be taken by whoever admires you, looks and glances will be exchanged, smiles and tender words, at first hesitatingly exchanged, but soon more boldly given and received. Far be it from me to describe the end, but this much I will say, nothing said or done by young men and women under such circumstances but is perilous. One act of levity leads to another, as the links in a chain." They who tamper with such things will fall into the trap. They fancy that they only mean to amuse themselves, but will not go too far. Little you know, forsooth! The tiny spark will burst into a flame, and, overpowering your heart, it will reduce your good resolutions to ashes, and your reputation to smoke. "Who will pity a charmer that is bitten with a serpent?" asks the Wise Man; [104] and with him I ask, Do you, in your folly, imagine that you can lightly handle love as you please? You think to trifle with it, but it will sting you cruelly, and then every one will mock you, and laugh at your foolish pretension to harbour a venomous serpent in your bosom, which has poisoned and lost alike your honour and your soul. What fatal blindness this to stake all that is most precious to man! Yes, I say it advisedly, for God desires to have us only for the sake of our soul, or the soul through our will, and our will for love's sake. Surely we have not by any means a sufficient store of love to offer God, and yet in our madness and folly we lavish and waste it on vain frivolous objects, as though we had enough and to spare. Our Dear Lord, Who demands nought save our love in return for our creation, preservation and redemption, will require a strict account of the senseless way in which we have frittered and wasted it. If He will call us to account for idle words, how will it be with respect to idle, foolish, pernicious friendships? Husbandmen know that the walnut tree is very harmful in a vineyard or field, because it absorbs the fatness of the land and draws it away from the other crops; its thick foliage overshadows and deprives them of sunshine; and, moreover, it attracts passers-by, who tread down and spoil all that is around while striving to gather its fruit. So with these foolish love affairs and the soul; they engross it, so that it is unable to bring forth good works; their superfluous foliage--flirtations, dallyings and idle talk--consume profitable time; and, moreover, they lead to so many temptations, distractions, suspicions, and the like, that the heart becomes altogether crushed and spoiled. Such follies not only banish Heavenly Love, they likewise drive out the fear of God, enervate the mind, and damage reputation. They may be the plaything of courts, but assuredly they are as a plague spot of the heart.[105]

Footnotes:

104. Ecclus. xii. 13.
105. "C'est en un mot le jouet des cours, mais la peste des coeurs."

CHAPTER XIX - Of Real Friendship

DO you, my child, love every one with the pure love of charity, but have no friendship save with those whose intercourse is good and true, and the purer the bond which unites you so much higher will your friendship be. If your intercourse is based on science it is praiseworthy, still more if it arises from a participation in goodness, prudence, justice and the like; but if the bond of your mutual liking be charity, devotion and Christian perfection, God knows how very precious a friendship it is! Precious because it comes from God, because it tends to God, because God is the link that binds you, because it will last for ever in Him. Truly it is a blessed thing to love on earth as we hope to love in Heaven, and to begin that friendship here which is to endure for ever there. I am not now speaking of simple charity, a love due to all mankind, but of that spiritual friendship which binds souls together, leading them to share devotions and spiritual interests, so as to have but one mind between them. Such as these may well cry out, "Behold, how good and joyful a thing it is, brethren, to dwell together in unity!" [106] Even so, for the "precious ointment" of devotion trickles continually from one heart to the other, so that truly we may say that to such friendship the Lord promises His Blessing and life for evermore. To my mind all other friendship is but as a shadow with respect to this, its links mere fragile glass compared to the golden bond of true devotion. Do you form no other friendships. I say "form," because you have no right to cast aside or neglect the natural bonds which draw you to relations, connexions, benefactors or neighbours. My rules apply to those you deliberately choose to make. There are some who will tell you that you should avoid all special affection or friendship, as likely to engross the heart, distract the mind, excite jealousy, and what not. But they are confusing things. They have read in the works of saintly and devout writers that individual friendships and special intimacies are a great hindrance in the religious life, and therefore they suppose it to be the same with all the world, which is not at all the case. Whereas in a well-regulated community every one's aim is true devotion, there is no need for individual intercourse, which might exceed due limits;--in the world those who aim at a devout life require to be united one with another by a holy friendship, which excites, stimulates and encourages them in well-doing. Just as men traversing a plain have no need to hold one another up, as they have who are amid slippery mountain paths, so religious do not need the stay of individual friendships; but those who are living in the world require such for strength and comfort amid the difficulties which beset them. In the world all have not one aim, one mind, and therefore we must take to us congenial friends, nor is there any undue partiality in such attachments, which are but as the separation of good from evil, the sheep from the goats, the bee from the drone--a necessary separation.

No one can deny that our Dear Lord loved S. John, Lazarus, Martha, Magdalene, with a specially tender friendship, since we are told so in Holy Scripture; and we know that S. Paul dearly loved S. Mark, S. Petronilla, as S. Paul Timothy and Thecla. [107] S. Gregory Nazianzen boasts continually of his friendship with the great S. Basil, of which he says: "It seemed as though with two bodies we had but one soul, and if we may not believe those who say that all things are in all else, at least one must affirm that we were two in one, and one in two --the only object that both had being to grow in holiness, and to mould our present life to our future hopes, thereby forsaking this mortal world before our death." And S. Augustine says that S. Ambrose loved S. Monica by reason of her many virtues, and that she in return loved him as an Angel of God.

What need to affirm so unquestionable a fact! S. Jerome, S. Augustine, S. Gregory, S. Bernard, and all the most notable servants of God, have had special friendships, which in nowise hindered their perfection. S. Paul, in describing evil men, says that they were "without natural affection," [108] i.e. without friendship. And S. Thomas, in common with other philosophers, acknowledges that friendship is a virtue, and he certainly means individual friendships, because he says that we cannot bestow perfect friendship on many persons. So we see that the highest grace does not lie in being without friendships, but in having none which are not good, holy and true.

Footnotes:

106. Ps. cxxxiii. 1.
107. S. Thecla (V.M.) was a native of Lycaonia, converted (so say S. Augustine, S. Ambrose, S. Epiphanius, and others of the Fathers) by S. Paul, who kindled so strong a love of virginity in her heart that she broke off her intended marriage, and devoted herself to Christ. She is said to have followed S. Paul in several of his journeys, and a very ancient Martyrology, which bears the name of S. Jerome,

published by Florentinus, says that she was miraculously delivered unhurt from the persecutors' flames at Rome. It seems doubtful whether she died a natural or a martyr's death. The first Christian Emperors built a great Church at Seleucia, where she died.

108. Rom. i. 31.

CHAPTER XX - Of the Difference between True and False Friendship

TAKE notice, my child, that the honey of Heraclyum, which is so poisonous, altogether resembles that which is wholesome, and there is great danger of mistaking one for the other, or of mixing them, for the virtue of one would not counteract the harmfulness of the other. We must be on our guard not to be deceived in making friendships, especially between persons of the opposite sexes, for not unfrequently Satan deludes those who love one another. They may begin with a virtuous affection, but if discretion be lacking, frivolity will creep in, and then sensuality, till their love becomes carnal: even in spiritual love there is a danger if people are not on the watch, although it is not so easy to be deluded therein, inasmuch as the very purity and transparency of spiritual affection show Satan's stains more promptly. Consequently, when he seeks to interpose, he does it stealthily, and strives to insinuate impurity almost imperceptibly.

You may distinguish between worldly friendship and that which is good and holy, just as one distinguishes that poisonous honey from what is good--it is sweeter to the taste than ordinary honey, owing to the aconite infused;--and so worldly friendship is profuse in honeyed words, passionate endearments, commendations of beauty and sensual charms, while true friendship speaks a simple honest language, lauding nought save the Grace of God, its one only foundation. That strange honey causes giddiness; and so false friendship upsets the mind, makes its victim to totter in the ways of purity and devotion, inducing affected, mincing looks, sensual caresses, inordinate sighings, petty complaints of not being loved, slight but questionable familiarities, gallantries, embraces, and the like, which are sure precursors of evil; whereas true friendship is modest and straightforward in every glance, loving and pure in caresses, has no sighs save for Heaven, no complaints save that God is not loved sufficiently. That honey confuses the sight, and worldly friendship confuses the judgment, so that men think themselves right while doing evil, and assume their excuses and pretexts to be valid reasoning. They fear the light and love darkness; but true friendship is clear-sighted, and hides nothing--rather seeks to be seen of good men. Lastly, this poisonous honey leaves an exceeding bitter taste behind; and so false friendship turns to evil desires, upbraidings, slander, deceit, sorrow, confusion and jealousies, too often ending in downright sin; but pure friendship is always the same--modest, courteous and loving--knowing no change save an increasingly pure and perfect union, a type of the blessed friendships of Heaven.

When young people indulge in looks, words or actions which they would not like to be seen by their parents, husbands or confessors, it is a sure sign that they are damaging their conscience and their honour. Our Lady was troubled [109] when the Angel appeared to her in human form, because she was alone, and he spoke to her with flattering although heavenly words. O Saviour of the world, if purity itself fears an Angel in human shape, how much more need that our impurity should fear men, although they take the likeness of an Angel, if they speak words of earthliness and sensuality!

Footnote:

109. S. Luke i. 29.

CHAPTER XXI - Remedies against Evil Friendships

HOW are you to meet the swarm of foolish attachments, triflings, and undesirable inclinations which beset you? By turning sharply away, and thoroughly renouncing such vanities, flying to the Saviour's Cross, and clasping His Crown of thorns to your heart, so that these little foxes may not spoil your vines. [110] Beware of entering into any manner of treaty with the Enemy; do not delude yourself by listening to him while intending to reject him. For God's Sake, my daughter, be firm on all such occasions; the heart and ear are closely allied, and just as you would vainly seek to check the downward course of a mountain torrent, so difficult will you find it to keep the smooth words which enter in at the ear from finding their way down into the heart. Alcmeon says (what indeed Aristotle denies) that the goat breathes through its ears, not its nostrils. I know not whether this be so, but one thing I know, that our heart breathes through the ear, and that while it exhales its own thoughts through the mouth, it inhales those of others by the ear. Let us then carefully guard our ears against evil words which would speedily infect the heart. Never hearken to any indiscreet conversation whatsoever--never mind if you seem rude and uncourteous in rejecting all such. Always bear in mind that you have dedicated your heart to God, and offered your love to Him; so that it were sacrilege to deprive Him of one particle thereof. Do you rather renew the offering continually by fresh resolutions, entrenching yourself therein as in a fortress;--cry out to God, He will succour you, and His Love will shelter you, so that all your love may be kept for Him only.

If unhappily you are already entangled in the nets of any unreal affection, truly it is hard to set you free! But place yourself before His Divine Majesty, acknowledge the depth of your wretchedness, your weakness and vanity, and then with all the earnestness of purpose you can muster, arrest the budding evil, abjure your own empty promises, and renounce those you have received, and resolve with a firm, absolute will never again to indulge in any trifling or dallying with such matters.

If you can remove from the object of your unworthy affection, it is most desirable to do so. He who has been bitten by a viper cannot heal his wound in the presence of another suffering from the like injury, and so one bitten with a false fancy will not shake it off while near to his fellow-victim. Change of scene is very helpful in quieting the excitement and restlessness of sorrow or love. S. Ambrose tells a story in his Second Book on Penitence, of a young man, who coming home after a long journey quite cured of a foolish attachment, met the unworthy object of his former passion, who stopped him, saying, "Do you not know me, I am still myself?" "That may be," was the answer, "but I am not myself:"--so thoroughly and happily was he changed by absence. And S. Augustine tells us how, after the death of his dear friend, he soothed his grief by leaving Tagaste and going to Carthage.

But what is he to do, who cannot try this remedy? To such I would say, abstain from all private intercourse, all tender glances and smiles, and from every kind of communication which can feed the unholy flame. If it be necessary to speak at all, express clearly and tersely the eternal renunciation on which you have resolved. I say unhesitatingly to whosoever has become entangled in any such worthless love affairs, Cut it short, break it off--do not play with it, or pretend to untie the knot; cut it through, tear it asunder. There must be no dallying with an attachment which is incompatible with the Love of God.

But, you ask, after I have thus burst the chains of my unholy bondage, will no traces remain, and shall I not still carry the scars on my feet--that is, in my wounded affections? Not so, my child, if you have attained a due abhorrence of the evil; in that case all you will feel is an exceeding horror of your unworthy affection, and all appertaining thereto; no thought will linger in your breast concerning it save a true love of God. Or if, by reason of the imperfection of your repentance, any evil inclinations still hover round you, seek such a mental solitude as I have already described, retire into it as much as possible, and then by repeated efforts and ejaculations renounce your evil desires; abjure them heartily; read pious books more than is your wont; go more frequently to Confession and Communion; tell your director simply and humbly all that tempts and troubles you, if you can, or at all events take counsel with some faithful, wise friend. And never doubt but that God will set you free from all evil passions, if you are stedfast and devout on your part. Perhaps you will say that it is unkind, ungrateful, thus pitilessly to break off a friendship. Surely it were a happy unkindness which is acceptable to God; but of a truth, my child, you are committing no unkindness, rather conferring a great benefit on the person you love, for you break his chains as well as your own, and although at the moment he may not appreciate his gain, he will do so by and by, and will join you in thanksgiving, "Thou, Lord, hast broken my bonds in sunder. I will offer to Thee the sacrifice of thanksgiving, and will call upon the Name of the Lord."[111]

Footnotes:

110. Cant. ii. 15.
111. Ps. cxvi. 14, 15.

CHAPTER XXII - Further Advice concerning Intimacies

FRIENDSHIP demands very close correspondence between those who love one another, otherwise it can never take root or continue. And together with the interchange of friendship, other things imperceptibly glide in, and a mutual giving and receiving of emotions and inclinations takes place; especially when we esteem the object of our love very highly, because then we so entirely open our heart to him, that his influence rules us altogether, whether for good or evil. The bees which make that oriental honey of which I spoke, seek to gather nought save honey, but with it they suck up the poisonous juices of the aconite on which they light. So here, my child, we must bear in mind what our Saviour said about putting out our money to the exchangers; [112] we must seek to make a good exchange, not receiving bad money and good alike, and learning to distinguish that which is valuable from what is worthless, since scarcely any one is free from some imperfection, nor is there any reason why we should adopt all our friend's faults as well as his friendship. Of course we should love him notwithstanding his faults, but without loving those faults; true friendship implies an interchange of what is good, not what is evil. As men who drag the river Tagus sift the gold from its sands and throw the latter back upon the shore, so true friends should sift the sand of imperfections and reject it. S. Gregory Nazianzen tells us how certain persons who loved and admired S. Basil were led to imitate even his external blemishes, his slow, abstracted manner of speaking, the cut of his beard, and his peculiar gait. And so we see husbands and wives, children, friends, who, by reason of their great affection for one another, acquire--either accidentally or designedly--many foolish little ways and tricks peculiar to each. This ought not to be; for every one has enough imperfections of their own without adding those of anybody else, and friendship requires no such thing; on the contrary, it rather constrains us to help one another in getting rid of all sorts of imperfections. Of course we should bear with our friend's infirmities, but we should not encourage them, much less copy them.

Of course I am speaking of imperfections only, for, as to sins, we must neither imitate or tolerate these in our friends. That is but a sorry friendship which would see a friend perish, and not try to save him; would watch him dying of an abscess without daring to handle the knife of correction which would save him. True and living friendship cannot thrive amid sin. There is a tradition that the salamander extinguishes any fire into which it enters, and so sin destroys friendship. Friendship will banish a casual sin by brotherly correction, but if the sin be persistent, friendship dies out,--it can only live in a pure atmosphere. Much less can true friendship ever lead any one into sin; our friend becomes an enemy if he seeks to do so, and deserves to lose our friendship, and there is no surer proof of the hollowness of friendship than its profession between evil-doers. If we love a vicious person, our friendship will be vicious too; it will be like those to whom it is given.

Those who draw together for mere temporal profit, have no right to call their union friendship; it is not for love of one another that they unite, but for love of gain.

There are two sayings in Holy Scripture on which all Christian friendship should be built:--that of the Wise Man, "Whoso feareth the Lord shall direct his friendship aright;" [113] and that of S. James, "The friendship of the world is enmity with God." [114]

Footnotes:

112. S. Matt. xxv. 27.
113. Ecclus. vi. 17.
114. S. James iv. 4.

CHAPTER XXIII - On The Practice of Bodily Mortification

IT has been said that if one writes a word on an almond, and then replace it carefully in its husk, and sow it, all the fruit borne by that tree will be marked by the word so inscribed. For my own part, I never could approve of beginning to reform any one by merely external things,--dress, the arrangement of hair, and outward show. On the contrary, it seems to me that one should begin from within. "Turn ye to Me with all your heart;" [115] "My son, give Me thine heart; " [116] for as the heart is the fount whence all our actions spring, they will be according to what it is. And the Heavenly Bridegroom, calling the soul, says, "Set Me as a seal upon thine heart, as a seal upon thine arm." [117] Yes verily, for whosoever has Jesus Christ in his heart will soon show it in all his external actions. Therefore, my daughter, above all things I would write that precious and Holy Name JESUS in your heart, certain that having done so, your life--like the almond tree in the fable--will bear the stamp of that Saving Name in every act; and if the Dear Lord dwells within your heart, He will live in your every action, and will be traced in every member and part of you, so that you will be able to say with S. Paul, "I live, yet not I, but Christ liveth in me." [118] In a word, whosoever gains the heart has won the whole man. But this heart needs to be trained in its external conduct, so that it may display not merely a true devotion, but also wisdom and discretion. To this end I would make one or two suggestions.

If you are able to fast, you will do well to observe some days beyond what are ordered by the Church, for besides the ordinary effect of fasting in raising the mind, subduing the flesh, confirming goodness, and obtaining a heavenly reward, it is also a great matter to be able to control greediness, and to keep the sensual appetites and the whole body subject to the law of the Spirit; and although we may be able to do but little, the enemy nevertheless stands more in awe of those whom he knows can fast. The early Christians selected Wednesday, Friday and Saturday as days of abstinence. Do you follow therein according as your own devotion and your director's discretion may appoint.

I am prepared to say with S. Jerome (to the pious Leta) that I disapprove of long and immoderate fasting, especially for the young. I have learnt by experience that when the colt grows weary it turns aside, and so when young people become delicate by excessive fasting, they readily take to self-indulgence. The stag does not run with due speed either when over fat or too thin, and we are in peril of temptation both when the body is overfed or underfed; in the one case it grows indolent, in the other it sinks through depression, and if we cannot bear with it in the first case, neither can it bear with us in the last. A want of moderation in the use of fasting, discipline and austerity has made many a one useless in works of charity during the best years of his life, as happened to S. Bernard, who repented of his excessive austerity. Those who misuse the body at the outset will have to indulge it overmuch at last. Surely it were wiser to deal sensibly with it, and treat it according to the work and service required by each man's state of life.

Fasting and labour both exhaust and subdue the body. If your work is necessary or profitable to God's Glory, I would rather see you bear the exhaustion of work than of fasting. Such is the mind of the Church, who dispenses those who are called to work for God or their neighbour even from her prescribed fasts. One man finds it hard to fast, another finds it as hard to attend the sick, to visit prisons, to hear confessions, preach, minister to the afflicted, pray, and the like. And the last hardship is better than the other; for while it subdues the flesh equally, it brings forth better fruit. And as a general rule it is better to preserve more bodily strength than is absolutely necessary, than to damage it more than is necessary. Bodily strength can always be lowered if needful, but we cannot restore it at will. It seems to me that we ought to have in great reverence that which our Saviour and Redeemer Jesus Christ said to His disciples, "Eat such things as are set before you." [119] To my mind there is more virtue in eating whatever is offered you just as it comes, whether you like it or not, than in always choosing what is worst; for although the latter course may seem more ascetic, the former involves greater submission of will, because by it you give up not merely your taste, but your choice; and it is no slight austerity to hold up one's likings in one's hand, and subject them to all manner of accidents. Furthermore, this kind of mortification makes no show, inconveniences no one, and is admirably adapted to social life. To be always discarding one dish for another, examining everything, suspicious as to everything, making a fuss over every morsel--all this to my mind is contemptible, and implies too much thought of meats and platters. To my mind there was more austerity in S. Bernard's drinking oil by mistake for wine or water than if he had deliberately drunk wormwood, for it showed that he was not thinking of what he drank. And the real meaning of those sacred words, "Eat such things as are set before you," lies in such an indifference to what one eats and drinks. I should make an exception of any food which is unwholesome, or likely to be injurious to the mind's energies, such as certain hot, spiced, or stimulating dishes; as also on certain occasions when nature requires to be refreshed and invigorated in order to perform the work needful for God's Glory. At all times a constant habitual moderation is better than occasional excessive abstinence, alternated with great indulgence. The discipline has a surprising effect in rousing the taste for devotion, if used moderately. The body is greatly subdued by the use of the hair shirt, but it is not fit for ordinary people, married persons, those who are delicate, or who have to bear considerable fatigue. On certain days of special penitence it may be used, subject to the counsel of a judicious confessor.

Every one must take so much of the night for sleep, as his constitution, and the profitable performance of his day's work, requires. Holy Scripture continually teaches us that the morning is the best and most profitable part of the day, and so do the examples of the Saints and our natural reason. Our Lord Himself is called the Sun, risinig upon the earth, and our Lady the Day-star; and so I think it is wise to go to sleep early at night in order to be ready to waken and rise early. Moreover, that is the pleasantest, the freshest, and the freest hour of the day,--the very birds stimulate us to rise and sing God's praises. Early rising promotes both health and holiness.

Balaam saddled his ass and went to meet Balak, but his heart was not right with God, and therefore the Angel of the Lord stood in the way, with a sword in his hand to kill him, had not the ass three times turned out of the way as though she were restive; whereat Balaam smote her with his staff, until at last she fell down beneath him, and her mouth being miraculously opened, she said unto him, "What have I done unto thee that thou hast smitten me these three times?" Then Balaam's eyes were opened, and he saw the Angel, who said to him, "Wherefore hast thou smitten thine ass? unless she had turned from me surely now I had slain thee, and saved her alive." Then Balaam said to the Angel of the Lord, "I have sinned, for I knew not that thou stoodest in the way against me." [120] Do you see, my daughter, it was Balaam who did wrong, but he beat the poor ass, who was not to blame. It is often so with us. A woman's husband or child is ill, and forthwith she has recourse to fasting, the discipline, and hair shirt, even as David did on a like occasion. [121] But, dear friend, you are smiting the ass! you afflict your body, which can do nothing when God stands before you with His sword unsheathed. Rather correct your heart, which idolises your husband, and has indulged your child, letting him give way to pride, vanity, and ambition. Or, again, a man falls often into fleshly sins, and the voice of conscience stands before him in the way, rousing him to a holy fear. Then recollecting himself, he begins to abuse his flesh for betraying him, he deals out strict fasts, severe discipline, and the like, to it, and meanwhile the poor flesh might cry out like Balaam's ass, Why smitest thou me? It is you yourself, O my soul, that are guilty. Wherefore do you force me into evil, using my eyes, and hands, and lips for unholy purposes, and tormenting me with evil imaginations? Do you entertain only good thoughts, and I shall feel no unholy impulses, frequent none save pious people, and I shall not be kindled with guilty fire. You cast me yourself into the flames, and bid me not to burn! you fill my eyes with smoke, and wonder that they are inflamed! But God bids you deal chiefly with your heart, for that is the chief offender. When a man suffers from the itch, there is less need to bathe him, and cleanse the surface, than to purify his blood; and so, in order to purge our vices, no doubt it is well to mortify the flesh, but above all it is necessary to purify the affections and renew the heart. Make it a rule then never to undertake any bodily austerities without the advice of your spiritual guide.

Footnotes:

115. Joel ii. 12.
116. Prov. xxiii. 26.
117. Cant. viii. 6.
118. Gal. ii. 20.
119. S. Luke x. 8.
120. Numb. xxii.
121. 2 Sam. xii. 16.

CHAPTER XXIV - Of Society and Solitude

EITHER to seek or to shun society is a fault in one striving to lead a devout life in the world, such as I am now speaking of. To shun society implies indifference and contempt for one's neighbours; and to seek it savours of idleness and uselessness. We are told to love one's neighbour as one's self. In token that we love him, we must not avoid being with him, and the test of loving one's self is to be happy when alone. "Think first on thyself," says S. Bernard, "and then on other men." So that, if nothing obliges you to mix in society either at home or abroad, retire within yourself, and hold converse with your own heart. But if friends come to you, or there is fitting cause for you to go forth into society, then, my daughter, by all means go, and meet your neighbour with a kindly glance and a kindly heart.

Bad society is all such intercourse with others as has an evil object, or when those with whom we mix are vicious, indiscreet, or profligate. From such as these turn away, like the bee from a dunghill. The breath and saliva of those who have been bitten by a mad dog is dangerous, especially to children or delicate people, and in like manner it is perilous to associate with vicious, reckless people, above all to those whose devotion is still weakly and unstable.

There is a kind of social intercourse which merely tends to refresh us after more serious labour, and although it would not be well to indulge in this to excess, there is no harm in enjoying it during your leisure hours.

Other social meetings are in compliance with courtesy, such as mutual visits, and certain assemblies with a view to pay respect to one another. As to these, without being a slave to them, it is well not to despise them altogether, but to bear one's own due part in them quietly, avoiding rudeness and frivolity. Lastly, there is a profitable society;--that of good devout people, and it will always be very good for you to meet with them. Vines grown amid olivetrees are wont to bear rich grapes, and he who frequents the society of good people will imbibe some of their goodness. The bumble bee makes no honey alone, but if it falls among bees it works with them. Our own devout life will be materially helped by intercourse with other devout souls.

Simplicity, gentleness and modesty are to be desired in all society;--there are some people who are so full of affectation in whatever they do that every one is annoyed by them. A man who could not move without counting his steps, or speak without singing, would be very tiresome to everybody, and just so any one who is artificial in all he does spoils the pleasure of society; and moreover such people are generally more or less self-conceited. A quiet cheerfulness should be your aim in society. S. Romuald and S. Anthony are greatly lauded because, notwithstanding their asceticism, their countenance and words were always courteous and cheerful. I would say to you with S. Paul, "Rejoice with them that do rejoice;" [122] and again, "Rejoice in the Lord alway: let your moderation be known unto all men." [123] And if you would rejoice in the Lord, the cause of your joy must not only be lawful, but worthy; and remember this, because there are lawful things which nevertheless are not good; and in order that your moderation may be known, you must avoid all that is impertinent and uncivil, which is sure to be wrong. Depreciating this person, slandering another, wounding a third, stimulating the folly of a fourth--all such things, however amusing, are foolish and impertinent.

I have already spoken of that mental solitude into which you can retire when amid the greatest crowd, and furthermore you should learn to like a real material solitude. Not that I want you to fly to a desert like S. Mary of Egypt, S. Paul, S. Anthony, Arsenius, or the other hermits, but it is well for you to retire sometimes within your own chamber or garden, or wheresoever you can best recollect your mind, and refresh your soul with good and holy thoughts, and some spiritual reading, as the good Bishop of Nazianzum tells us was his custom. "I was walking alone," he says, "at sunset, on the seashore, a recreation I am wont to take in order somewhat to lay aside my daily worries." And S. Augustine says that he often used to go into S. Ambrose' room--his door was open to every one,--and after watching him absorbed in reading for a time, he would retire without speaking, fearing to interrupt the Bishop, who had so little time for refreshing his mind amid the burden of his heavy duties. And we read how when the disciples came to Jesus, and told Him all they had been doing and preaching, He said to them, "Come ye yourselves apart into a desert place, and rest awhile." [124]

Footnotes:

[122] Rom. xii. 15.
[123] Phil. iv. 4, 5.
[124] S. Mark vi. 30, 31.

CHAPTER XXV - On Modesty in Dress

S. PAUL expresses his desire that all Christian women should wear "modest apparel, with shamefacedness and sobriety;" [125] --and for that matter he certainly meant that men should do so likewise. Now, modesty in dress and its appurtenances depends upon the quality, the fashion and the cleanliness thereof. As to cleanliness, that should be uniform, and we should never, if possible, let any part of our dress be soiled or stained. External seemliness is a sort of indication of inward good order, and God requires those who minister at His Altar, or minister in holy things, to be attentive in respect of personal cleanliness. As to the quality and fashion of clothes, modesty in these points must depend upon various circumstances, age, season, condition, the society we move in, and the special occasion. Most people dress better on a high festival than at other times; in Lent, or other penitential seasons, they lay aside all gay apparel; at a wedding they wear wedding garments, at a funeral, mourning garb; and at a king's court the dress which would be unsuitable at home is suitable. A wife may and should adorn herself according to her husband's wishes when he is present;--if she does as much in his absence one is disposed to ask in whose eyes she seeks to shine? We may grant somewhat greater latitude to maidens, who may lawfully desire to attract many, although only with the view of ultimately winning one in holy matrimony. Neither do I blame such widows as purpose to marry again for adorning themselves, provided they keep within such limits as are seemly for those who are at the head of a family, and who have gone through the sobering sorrows of widowhood. But for those who are widows indeed, in heart as well as outwardly, humility, modesty and devotion are the only suitable ornaments. If they seek to attract men's admiration they are not widows indeed, and if they have no such intention, why should they wear its tokens? Those who do not mean to entertain guests should take down their signboard. So, again, every one laughs at old women who affect youthful graces,--such things are only tolerable in the young.

Always be neat, do not ever permit any disorder or untidiness about you. There is a certain disrespect to those with whom you mix in slovenly dress; but at the same time avoid all vanity, peculiarity, and fancifulness. As far as may be, keep to what is simple and unpretending--such dress is the best adornment of beauty and the best excuse for ugliness. S. Peter bids women not to be over particular in dressing their hair. Every one despises a man as effeminate who lowers himself by such things, and we count a vain woman as wanting in modesty, or at all events what she has becomes smothered among her trinkets and furbelows. They say that they mean no harm, but I should reply that the devil will contrive to get some harm out of it all. For my own part I should like my devout man or woman to be the best dressed person in the company, but the least fine or splendid, and adorned, as S. Peter says, with "the ornament of a meek and quiet spirit." [126] S. Louis said that the right thing is for every one to dress according to his position, so that good and sensible people should not be able to say they are over-dressed, or younger gayer ones that they are under-dressed. But if these last are not satisfied with what is modest and seemly, they must be content with the approbation of the elders.

Footnotes:

125. 1 Tim. ii. 9.
126. 1 Pet. iii. 3.

CHAPTER XXVI - Of Conversation; and, first, how to Speak of God

PHYSICIANS judge to a great extent as to the health or disease of a man by the state of his tongue, and our words are a true test of the state of our soul. "By thy words thou shalt be justified, and by thy words thou shalt be condemned," [127] the Saviour says. We are apt to apply the hand quickly to the place where we feel pain, and so too the tongue is quick to point out what we love.

If you love God heartily, my child, you will often speak of Him among your relations, household and familiar friends, and that because "the mouth of the righteous speaketh wisdom, and his tongue talketh of judgment." [128] Even as the bee touches nought save honey with his tongue, so should your lips be ever sweetened with your God, knowing nothing more pleasant than to praise and bless His Holy Name,--as we are told that when S. Francis uttered the Name of the Lord, he seemed to feel the sweetness lingering on his lips, and could not let it go. But always remember, when you speak of God, that He is God; and speak reverently and with devotion,--not affectedly or as if you were preaching, but with a spirit of meekness, love, and humility; dropping honey from your lips (like the Bride in the Canticles [129]) in devout and pious words, as you speak to one or another around, in your secret heart the while asking God to let this soft heavenly dew sink into their minds as they hearken. And remember very specially always to fulfil this angelic task meekly and lovingly, not as though you were reproving others, but rather winning them. It is wonderful how attractive a gentle, pleasant manner is, and how much it wins hearts.

Take care, then, never to speak of God, or those things which concern Him, in a merely formal, conventional manner; but with earnestness and devotion, avoiding the affected way in which some professedly religious people are perpetually interlarding their conversation with pious words and sayings, after a most unseasonable and unthinking manner. Too often they imagine that they really are themselves as pious as their words, which probably is not the case.

Footnotes:

127. S. Matt. xii. 37.
128. Ps. xxxvii. 30.
129. Cant. iv. 11.

CHAPTER XXVII - Of Unseemly Words, and the Respect due to Others

SAINT JAMES says, "If any man offend not in word, the same is, a perfect man." [130] Beware most watchfully against ever uttering any unseemly expression; even though you may have no evil intention, those who hear it may receive it with a different meaning. An impure word falling upon a weak mind spreads its infection like a drop of oil on a garment, and sometimes it will take such a hold of the heart, as to fill it with an infinitude of lascivious thoughts and temptations. The body is poisoned through the mouth, even so is the heart through the ear; and the tongue which does the deed is a murderer, even when the venom it has infused is counteracted by some antidote preoccupying the listener's heart. It was not the speaker's fault that he did not slay that soul. Nor let any one answer that he meant no harm. Our Lord, Who knoweth the hearts of men, has said, "Out of the abundance of the heart the mouth speaketh." [131] And even if we do mean no harm, the Evil One means a great deal, and he will use those idle words as a sharp weapon against some neighbour's heart. It is said that those who eat the plant called Angelica always have a sweet, pleasant breath; and those who cherish the angelic virtues of purity and modesty, will always speak simply, courteously, and modestly. As to unclean and light-minded talk, S. Paul says such things should not even be named [132] among us, for, as he elsewhere tells us, "Evil communications corrupt good manners." [133]

Those impure words which are spoken in disguise, and with an affectation of reserve, are the most harmful of all; for just as the sharper the point of a dart, so much deeper it will pierce the flesh, so the sharper an unholy word, the more it penetrates the heart. And as for those who think to show themselves knowing when they say such things, they do not even understand the first object of mutual intercourse among men, who ought rather to be like a hive of bees gathering to make honey by good and useful conversation, than like a wasps' nest, feeding on corruption. If any impertinent person addresses you in unseemly language, show that you are displeased by turning away, or by whatever other method your discretion may indicate.

One of the most evil dispositions possible is that which satirises and turns everything to ridicule. God abhors this vice, and has sometimes punished it in a marked manner. Nothing is so opposed to charity, much more to a devout spirit, as contempt and depreciation of one's neighbour, and where satire and ridicule exist contempt must be. Therefore contempt is a grievous sin, and our spiritual doctors have well said that ridicule is the greatest sin we can commit in word against our neighbour, inasmuch as when we offend him in any other way, there may still be some respect for him in our heart, but we are sure to despise those whom we ridicule.

There is a light-hearted talk, full of modest life and gaiety, which the Greeks called Eutrapelia, and which we should call good conversation, by which we may find an innocent and kindly amusement out of the trifling occurrences which human imperfections afford. Only beware of letting this seemly mirth go too far, till it becomes ridicule. Ridicule excites mirth at the expense of one's neighbour; seemly mirth and playful fun never lose sight of a trustful, kindly courtesy, which can wound no one. When the religious around him would fain have discussed serious matters with S. Louis at meal-times, he used to say, "This is not the time for grave discussion, but for general conversation and cheerful recreation,"-- out of consideration for his courtiers. But, my daughter, let our recreation always be so spent, that we may win all eternity through devotion.

Footnotes:

130. S. James iii. 2.
131. S. Matt. xii. 34.
132. Eph. v. 3.
133. 1 Cor. xv. 33.

CHAPTER XXVIII - Of Hasty Judgments

JUDGE not, and ye shall not be judged," said the Saviour of our souls; "condemn not, and ye shall not be condemned:" [134] and the Apostle S. Paul, "Judge nothing before the time, until the Lord come, Who both will bring to light the hidden things of darkness, and will make manifest the counsels of the hearts." [135] Of a truth, hasty judgments are most displeasing to God, and men's judgments are hasty, because we are not judges one of another, and by judging we usurp our Lord's own office. Man's judgment is hasty, because the chief malice of sin lies in the intention and counsel of the heart, which is shrouded in darkness to us. Moreover, man's judgments are hasty, because each one has enough to do in judging himself, without undertaking to judge his neighbour. If we would not be judged, it behoves us alike not to judge others, and to judge ourselves. Our Lord forbids the one, His Apostle enjoins the other, saying, "If we would judge ourselves, we should not be judged." [136] But alas! for the most part we precisely reverse these precepts, judging our neighbour, which is forbidden on all sides, while rarely judging ourselves, as we are told to do.

We must proceed to rectify rash judgments, according to their cause. Some hearts there are so bitter and harsh by nature, that everything turns bitter under their touch; men who, in the Prophet's words, "turn judgment to wormwood, and leave off righteousness in the earth." [137] Such as these greatly need to be dealt with by some wise spiritual physician, for this bitterness being natural to them, it is hard to conquer; and although it be rather an imperfection than a sin, still it is very dangerous, because it gives rise to and fosters rash judgments and slander within the heart. Others there are who are guilty of rash judgments less out of a bitter spirit than from pride, supposing to exalt their own credit by disparaging that of others. These are self-sufficient, presumptuous people, who stand so high in their own conceit that they despise all else as mean and worthless. It was the foolish Pharisee who said, "I am not as other men are." [138] Others, again, have not quite such overt pride, but rather a lurking little satisfaction in beholding what is wrong in others, in order to appreciate more fully what they believe to be their own superiority. This satisfaction is so well concealed, so nearly imperceptible, that it requires a clear sight to discover it, and those who experience it need that it be pointed out to them. Some there are who seek to excuse and justify themselves to their own conscience, by assuming readily that others are guilty of the same faults, or as great ones, vainly imagining that the sin becomes less culpable when shared by many. Others, again, give way to rash judgments merely because they take pleasure in a philosophic analysis and dissection of their neighbours' characters; and if by ill luck they chance now and then to be right, their presumption and love of criticism strengthens almost incurably.

Then there are people whose judgment is solely formed by inclination; who always think well of those they like, and ill of those they dislike. To this, however, there is one rare exception, which nevertheless we do sometimes meet, when an excessive love provokes a false judgment concerning its object; the hideous result of a diseased, faulty, restless affection, which is in fact jealousy; an evil passion capable, as everybody knows, of condemning others of perfidy and adultery upon the most trivial and fanciful ground. In like manner, fear, ambition, and other moral infirmities often tend largely to produce suspicion and rash judgments.

What remedy can we apply? They who drink the juice of the Ethiopian herb Ophiusa imagine that they see serpents and horrors everywhere; and those who drink deep of pride, envy, ambition, hatred, will see harm and shame in every one they look upon. The first can only be cured by drinking palm wine, and so I say of these latter,--Drink freely of the sacred wine of love, and it will cure you of the evil tempers which lead you to these perverse judgments. So far from seeking out that which is evil, Love dreads meeting with it, and when such meeting is unavoidable, she shuts her eyes at the first symptom, and then in her holy simplicity she questions whether it were not merely a fantastic shadow which crossed her path rather than sin itself. Or if Love is forced to recognise the fact, she turns aside hastily, and strives to forget what she has seen. Of a truth, Love is the great healer of all ills, and of this above the rest. Everything looks yellow to a man that has the jaundice; and it is said that the only cure is through the soles of the feet. Most assuredly the sin of rash judgments is a spiritual jaundice, which makes everything look amiss to those who have it; and he who would be cured of this malady must not be content with applying remedies to his eyes or his intellect, he must attack it through the affections, which are as the soul's feet. If your affections are warm and tender, your judgment will not be harsh; if they are loving, your judgment will be the same. Holy Scripture offers us three striking illustrations. Isaac, when in the Land of Gerar, gave out that Rebecca was his sister, but when Abimelech saw their familiarity, he at once concluded that she was his wife. [139] A malicious mind would rather have supposed that there was some unlawful connection between them, but Abimelech took the most charitable view of the case that was possible. And so ought we always to judge our neighbour as charitably as may be; and if his actions are many-sided, we should accept the best. Again, when S. Joseph found that the Blessed Virgin was with child, [140] knowing her to be pure and holy, he could not believe that there was any sin in her, and he left all judgment to God, although there was strong presumptive evidence on which to condemn her. And the Holy Spirit speaks of S. Joseph as "a just man." When a just man cannot see any excuse for what is done by a person in whose general worth he believes, he still refrains from judging him, and leaves all to God's Judgment. Again, our Crucified Saviour, while He could not wholly ignore the sin of those who Crucified Him, yet made what excuse He might for them, pleading their ignorance. [141] And so when we cannot find any excuse for sin, let us at least claim what compassion we may for it, and impute it to the least damaging motives we can find, as ignorance or infirmity.

Are we never, then, to judge our neighbour? you ask. Never, my child. It is God Who judges criminals brought before a court of law. He uses magistrates to convey His sentence to us; they are His interpreters, and have only to proclaim His law. If they go beyond this, and are led by their own passions, then they do themselves judge, and for so doing they will be judged. It is forbidden to all men alike, as men, to judge one another.

We do not necessarily judge because we see or are conscious of something wrong. Rash judgment always presupposes something that is not clear, in spite of which we condemn another. It is not wrong to have doubts concerning a neighbour, but we ought to be very watchful lest even our doubts or suspicions be rash and hasty. A malicious person seeing Jacob kiss Rachel at the well-side, [142] or Rebecca accepting jewels from Eleazer, [143] a stranger, might have suspected them of levity, though falsely and unreasonably. If an action is in itself indifferent, it is a rash suspicion to imagine that it means evil, unless there is strong circumstantial evidence to prove such to be the case. And it is a rash judgment when we draw condemnatory inferences from an action which may be blameless.

Those who keep careful watch over their conscience are not often liable to form rash judgments, for just as when the clouds lower the bees make for the shelter of their hive, so really good people shrink back into themselves, and refuse to be mixed up with the clouds and fogs of their neighbour's questionable doings, and rather than meddle with others, they consecrate their energies on their own improvement and good resolutions.

No surer sign of an unprofitable life than when people give way to censoriousness and inquisitiveness into the lives of other men. Of course exception must be made as to those who are responsible for others, whether in family or public life;--to all such it becomes a matter of conscience to watch over the conduct of their fellows. Let them fulfil their duty lovingly, and let them also give heed to restrain themselves within the bounds of that duty.

Footnotes:

134. S. Luke vi. 37.
135. 1 Cor. iv. 5.
136. 1 Cor. xi. 31.
137. Amos v. 7.
138. S. Luke xviii. 11.
139. Gen. xxvi.
140. S. Matt. i.
141. S. Luke xxiii. 34.
142. Gen. xxix. 11.
143. Gen. xxiv. 22.

CHAPTER XXIX - On Slander

FROM rash judgments proceed mistrust, contempt for others, pride, and self-sufficiency, and numberless other pernicious results, among which stands forth prominently the sin of slander, which is a veritable pest of society. Oh, wherefore can I not take a live coal from God's Altar, and touch the lips of men, so that their iniquity may be taken away and their sin purged, even as the Seraphim purged the lips of Isaiah. [144] He who could purge the world of slander would cleanse it from a great part of its sinfulness!

He who unjustly takes away his neighbour's good name is guilty of sin, and is bound to make reparation, according to the nature of his evil speaking; since no man can enter into Heaven cumbered with stolen goods, and of all worldly possessions the most precious is a good name. Slander is a kind of murder; for we all have three lives--a spiritual life, which depends upon the Grace of God; a bodily life, depending on the soul; and a civil life, consisting in a good reputation. Sin deprives us of the first, death of the second, and slander of the third. But the slanderer commits three several murders with his idle tongue: he destroys his own soul and that of him who hearkens, as well as causing civil death to the object of his slander; for, as S. Bernard says, the Devil has possession both of the slanderer and of those who listen to him, of the tongue of the one, the ear of the other. And David says of slanderers, "They have sharpened their tongues like a serpent; adders' poison is under their lips." [145] Aristotle says that, like the forked, two-edged tongue of the serpent, so is that of the slanderer, who at one dart pricks and poisons the ear of those who hear him, and the reputation of him who is slandered.

My daughter, I entreat you never speak evil of any, either directly or indirectly; beware of ever unjustly imputing sins or faults to your neighbour, of needlessly disclosing his real faults, of exaggerating such as are overt, of attributing wrong motives to good actions, of denying the good that you know to exist in another, of maliciously concealing it, or depreciating it in conversation. In all and each of these ways you grievously offend God, although the worst is false accusation, or denying the truth to your neighbour's damage, since therein you combine his harm with falsehood.

Those who slander others with an affectation of good will, or with dishonest pretences of friendliness, are the most spiteful and evil of all. They will profess that they love their victim, and that in many ways he is an excellent man, but all the same, truth must be told, and he was very wrong in such a matter; or that such and such a woman is very virtuous generally, but and so on. Do you not see through the artifice? He who draws a bow draws the arrow as close as he can to himself, but it is only to let it fly more forcibly; and so such slanderers appear to be withholding their evil-speaking, but it is only to let it fly with surer aim and go deeper into the listeners' minds. Witty slander is the most mischievous of all; for just as some poisons are but feeble when taken alone, which become powerful when mixed with wine, so many a slander, which would go in at one ear and out at the other of itself, finds a resting-place in the listener's brain when it is accompanied with amusing, witty comments. "The poison of asps is under their lips." The asp's bite is scarcely perceptible, and its poison at first only causes an irritation which is scarcely disagreeable, so that the heart and nervous system dilate and receive that poison, against which later on there is no remedy.

Do not pronounce a man to be a drunkard although you may have seen him drunk, or an adulterer, because you know he has sinned; a single act does not stamp him for ever. The sun once stood still while Joshua and the children of Israel avenged themselves upon their enemies; [146] and another time it was darkened at mid-day when the Lord was crucified; [147] but no one would therefore say that it was stationary or dark. Noah was drunk once, and Lot, moreover, was guilty of incest, yet neither man could be spoken of as habitually given to such sins; neither would you call S. Paul a man of blood or a blasphemer, because he had blasphemed and shed blood before he became a Christian. Before a man deserves to be thus stigmatised, he must have formed a habit of the sin he is accused of, and it is unfair to call a man passionate or a thief, because you have once known him steal or fly into a passion. Even when a man may have persisted long in sin, you may say what is untrue in calling him vicious. Simon the leper called Magdalene a sinner, because she had once lived a life of sin; but he lied, for she was a sinner no longer, but rather a very saintly penitent, and so our Lord Himself undertook her defence. [148]

The Pharisee looked upon the publican as a great sinner,--probably as unjust, extortionate, adulterous; [149] but how mistaken he was, inasmuch as the condemned publican was even then justified! If God's Mercy is so great, that one single moment is sufficient for it to justify and save a man, what assurance have we that he who yesterday was a sinner is the same to-day? Yesterday may not be the judge of to-day, nor to-day of yesterday: all will be really judged at the Last Great Day. In short, we can never affirm a man to be evil without running the risk of lying. If it be absolutely necessary to speak, we may say that he was guilty of such an act, that he led an evil life at such and such a time, or that he is doing certain wrong at the present day; but we have no right to draw deductions for to-day from yesterday, nor of yesterday from today; still less to speak with respect to the future.

But while extremely sensitive as to the slightest approach to slander, you must also guard against an extreme into which some people fall, who, in their desire to speak evil of no one, actually uphold and speak well of vice. If you have to do with one who is unquestionably a slanderer, do not excuse him under the expressions of frank and free-spoken; do not call one who is notoriously vain, liberal and elegant; do not call dangerous levities mere simplicity; do not screen disobedience under the name of zeal, or arrogance of frankness, or evil intimacy of friendship. No, my child, we must never, in our wish to shun slander, foster or flatter vice in others; but we must call evil evil, and sin sin, and so doing we shall serve God's Glory, always bearing in mind the following rules.

If you would be justified in condemning a neighbour's sin, you must be sure that it is needful either for his good or that of others to do so. For instance, if light, unseemly conduct is spoken of before young people in a way calculated to injure their purity, and you pass it over, or excuse it, they may be led to think lightly of evil, and to imitate it; and therefore you are bound to condemn all such things freely and at once, unless it is obvious that by reserving your charitable work of reprehension to a future time, you can do it more profitably.

Furthermore, on such occasions it is well to be sure that you are the most proper person among those present to express your opinion, and that your silence would seem in any way to condone the sin. If you are one of the least important persons present, it is probably not your place to censure; but supposing it to be your duty, be most carefully just in what you say,--let there not be a word too much or too little. For instance, you censure the intimacy of certain people, as dangerous and indiscreet. Well, but you must hold the scales with the most exact justice, and not exaggerate in the smallest item. If there be only a slight appearance of evil, say no more than that; if it be a question of some trifling imprudence, do not make it out to be more; if there be really neither imprudence nor positive appearance of evil, but only such as affords a pretext for malicious slander, either say simply so much, or, better still, say nothing at all. When you speak of your neighbour, look upon your tongue as a sharp razor in the surgeon's hand, about to cut nerves and tendons; it should be used so carefully, as to insure that no particle more or less than the truth be said. And finally, when you are called upon to blame sin, always strive as far as possible to spare the sinner.

Public, notorious sinners may be spoken of freely, provided always even then that a spirit of charity and compassion prevail, and that you do not speak of them with arrogance or presumption, or as though you took pleasure in the fall of others. To do this is the sure sign of a mean ungenerous mind. And, of course, you must speak freely in condemnation of the professed enemies of God and His Church, heretics and schismatics,--it is true charity to point out the wolf wheresoever he creeps in among the flock. Most people permit themselves absolute latitude in criticising and censuring rulers, and in calumniating nationalities, according to their own opinions and likings. But do you avoid this fault; it is displeasing to God, and is liable to lead you into disputes and quarrels. When you hear evil of any one, cast any doubt you fairly can upon the accusation; or if that is impossible, make any available excuse for the culprit; and where even that may not be, be yet pitiful and compassionate, and remind those with whom you are speaking that such as stand upright do so solely through God's Grace. Do your best kindly to check the scandal-bearer, and if you know anything favourable to the person criticised, take pains to mention it.

Footnotes:

144. Isa. vi. 6, 7.
145. Ps. cxl. 3.
146. Josh. x. 13.
147. S. Luke xxiii. 44.
148. S. Luke vii. 37-39.
149. S. Luke xviii. 11.

CHAPTER XXX - Further Counsels as to Conversation

LET your words be kindly, frank, sincere, straightforward, simple and true; avoid all artifice, duplicity and pretence, remembering that, although it is not always well to publish abroad everything that may be true, yet it is never allowable to oppose the truth. Make it your rule never knowingly to say what is not strictly true, either accusing or excusing, always remembering that God is the God of Truth. If you have unintentionally said what is not true, and it is possible to correct yourself at once by means of explanation or reparation, do so. A straightforward excuse has far greater weight than any falsehood.

It may be lawful occasionally to conceal or disguise the truth, but this should never be done save in such special cases as make this reserve obviously a necessity for the service and glory of God. Otherwise all such artifice is dangerous; and we are told in Holy Scripture that God's Holy Spirit will not abide with the false or double-minded. Depend upon it there is no craft half so profitable and successful as simplicity. Worldly prudence and artifice belong to the children of this world; but the children of God go straight on with a single heart and in all confidence;--falsehood, deceit and duplicity are sure signs of a mean, weak mind.

In the Fourth Book of his Confessions, S. Augustine spoke in very strong terms of his passionate devotion to a friend, saying that they had but as one soul, and that after his friend's death his life was a horror to him, although he feared to die. But later on these expressions seemed unreal and affected to him, and he withdrew them in his Retractations. [150] You see how sensitive that great mind was to unreality or affectation. Assuredly straightforward honesty and sincerity in speech is a great beauty in the Christian life. "I said I will take heed to my ways, that I offend not in my tongue." [151] "Set a watch, O Lord, before my mouth, and keep the door of my lips." [152]

It was a saying of S. Louis, that one should contradict nobody, unless there was sin or harm in consenting; and that in order to avoid contention and dispute. At any rate, when it is necessary to contradict anybody, or to assert one's own opinion, it should be done gently and considerately, without irritation or vehemence. Indeed, we gain nothing by sharpness or petulance.

The silence, so much commended by wise men of old, does not refer so much to a literal use of few words, as to not using many useless words. On this score, we must look less to the quantity than the quality, and, as it seems to me, our aim should be to avoid both extremes. An excessive reserve and stiffness, which stands aloof from familiar friendly conversation, is untrusting, and implies a certain sort of contemptuous pride; while an incessant chatter and babble, leaving no opportunity for others to put in their word, is frivolous and troublesome.

S. Louis objected to private confidences and whisperings in society, especially at table, lest suspicion should be aroused that scandal was being repeated. "Those who have anything amusing or pleasant to say," he argued, "should let everybody share the entertainment, but if they want to speak of important matters, they should wait a more suitable time."

Footnotes:

150. "My dearest Nebridius . . . I wondered that others subject to death should live, since he whom I loved, as if he should never die, was dead; and I wondered yet more that myself, who was to him as a second self, could live, he being dead. . . . I felt that my soul and his soul were one soul in two bodies, and therefore my life was a horror to me, because I would not live halved, and therefore perchance I feared to die, lest he whom I had much loved should die wholly."--Confessions, Oxf. Trans. Bk. iv. p. 52. ". . . which seems to me rather an empty declamation than a grave confession."--Retract., Bk. ii. c. 6.

151. Ps. xxxix. 1.

152. Ps. cxli. 3.

CHAPTER XXXI - Of Amusements and Recreations: what are allowable

WE must needs occasionally relax the mind, and the body requires some recreation also. Cassian relates how S. John the Evangelist was found by a certain hunter amusing himself by caressing a partridge, which sat upon his wrist. The hunter asked how a man of his mental powers could find time for so trifling an occupation. In reply, S. John asked why he did not always carry his bow strung? The man answered, Because, if always bent, the bow would lose its spring when really wanted. "Do not marvel then," the Apostle replied, "if I slacken my mental efforts from time to time, and recreate myself, in order to return more vigorously to contemplation." It is a great mistake to be so strict as to grudge any recreation either to others or one's self.

Walking, harmless games, music, instrumental or vocal, field sports, etc., are such entirely lawful recreations that they need no rules beyond those of ordinary discretion, which keep every thing within due limits of time, place, and degree. So again games of skill, which exercise and strengthen body or mind, such as tennis, rackets, running at the ring, chess, and the like, are in themselves both lawful and good. Only one must avoid excess, either in the time given to them, or the amount of interest they absorb; for if too much time be given up to such things, they cease to be a recreation and become an occupation; and so far from resting and restoring mind or body, they have precisely the contrary effect. After five or six hours spent over chess, one's mind is spent and weary, and too long a time given to tennis results in physical exhaustion; or if people play for a high stake, they get anxious and discomposed, and such unimportant objects are unworthy of so much care and thought. But, above all, beware of setting your heart upon any of these things, for however lawful an amusement may be, it is wrong to give one's heart up to it. Not that I would not have you take pleasure in what you are doing,--it were no recreation else,--but I would not have you engrossed by it, or become eager or over fond of any of these things.

CHAPTER XXXII - Of Forbidden Amusements

DICE, cards, and the like games of hazard, are not merely dangerous amusements, like dancing, but they are plainly bad and harmful, and therefore they are forbidden by the civil as by the ecclesiastical law. What harm is there in them? you ask. Such games are unreasonable:--the winner often has neither skill nor industry to boast of, which is contrary to reason. You reply that this is understood by those who play. But though that may prove that you are not wronging anybody, it does not prove that the game is in accordance with reason, as victory ought to be the reward of skill or labour, which it cannot be in mere games of chance. Moreover, though such games may be called a recreation, and are intended as such, they are practically an intense occupation. Is it not an occupation, when a man's mind is kept on the stretch of close attention, and disturbed by endless anxieties, fears and agitations? Who exercises a more dismal, painful attention than the gambler? No one must speak or laugh,--if you do but cough you will annoy him and his companions. The only pleasure in gambling is to win, and this cannot be a satisfactory pleasure, since it can only be enjoyed at the expense of your antagonist. Once, when he was very ill, S. Louis heard that his brother the Comte d'Anjou and Messire Gautier de Nemours were gambling, and in spite of his weakness the King tottered into the room where they were, and threw dice and money and everything out of the window, in great indignation. And the pure and pious Sara, in her appeal to God, declared that she had never had dealings with gamblers. [153]

Footnote:

153. It is not very clear what S. Francis means by this. In the English version, Sara only says, "Thou knowest, Lord . . . that I never polluted my name, nor the name of my father" (Tobit iii. 15). In the Vulgate the words are "Numquam cum ludentibus miscui me; neque cum his, qui in levitate ambulant, participem me praebui" (iii. 17).

CHAPTER XXXIII - Of Balls, and other Lawful but Dangerous Amusements

DANCES and balls are things in themselves indifferent, but the circumstances ordinarily surrounding them have so generally an evil tendency, that they become full of temptation and danger. The time of night at which they take place is in itself conducive to harm, both as the season when people's nerves are most excited and open to evil impressions; and because, after being up the greater part of the night, they spend the mornings afterwards in sleep, and lose the best part of the day for God's Service. It is a senseless thing to turn day into night, light into darkness, and to exchange good works for mere trifling follies. Moreover, those who frequent balls almost inevitably foster their Vanity, and vanity is very conducive to unholy desires and dangerous attachments.

I am inclined to say about balls what doctors say of certain articles of food, such as mushrooms and the like--the best are not good for much; but if eat them you must, at least mind that they are properly cooked. So, if circumstances over which you have no control take you into such places, be watchful how you prepare to enter them. Let the dish be seasoned with moderation, dignity and good intentions. The doctors say (still referring to the mushrooms), eat sparingly of them, and that but seldom, for, however well dressed, an excess is harmful. So dance but little, and that rarely, my daughter, lest you run the risk of growing over fond of the amusement.

Pliny says that mushrooms, from their porous, spongy nature, easily imbibe meretricious matter, so that if they are near a serpent, they are infected by its poison. So balls and similar gatherings are wont to attract all that is bad and vicious; all the quarrels, envyings, slanders, and indiscreet tendencies of a place will be found collected in the ballroom. While people's bodily pores are opened by the exercise of dancing, the heart's pores will be also opened by excitement, and if any serpent be at hand to whisper foolish words of levity or impurity, to insinuate unworthy thoughts and desires, the ears which listen are more than prepared to receive the contagion.

Believe me, my daughter, these frivolous amusements are for the most part dangerous; they dissipate the spirit of devotion, enervate the mind, check true charity, and arouse a multitude of evil inclinations in the soul, and therefore I would have you very reticent in their use.

To return to the medical simile;--it is said that after eating mushrooms you should drink some good wine. So after frequenting balls you should frame pious thoughts which may counteract the dangerous impressions made by such empty pleasures on your heart. Bethink you, then--1. That while you were dancing, souls were groaning in hell by reason of sins committed when similarly occupied, or in consequence thereof.

2. Remember how, at the selfsame time, many religious and other devout persons were kneeling before God, praying or praising Him. Was not their time better spent than yours?

3. Again, while you were dancing, many a soul has passed away amid sharp sufferings; thousands and tens of thousands were lying all the while on beds of anguish, some perhaps untended, unconsoled, in fevers, and all manner of painful diseases. Will you not rouse yourself to a sense of pity for them? At all events, remember that a day will come when you in your turn will lie on your bed of sickness, while others dance and make merry.

4. Bethink you that our Dear Lord, Our Lady, all the Angels and Saints, saw all that was passing. Did they not look on with sorrowful pity, while your heart, capable of better things, was engrossed with such mere follies?

5. And while you were dancing time passed by, and death drew nearer. Trifle as you may, the awful dance of death [154] must come, the real pastime of men, since therein they must, whether they will or no, pass from time to an eternity of good or evil. If you think of the matter quietly, and as in God's Sight, He will suggest many a like thought, which will steady and strengthen your heart.

Footnote:

154. S. Francis de Sales doubtless had in his thoughts the then common pictorial representations of the Dance of Death, with which (although to our own modern ideas there would be almost irreverence if reproduced) we are familiar through Holbein's celebrated Dance, and others. The old covered bridge at Lucerne is one of the most striking illustrations.

CHAPTER XXXIV - When to use such Amusements rightly

IF you would dance or play rightly, it must be done as a recreation, not as a pursuit, for a brief space of time, not so as make you unfit for other things, and even then but seldom. If it is a constant habit, recreation turns into occupation. You will ask when it is right to dance or play? The occasions on which it is right to play at questionable games are rare; ordinary games and dances may be indulged in more frequently. But let your rule be to do so chiefly when courteous consideration for others among whom you are thrown requires it, subject to prudence and discretion; for consideration towards others often sanctions things indifferent or dangerous, and turns them to good, taking away what is evil. Thus certain games of chance, bad in themselves, cease to be so to you, if you join in them merely out of a due courtesy. I have been much comforted by reading in the Life of S. Carlo Borromeo, how he joined in certain things to please the Swiss, concerning which ordinarily he was very strict; as also how S. Ignatius Loyola, when asked to play, did so. As to S. Elizabeth of Hungary, she both played and danced occasionally, when in society, without thereby hindering her devotion, which was so firmly rooted that, like the rocks of a mountain lake, it stood unmoved amid the waves and storms of pomp and vanity which it encountered.

Great fires are fanned by the wind, but a little one is soon extinguished if left without shelter.

CHAPTER XXXV - We must be Faithful in Things Great and Small

THE Bridegroom of the Canticles says that the Bride has ravished His heart with "one of her eyes, one lock of her hair." [155] In all the human body no part is nobler either in mechanism or activity than the eye, none more unimportant than the hair. And so the Divine Bridegroom makes us to know that He accepts not only the great works of devout people, but every poor and lowly offering too; and that they who would serve Him acceptably must give heed not only to lofty and important matters, but to things mean and little, since by both alike we may win His Heart and Love.

Be ready then, my child, to bear great afflictions for your Lord, even to martyrdom itself; resolve to give up to Him all that you hold most precious, if He should require it of you;--father, mother, husband, wife, or child; the light of your eyes; your very life; for all such offering your heart should be ready. But so long as God's Providence does not send you these great and heavy afflictions; so long as He does not ask your eyes, at least give Him your hair. I mean, take patiently the petty annoyances, the trifling discomforts, the unimportant losses which come upon all of us daily; for by means of these little matters, lovingly and freely accepted, you will give Him your whole heart, and win His. I mean the acts of daily forbearance, the headache, or toothache, or heavy cold; the tiresome peculiarities of husband or wife, the broken glass, the loss of a ring, a handkerchief, a glove; the sneer of a neighbour, the effort of going to bed early in order to rise early for prayer or Communion, the little shyness some people feel in openly performing religious duties; and be sure that all of these sufferings, small as they are, if accepted lovingly, are most pleasing to God's Goodness, Which has promised a whole ocean of happiness to His children in return for one cup of cold water. And, moreover, inasmuch as these occasions are for ever arising, they give us a fertile field for gathering in spiritual riches, if only we will use them rightly.

When I read in the Life of S. Catherine of Sienna of her ecstasies and visions, her wise sayings and teaching, I do not doubt but that she "ravished" her Bridegroom's heart with this eye of contemplation; but I must own that I behold her with no less delight in her father's kitchen, kindling the fire, turning the spit, baking the bread, cooking the dinner, and doing all the most menial offices in a loving spirit which looked through all things straight to God. Nor do I prize the lowly meditations she was wont to make while so humbly employed less than the ecstasies with which she was favoured at other times, probably as a reward for this very humility and lowliness. Her meditations would take the shape of imagining that all she prepared for her father was prepared for Our Lord, as by Martha; her mother was a symbol to her of Our Lady, her brothers of the Apostles, and thus she mentally ministered to all the Heavenly Courts, fulfilling her humble ministrations with an exceeding sweetness, because she saw God's Will in each. Let this example, my daughter, teach you how important it is to dedicate all we do, however trifling, to His service. And to this end I earnestly counsel you to imitate that "virtuous woman" whom King Solomon lauds, [156] who "layeth her hands" to all that is good and noble, and yet at the same time to the spindle and distaff. Do you seek the higher things, such as prayer and meditation, the Sacraments leading souls to God and kindling good thoughts in them, in a word, by all manner of good works according to your vocation; but meanwhile do not neglect your spindle and distaff. I mean, cultivate those lowly virtues which spring like flowers round the foot of the Cross, such as ministering to the poor and sick, family cares, and the duties arising therefrom, and practical diligence and activity; and amid all these things cultivate such spiritual thoughts as S. Catherine intermingled with her work.

Great occasions for serving God come seldom, but little ones surround us daily; and our Lord Himself has told us that "he that is faithful in that which is least is faithful also in much." [157] If you do all in God's Name, all you do will be well done, whether you eat, drink or sleep, whether you amuse yourself or turn the spit, so long as you do all wisely, you will gain greatly as in God's Sight, doing all because He would have you do it.

Footnotes:

155. Cant. iv. 9. In the English version this passage stands as "one chain of her neck;" but in the Vulgate it is "uno crine colli tui."

156. Prov. xxxi. Those who desire a helpful book will find one in Mgr. Landriot's "Femme Forte," a series of lectures on this chapter of Holy Scripture, which, as well as his "Femme Picuse" is largely imbued with the spirit of S. Francis de Sales, who is frequently quoted in both.

157. S. Luke xvi. 10.

CHAPTER XXXVI - Of a Well-Balanced, Reasonable Mind

REASON is the special characteristic of man, and yet it is a rare thing to find really reasonable men, all the more that self-love hinders reason, and beguiles us insensibly into all manner of trifling, but yet dangerous acts of injustice and untruth, which, like the little foxes in the Canticles, [158] spoil our vines, while, just because they are trifling, people pay no attention to them, and because they are numerous, they do infinite harm. Let me give some instances of what I mean.

We find fault with our neighbour very readily for a small matter, while we pass over great things in ourselves. We strive to sell dear and buy cheap. We are eager to deal out strict justice to others, but to obtain indulgence for ourselves. We expect a good construction to be put on all we say, but we are sensitive and critical as to our neighbour's words. We expect him to let us have whatever we want for money, when it would be more reasonable to let him keep that which is his, if he desires to do so, and leave us to keep our gold. We are vexed with him because he will not accommodate us, while perhaps he has better reason to be vexed with us for wanting to disturb him. If we have a liking for any one particular thing, we despise all else, and reject whatever does not precisely suit our taste. If some inferior is unacceptable to us, or we have once caught him in error, he is sure to be wrong in our eyes whatever he may do, and we are for ever thwarting, or looking coldly on him, while, on the other hand, some one who happens to please us is sure to be right. Sometimes even parents show unfair preference for a child endowed with personal gifts over one afflicted with some physical imperfection. We put the rich before the poor, although they may have less claim, and be less worthy; we even give preference to well-dressed people. We are strict in exacting our own rights, but expect others to be yielding as to theirs;--we complain freely of our neighbours, but we do not like them to make any complaints of us. Whatever we do for them appears very great in our sight, but what they do for us counts as nothing. In a word, we are like the Paphlagonian partridge, which has two hearts; for we have a very tender, pitiful, easy heart towards ourselves, and one which is hard, harsh and strict towards our neighbour. We have two scales, one wherein to measure our own goods to the best advantage, and the other to weigh our neighbours' to the worst. Holy Scripture tells us that lying lips are an abomination unto the Lord, [159] and the double heart, with one measure whereby to receive, and another to give, is also abominable in His Sight.

Be just and fair in all you do. Always put yourself in your neighbour's place, and put him into yours, and then you will judge fairly. Sell as you would buy, and buy as you would sell, and your buying and selling will alike be honest. These little dishonesties seem unimportant, because we are not obliged to make restitution, and we have, after all, only taken that which we might demand according to the strict letter of the law; but, nevertheless, they are sins against right and charity, and are mere trickery, greatly needing correction--nor does any one ever lose by being generous, noble-hearted and courteous. Be sure then often to examine your dealings with your neighbour, whether your heart is right towards him, as you would have his towards you, were things reversed--this is the true test of reason. When Trajan was blamed by his confidential friends for making the Imperial presence too accessible, he replied, "Does it not behove me to strive to be such an emperor towards my subjects as I should wish to meet with were I a subject?"

Footnotes:

158. Cant. ii. 15.
159. Prov. xii. 22.

CHAPTER XXXVII - Of Wishes

EVERYBODY grants that we must guard against the desire for evil things, since evil desires make evil men. But I say yet further, my daughter, do not desire dangerous things, such as balls or pleasures, office or honour, visions or ecstacies. Do not long after things afar off; such, I mean, as cannot happen till a distant time, as some do who by this means wear themselves out and expend their energies uselessly, fostering a dangerous spirit of distraction. If a young man gives way to overweening longings for an employment he cannot obtain yet a while, what good will it do him? If a married woman sets her heart on becoming a religious, or if I crave to buy my neighbour's estate, he not being willing to sell it, is it not mere waste of time? If, when sick, I am restlessly anxious to preach or celebrate, to visit other sick people, or generally to do work befitting the strong, is it not an unprofitable desire, inasmuch as I have no power to fulfil it? and meanwhile these useless wishes take the place of such as I ought to have,--namely, to be patient, resigned, self-denying, obedient, gentle under suffering,--which are what God requires of me under the circumstances. We are too apt to be like a sickly woman, craving ripe cherries in autumn and grapes in spring. I can never think it well for one whose vocation is clear to waste time in wishing for some different manner of life than that which is adapted to his duty, or practices unsuitable to his present position--it is mere idling, and will make him slack in his needful work. If I long after a Carthusian solitude, I am losing my time, and such longing usurps the place of that which I ought to entertain--to fulfil my actual duties rightly. No indeed, I would not even have people wish for more wit or better judgment, for such desires are frivolous, and take the place of the wish every one ought to possess of improving what he has. We ought not to desire ways of serving God which He does not open to us, but rather desire to use what we have rightly. Of course I mean by this, real earnest desires, not common superficial wishes, which do no harm if not too frequently indulged.

Do not desire crosses, unless you have borne those already laid upon you well--it is an abuse to long after martyrdom while unable to bear an insult patiently. The Enemy of souls often inspires men with ardent desires for unattainable things, in order to divert their attention from present duties, which would be profitable however trifling in themselves. We are apt to fight African monsters in imagination, while we let very petty foes vanquish us in reality for want of due heed.

Do not desire temptations, that is temerity, but prepare your heart to meet them bravely, and to resist them when they come.

Too great variety and quantity of food loads the stomach, and (especially when it is weakly) spoils the digestion. Do not overload your soul with innumerable longings, either worldly, for that were destruction,--or even spiritual, for these only cumber you. When the soul is purged of the evil humours of sin, it experiences a ravenous hunger for spiritual things, and sets to work as one famished at all manner of spiritual exercises;--mortification, penitence, humility, charity, prayer. Doubtless such an appetite is a good sign, but it behoves you to reflect whether you are able to digest all that you fain would eat. Make rather a selection from all these desires, under the guidance of your spiritual father, of such as you are able to perform, and then use them as perfectly as you are able. When you have done this, God will send you more, to be fulfilled in their turn, and so you will not waste time in unprofitable wishes. Not that I would have you lose any good desires, but rather treat them methodically, putting them aside in one corner of your heart till due time comes, while you carry out such as are ripe for action. And this counsel I give to worldly people as well as those who are spiritual, for without heeding it no one can avoid anxiety and over-eagerness.

CHAPTER XXXVIII - Counsels to Married People

MARRIAGE is a great Sacrament both in Jesus Christ and His Church, and one to be honoured to all, by all and in all. To all, for even those who do not enter upon it should honour it in all humility. By all, for it is holy alike to poor as to rich. In all, for its origin, its end, its form and matter are holy. It is the nursery of Christianity, whence the earth is peopled with faithful, till the number of the elect in Heaven be perfected; so that respect for the marriage tie is exceedingly important to the commonwealth, of which it is the source and supply.

Would to God that His Dear Son were bidden to all weddings as to that of Cana! Truly then the wine of consolation and blessing would never be lacking; for if these are often so wanting, it is because too frequently now men summon Adonis instead of our Lord, and Venus rather than Our Lady. He who desires that the young of his flock should be like Jacob's, fair and ring-straked, must set fair objects before their eyes; and he who would find a blessing in his marriage, must ponder the holiness and dignity of this Sacrament, instead of which too often weddings become a season of mere feasting and disorder.

Above all, I would exhort all married people to seek that mutual love so commended to them by the Holy Spirit in the Bible. It is little to bid you love one another with a mutual love,---turtle-doves do that; or with human love,--the heathen cherished such love as that. But I say to you in the Apostle's words: "Husbands, love your wives, even as Christ also loved the Church. Wives, submit yourselves to your husbands as unto the Lord." [160] It was God Who brought Eve to our first father Adam, and gave her to him to wife; and even so, my friends, it is God's Invisible Hand Which binds you in the sacred bonds of marriage; it is He Who gives you one to the other, therefore cherish one another with a holy, sacred, heavenly love.

The first effect of this love is the indissoluble union of your hearts. If you glue together two pieces of deal, provided that the glue be strong, their union will be so close that the stick will break more easily in any other part than where it is joined. Now God unites husband and wife so closely in Himself, that it should be easier to sunder soul from body than husband from wife; nor is this union to be considered as mainly of the body, but yet more a union of the heart, its affections and love.

The second effect of this love should be an inviolable fidelity to one another. In olden times finger-rings were wont to be graven as seals. We read of it in Holy Scripture, and this explains the meaning of the marriage ceremony, when the Church, by the hand of her priest, blesses a ring, and gives it first to the man in token that she sets a seal on his heart by this Sacrament, so that no thought of any other woman may ever enter therein so long as she, who now is given to him, shall live. Then the bridegroom places the ring on the bride's hand, so that she in her turn may know that she must never conceive any affection in her heart for any other man so long as he shall live, who is now given to her by our Lord Himself.

The third end of marriage is the birth and bringing up of children. And herein, O ye married people! are you greatly honoured, in that God, willing to multiply souls to bless and praise Him to all Eternity, He associates you with Himself in this His work, by the production of bodies into which, like dew from Heaven, He infuses the souls He creates as well as the bodies into which they enter.

Therefore, husbands, do you preserve a tender, constant, hearty love for your wives. It was that the wife might be loved heartily and tenderly that woman was taken from the side nearest Adam's heart. No failings or infirmities, bodily or mental, in your wife should ever excite any kind of dislike in you, but rather a loving, tender compassion; and that because God has made her dependent on you, and bound to defer to and obey you; and that while she is meant to be your helpmeet, you are her superior and her head. And on your part, wives, do you love the husbands God has given you tenderly, heartily, but with a reverential, confiding love, for God has made the man to have the predominance, and to be the stronger; and He wills the woman to depend upon him,--bone of his bone, flesh of his flesh,--taking her from out the ribs of the man, to show that she must be subject to his guidance. All Holy Scripture enjoins this subjection, which nevertheless is not grievous; and the same Holy Scripture, while it bids you accept it lovingly, bids your husband to use his superiority with great tenderness, lovingkindness, and gentleness. "Husbands, dwell with your wives according to knowledge, giving honour unto the wife as unto the weaker vessel." [161]

But while you seek diligently to foster this mutual love, give good heed that it do not turn to any manner of jealousy. Just as the worm is often hatched in the sweetest and ripest apple, so too often jealousy springs up in the most warm and loving hearts, defiling and ruining them, and if it is allowed to take root, it will produce dissension, quarrels, and separation. Of a truth, jealousy never arises where love is built up on true virtue, and therefore it is a sure sign of an earthly, sensual love, in which mistrust and inconstancy is soon infused. It is a sorry kind of friendship which seeks to strengthen itself by jealousy; for though jealousy may be a sign of strong, hot friendship, it is certainly no sign of a good, pure, perfect attachment; and that because perfect love implies absolute trust in the person loved, whereas jealousy implies uncertainty.

If you, husbands, would have your wives faithful, be it yours to set them the example. "How have you the face to exact purity from your wives," asks S. Gregory Nazianzen, "if you yourself live an impure life? or how can you require that which you do not give in return? If you would have them chaste, let your own conduct to them be chaste. S. Paul bids you possess your vessel in sanctification; but if, on the contrary, you teach them evil, no wonder that they dishonour you. And ye, O women! whose honour is inseparable from modesty and purity, preserve it jealously, and never allow the smallest speck to soil the whiteness of your reputation."

Shrink sensitively from the veriest trifles which can touch it; never permit any gallantries whatsoever. Suspect any who presume to flatter your beauty or grace, for when men praise wares they cannot purchase they are often tempted to steal; and if any one should dare to speak in disparagement of your husband, show that you are irrecoverably offended, for it is plain that he not only seeks your fall, but he counts you as half fallen, since the bargain with the new-comer is half made when one is disgusted with the first merchant.

Ladies both in ancient and modern times have worn pearls in their ears, for the sake (so says Pliny) of hearing them tinkle against each other. But remembering how that friend of God, Isaac, sent earrings as first pledges of his love to the chaste Rebecca, I look upon this mystic ornament as signifying that the first claim a husband has over his wife, and one which she ought most faithfully to keep for him, is her ear; so that no evil word or rumour enter therein, and nought be heard save the pleasant sound of true and pure words, which are represented by the choice pearls of the Gospel. Never forget that souls are poisoned through the ear as much as bodies through the mouth.

Love and faithfulness lead to familiarity and confidence, and Saints have abounded in tender caresses. Isaac and Rebecca, the type of chaste married life, indulged in such caresses, as to convince Abimelech that they must be husband and wife. The great S. Louis, strict as he was to himself, was so tender towards his wife, that some were ready to blame him for it; although in truth he rather deserved praise for subjecting his lofty, martial mind to the little details of conjugal love. Such minor matters will not suffice to knit hearts, but they tend to draw them closer, and promote mutual happiness.

Before giving birth to S. Augustine, S. Monica offered him repeatedly to God's Glory, as he himself tells us; and it is a good lesson for Christian women how to offer the fruit of their womb to God, Who accepts the free oblations of loving hearts, and promotes the desires of such faithful mothers: witness Samuel, S. Thomas Aquinas, S. Andrea di Fiesole, and others. [162] S. Bernard's mother, worthy of such a son, was wont to take her new-born babes in her arms to offer them to Jesus Christ, thenceforward loving them with a reverential love, as a sacred deposit from God; and so entirely was her offering accepted, that all her seven children became Saints. [163] And when children begin to use their reason, fathers and mothers should take great pains to fill their hearts with the fear of God. This the good Queen Blanche did most earnestly by S. Louis, her son: witness her oft-repeated words, "My son, I would sooner see you die than guilty of a mortal sin;" words which sank so deeply into the saintly monarch's heart, that he himself said there was no day on which they did not recur to his mind, and strengthen him in treading God's ways.

We call races and generations Houses; and the Hebrews were wont to speak of the birth of children as "the building up of the house;" as it is written of the Jewish midwives in Egypt, that the Lord "made them houses;" [164] whereby we learn that a good house is not reared so much by the accumulation of worldly goods, as by the bringing up of children in the ways of holiness and of God; and to this end no labour or trouble must be spared, for children are the crown of their parents. [165] Thus it was that S. Monica stedfastly withstood S. Augustine's evil propensities, and, following him across sea and land, he became more truly the child of her tears in the conversion of his soul, than the son of her body in his natural birth.

S. Paul assigns the charge of the household to the woman; and consequently some hold that the devotion of the family depends more upon the wife than the husband, who is more frequently absent, and has less influence in the house. Certainly King Solomon, in the Book of Proverbs, refers all household prosperity to the care and industry of that virtuous woman whom he describes. [166]

We read in Genesis that Isaac "entreated the Lord for his wife, because she was barren;" [167] or as the Hebrews read it, he prayed "over against" her,--on opposite sides of the place of prayer,--and his prayer was granted. That is the most fruitful union between husband and wife which is founded in devotion, to which they should mutually stimulate one another. There are certain fruits, like the quince, of so bitter a quality, that they are scarcely eatable, save when preserved; while others again, like cherries and apricots, are so delicate and soft, that they can only be kept by the same treatment. So the wife must seek that her husband be sweetened with the sugar of devotion, for man without religion is a rude, rough animal; and the husband will desire to see his wife devout, as without it her frailty and weakness are liable to tarnish and injury. S. Paul says that "the unbelieving husband is sanctified by the wife, and the unbelieving wife is sanctified by the husband;" [168] because in so close a tie one may easily draw the other to what is good. And how great is the blessing on those faithful husbands and wives who confirm one another continually in the Fear of the Lord!

Moreover, each should have such forbearance towards the other, that they never grow angry, or fall into discussion and argument. The bee will not dwell in a spot where there is much loud noise or shouting, or echo; neither will God's Holy Spirit dwell in a household where altercation and tumult, arguing and quarrelling, disturb the peace.

S. Gregory Nazianzen says that in his time married people were wont to celebrate the anniversary of their wedding, and it is a custom I should greatly approve, provided it were not a merely secular celebration; but if husbands and wives would go on that day to Confession and Communion, and commend their married life specially to God, renewing their resolution to promote mutual good by increased love and faithfulness, and thus take breath, so to say, and gather new vigour from the Lord to go on stedfastly in their vocation.

Footnotes:

160. Eph. v. 25, 22.

161. 1 Pet. iii. 7.

162. S. Francis de Sales himself is an instance, his mother having offered him up to God while yet unborn.

163. Cf. Marie Jenna's lovely poem, "L'aimeras-tu?" "Je ne veux plus d'enfants, si ce ne sont des saints."

164. Exod. i. 21.

165. Prov. xvii. 6.

166. Prov. xxxi.

167. Gen. xxv. 21.

168. 1 Cor. vii. 14.

CHAPTER XXXIX - The Sanctity of the Marriage Bed

THE marriage bed should be undefiled, as the Apostle tells us, [169] i.e. pure, as it was when it was first instituted in the earthly Paradise, wherein no unruly desires or impure thought might enter. All that is merely earthly must be treated as means to fulfil the end God sets before His creatures. Thus we eat in order to preserve life, moderately, voluntarily, and without seeking an undue, unworthy satisfaction therefrom. "The time is short," says S. Paul; "it remaineth that both they that have wives be as though they had not, and they that use this world, as not abusing it." [170]

Let every one, then, use this world according to his vocation, but so as not to entangle himself with its love, that he may be as free and ready to serve God as though he used it not. S. Augustine says that it is the great fault of men to want to enjoy things which they are only meant to use, and to use those which they are only meant to enjoy. We ought to enjoy spiritual things, and only use those which are material; but when we turn the use of these latter into enjoyment, the reasonable soul becomes degraded to a mere brutish level.

Footnotes:

169. Heb. xiii. 4.
170. 1 Cor. vii. 30, 31.

CHAPTER XL - Counsels to Widows

SAINT PAUL teaches us all in the person of S. Timothy when he says, "Honour widows that are widows indeed." [171] Now to be "a widow indeed" it is necessary:--

1. That the widow be one not in body only, but in heart also; that is to say, that she be fixed in an unalterable resolution to continue in her widowhood Those widows who are but waiting the opportunity of marrying again are only widowed in externals, while in will they have already laid aside their loneliness. If the "widow indeed" chooses to confirm her widowhood by offering herself by a vow to God, she will adorn that widowhood, and make her resolution doubly sure, for the remembrance that she cannot break her vow without danger of forfeiting Paradise, will make her so watchful over herself, that a great barrier will be raised against all kind of temptation that may assail her. S. Augustine strongly recommends Christian widows to take this vow, and the learned Origen goes yet further, for he advises married women to take a vow of chastity in the event of losing their husbands, so that amid the joys of married life they may yet have a share in the merits of a chaste widowhood. Vows render the actions performed under their shelter more acceptable to God, strengthen us to perform good works, and help us to devote to Him not merely those good works which are, so to say, the fruits of a holy will, but to consecrate that will itself, the source of all we do, to Him. By ordinary chastity we offer our body to God, retaining the power to return to sensual pleasure; but the vow of chastity is an absolute and irrevocable gift to Him, without any power to recall it, thereby making ourselves the happy slaves of Him Whose service is to be preferred to royal power. And as I greatly approve the counsels of the two venerable Fathers I have named, I would have such persons as are so favoured as to wish to embrace them, do so prudently, and in a holy, stedfast spirit, after careful examination of their own courage, having asked heavenly guidance, and taken the advice of some discreet and pious director, and then all will be profitably done.

2. Further, all such renunciation of second marriage must be done with a single heart, in order to fix the affections more entirely on God, and to seek a more complete union with Him. For if the widow retains her widowhood merely to enrich her children, or for any other worldly motive, she may receive the praise of men, but not that of God, inasmuch as nothing is worthy of His Approbation save that which is done for His Sake. Moreover, she who would be a widow indeed must be voluntarily cut off from all worldly delights. "She that liveth in pleasure is dead while she liveth," S. Paul says. [172] A widow who seeks to be admired and followed and flattered, who frequents balls and parties, who takes pleasure in dressing, perfuming and adorning herself, may be a widow in the body, but she is dead as to the soul. What does it matter, I pray you, whether the flag of Adonis and his profane love be made of white feathers or a net of crape? Nay, sometimes there is a conscious vanity in that black is the most becoming dress; and she who thereby endeavours to captivate men, and who lives in empty pleasure, is "dead while she liveth," and is a mere mockery of widowhood.

"The time of retrenchment is come, the voice of the turtle is heard in our land." [173] Retrenchment of worldly superfluity is required of whosoever would lead a devout life, but above all, it is needful for the widow indeed, who mourns the loss of her husband like a true turtle-dove. When Naomi returned from Moab to Bethlehem, those that had known her in her earlier and brighter days were moved, and said, "Is this Naomi? And she said unto them, Call me not Naomi (which means beautiful and agreeable), call me Mara, for the Almighty hath dealt very bitterly with me. I went out full, and the Lord hath brought me home again empty." [174] Even so the devout widow will not desire to be called or counted beautiful or agreeable, asking no more than to be that which God wills,--lowly and abject in His Eyes.

The lamp which is fed with aromatic oil sends forth a yet sweeter odour when it is extinguished; and so those women whose married love was true and pure, give out a stronger perfume of virtue and chastity when their light (that is, their husband) is extinguished by death. Love for a husband while living is a common matter enough among women, but to love him so deeply as to refuse to take another after his death, is a kind of love peculiar to her who is a widow indeed. Hope in God, while resting on a husband, is not so rare, but to hope in Him, when left alone and desolate, is a very gracious and worthy thing. And thus it is that widowhood becomes a test of the perfection of the virtues displayed by a woman in her married life.

The widow who has children requiring her care and guidance, above all in what pertains to their souls and the shaping of their lives, cannot and ought not on any wise to forsake them. S. Paul teaches this emphatically, and says that those who "provide not for their own, and specially for those of their own house, are worse than an infidel;" [175] but if her children do not need her care, then the widow should gather together all her affections and thoughts, in order to devote them more wholly to making progress in the love of God. If there is no call obliging her in conscience to attend to external secular matters (legal or other), I should advise her to leave them all alone, and to manage her affairs as quietly and peacefully as may be, even if such a course does not seem the most profitable. The fruit of disputes and lawsuits must be very great indeed before it can be compared in worth to the blessing of holy peace; not to say that those legal entanglements and the like are essentially distracting, and often open the way for enemies who sully the purity of a heart which should be solely devoted to God.

Prayer should be the widow's chief occupation: she has no love left save for God,--she should scarce have ought to say to any save God; and as iron, which is restrained from yielding to the attraction of the magnet when a diamond is near, darts instantly towards it so soon as the diamond is removed, so the widow's heart, which could not rise up wholly to God, or simply follow the leadings of His Heavenly Love during her husband's life, finds itself set free, when he is dead, to give itself entirely to Him, and cries out, with the Bride in the Canticles, "Draw me, I will run after Thee." [176] I will be wholly Thine, and seek nothing save the "savour of Thy good ointments."

A devout widow should chiefly seek to cultivate the graces of perfect modesty, renouncing all honours, rank, title, society, and the like vanities; she should be diligent in ministering to the poor and sick, comforting the afflicted, leading the young to a life of devotion, studying herself to be a perfect model of virtue to younger women. Necessity and simplicity should be the adornment of her garb, humility and charity of her actions, simplicity and kindliness of her words, modesty and purity of her eyes,--Jesus Christ Crucified the only Love of her heart.

Briefly, the true widow abides in the Church as a little March violet, [177] shedding forth an exquisite sweetness through the perfume of her devotion, ever concealing herself beneath the ample leaves of her heart's lowliness, while her subdued colouring indicates her mortification. She dwells in waste, uncultivated places, because she shrinks from the world's intercourse, and seeks to shelter her heart from the glare with which earthly longings, whether of honours, wealth, or love itself, might dazzle her. "Blessed is she if she so abide," says the holy Apostle. [178]

Much more could I say on this subject, but suffice it to bid her who seeks to be a widow indeed, read S. Jerome's striking Letters to Salvia, and the other noble ladies who rejoiced in being the spiritual children of such a Father. Nothing can be said more, unless it be to warn the widow indeed not to condemn or even censure those who do resume the married life, for there are cases in which God orders it thus to His Own greater Glory. We must ever bear in mind the ancient teaching, that in Heaven virgins, wives, and widows will know no difference, save that which their true hearts' humility assigns them.

Footnotes:

171. 1 Tim. v. 3.

172. 1 Tim. v. 6.

173. Cant. ii. 12. in the Vulgate, "Tempus putationis advenit; vox turturis audita est in terra nostra."

174. Ruth i. 20, 21.

175. 1 Tim. v. 8.

176. Cant. i. 3, 4.

177. "Quam gloriosa enim Ecclesia, et quanta virtutum multitudine, quasi florum varietate! Habet hortus ille Dominicus non solum rosas martyrum, sed et lilia virginum, et conjugatorum hederas, violasque viduarum Prorsus, Dilectissimi, nullum genus hominum de sua vocatione desperet: pro omnibus passus est Christus."--S. Aug. Serm. ccciv., In Laurent. Mart. iii. cap. 1-3. "How glorious is the Church, how countless her graces, varied as the flowers of earth in beauty! This garden of the Lord bears not only the martyr's rose, but the virgin's lily, the ivy wreath of wedded love, and the violet of widowhood. Therefore, beloved, let none despair of his calling, since Christ suffered for all."

178. 1 Cor. vii. 40. "Beatior autem erit si sic permanserit."--Vulgate.

CHAPTER XLI - One Word to Maidens

O YE virgins, I have but a word to say to you. If you look to married life in this life, guard your first love jealously for your husband. It seems to me a miserable fraud to give a husband a worn-out heart, whose love has been frittered away and despoiled of its first bloom instead of a true, whole-hearted love. But if you are happily called to be the chaste and holy bride of spiritual nuptials, and purpose to live a life of virginity, then in Christ's Name I bid you keep all your purest, most sensitive love for your Heavenly Bridegroom, Who, being Very Purity Himself, has a special love for purity; Him to Whom the first-fruits of all good things are due, above all those of love.

S. Jerome's Epistles will supply you with the needful counsels; and inasmuch as your state of life requires obedience, seek out a guide under whose direction you may wholly dedicate yourself, body and soul, to His Divine Majesty.

PART IV – CONTAINING NEEDFUL COUNSELS CONCERNING SOME ORDINARY TEMPTATIONS

CHAPTER I - We must not trifle with the Words of Worldly Wisdom

DIRECTLY that your worldly friends perceive that you aim at leading a devout life, they will let loose endless shafts of mockery and misrepresentation upon you; the more malicious will attribute your change to hypocrisy, designing, or bigotry; they will affirm that the world having looked coldly upon you, failing its favour you turn to God; while your friends will make a series of what, from their point of view, are prudent and charitable remonstrances. They will tell you that you are growing morbid; that you will lose your worldly credit, and will make yourself unacceptable to the world; they will prognosticate your premature old age, the ruin of your material prosperity; they will tell you that in the world you must live as the world does; that you can be saved without all this fuss; and much more of the like nature.

My daughter, all this is vain and foolish talk: these people have no real regard either for your bodily health or your material prosperity. "If ye were of the world," the Saviour has said, "the world would love his own; but because ye are not of the world, but I have chosen you out of the world, therefore the world hateth you." [179]

We have all seen men, and women too, pass the whole night, even several in succession, playing at chess or cards; and what can be a more dismal, unwholesome thing than that? But the world has not a word to say against it, and their friends are nowise troubled. But give up an hour to meditation, or get up rather earlier than usual to prepare for Holy Communion, and they will send for the doctor to cure you of hypochondria or jaundice! People spend every night for a month dancing, and no one will complain of being the worse; but if they keep the one watch of Christmas Eve, we shall hear of endless colds and maladies the next day! Is it not as plain as possible that the world is an unjust judge; indulgent and kindly to its own children, harsh and uncharitable to the children of God? We cannot stand well with the world save by renouncing His approval. It is not possible to satisfy the world's unreasonable demands: "John the Baptist came neither eating bread nor drinking wine; and ye say he hath a devil. The Son of Man is come eating and drinking, and ye say, Behold a gluttonous man, and a winebibber, the friend of publicans and sinners." [180] Even so, my child, if we give in to the world, and laugh, dance, and play as it does, it will affect to be scandalized; if we refuse to do so, it will accuse us of being hypocritical or morbid. If we adorn ourselves after its fashion, it will put some evil construction on what we do; if we go in plain attire, it will accuse us of meanness; our cheerfulness will be called dissipation; our mortification dulness; and ever casting its evil eye upon us, nothing we can do will please it. It exaggerates our failings, and publishes them abroad as sins; it represents our venial sins as mortal, and our sins of infirmity as malicious. S. Paul says that charity is kind, but the world is unkind; charity thinks no evil, but the world thinks evil of every one, and if it cannot find fault with our actions, it is sure at least to impute bad motives to them,--whether the sheep be black or white, horned or no, the wolf will devour them if he can. Do what we will, the world must wage war upon us. If we spend any length of time in confession, it will speculate on what we have so much to say about! if we are brief, it will suggest that we are keeping back something! It spies out our every act, and at the most trifling angry word, sets us down as intolerable. Attention to business is avarice, meekness mere silliness; whereas the wrath of worldly people is to be reckoned as generosity, their avarice, economy, their mean deeds, honourable. There are always spiders at hand to spoil the honey-bee's comb.

Let us leave the blind world to make as much noise as it may,--like a bat molesting the songbirds of day; let us be firm in our ways, unchangeable in our resolutions, and perseverance will be the test of our self-surrender to God, and our deliberate choice of the devout life.

The planets and a wandering comet shine with much the same brightness, but the comet's is a passing blaze, which does not linger long, while the planets cease not to display their brightness. Even so hypocrisy and real goodness have much outward resemblance; but one is easily known from the other, inasmuch as hypocrisy is short-lived, and disperses like a mist, while real goodness is firm and abiding. There is no surer groundwork for the beginnings of a devout life than the endurance of misrepresentation and calumny, since thereby we escape the danger of vainglory and pride, which are like the midwives of Egypt, who were bidden by Pharaoh to kill the male children born to Israel directly after their birth. We are crucified to the world, and the world must be as crucified to us. It esteems us as fools, let us esteem it as mad.

Footnotes:

179. S. John xv. 19.
180. S. Luke vii. 33, 34.

CHAPTER II - The need of a Good Courage

HOWEVER much we may admire and crave for light, it is apt to dazzle our eyes when they have been long accustomed to darkness; and on first visiting a foreign country, we are sure to feel strange among its inhabitants, however kindly or courteous they may be. Even so, my child, your changed life may be attended with some inward discomfort, and you may feel some reaction of discouragement and weariness after you have taken a final farewell of the world and its follies. Should it be so, I pray you take it patiently, for it will not last,--it is merely the disturbance caused by novelty; and when it is gone by, you will abound in consolations. At first you may suffer somewhat under the loss what you enjoyed among your vain, frivolous companions; but would you forfeit the eternal gifts of God for such things as these? The empty amusements which have engrossed you hitherto may rise up attractively before your imagination, and strive to win you back to rest in them; but are you bold enough to give up a blessed eternity for such deceitful snares? Believe me, if you will but persevere you will not fail to enjoy a sweetness so real and satisfying, that you will be constrained to confess that the world has only gall to give as compared with this honey, and that one single day of devotion is worth more than a thousand years of worldly life.

But you see before you the mountain of Christian perfection, which is very high, and you exclaim in fearfulness that you can never ascend it. Be of good cheer, my child. When the young bees first begin to live they are mere grubs, unable to hover over flowers, or to fly to the mountains, or even to the little hills where they might gather honey; but they are fed for a time with the honey laid up by their predecessors, and by degrees the grubs put forth their wings and grow strong, until they fly abroad and gather their harvest from all the country round. Now we are yet but as grubs in devotion, unable to fly at will, and attain the desired aim of Christian perfection; but if we begin to take shape through our desires and resolutions, our wings will gradually grow, and we may hope one day to become spiritual bees, able to fly. Meanwhile let us feed upon the honey left us in the teaching of so many holy men of old, praying God that He would grant us doves' wings, so that we may not only fly during this life, but find an abiding resting-place in Eternity.

CHAPTER III - Of Temptations, and the difference between experiencing them and consenting to them

PICTURE to yourself a young princess beloved of her husband, to whom some evil wretch should send a messenger to tempt her to infidelity. First, the messenger would bring forth his propositions. Secondly, the princess would either accept or reject the overtures. Thirdly, she would consent to them or refuse them. Even so, when Satan, the world, and the flesh look upon a soul espoused to the Son of God, they set temptations and suggestions before that soul, whereby--1. Sin is proposed to it. 2. Which proposals are either pleasing or displeasing to the soul. 3. The soul either consents, or rejects them. In other words, the three downward steps of temptation, delectation, and consent. And although the three steps may not always be so clearly defined as in this illustration, they are to be plainly traced in all great and serious sins.

If we should undergo the temptation to every sin whatsoever during our whole life, that would not damage us in the Sight of God's Majesty, provided we took no pleasure in it, and did not consent to it; and that because in temptation we do not act, we only suffer, and inasmuch as we take no delight in it, we can be liable to no blame. S. Paul bore long time with temptations of the flesh, but so far from displeasing God thereby, He was glorified in them. The blessed Angela di Foligni underwent terrible carnal temptations, which move us to pity as we read of them. S. Francis and S. Benedict both experienced grievous temptations, so that the one cast himself amid thorns, the other into the snow, to quench them, but so far from losing anything of God's Grace thereby, they greatly increased it.

Be then very courageous amid temptation, and never imagine yourself conquered so long as it is displeasing to you, ever bearing in mind the difference between experiencing and consenting to temptation, [181] --that difference being, that whereas they may be experienced while most displeasing to us, we can never consent to them without taking pleasure in them, inasmuch as pleasure felt in a temptation is usually the first step towards consent. So let the enemies of our salvation spread as many snares and wiles in our way as they will, let them besiege the door of our heart perpetually, let them ply us with endless proposals to sin,--so long as we abide in our firm resolution to take no pleasure therein, we cannot offend God any more than the husband of the princess in my illustration could be displeased with her because of the overtures made to her, so long as she was in no way gratified by them. Of course, there is one great difference between my imaginary princess and the soul, namely, that the former has it in her power to drive away the messenger of evil and never hear him more, while the latter cannot always refuse to experience temptation, although it be always in its power to refuse consent. But how long soever the temptation may persist, it cannot harm us so long as it is unwelcome to us.

But again, as to the pleasure which may be taken in temptation (technically called delectation), inasmuch as our souls have two parts, one inferior, the other superior, and the inferior does not always choose to be led by the superior, but takes its own line,--it not unfrequently happens that the inferior part takes pleasure in a temptation not only without consent from, but absolutely in contradiction to the superior will. It is this contest which S. Paul describes when he speaks of the "law in my members, warring against the law of my mind," [182] and of the "flesh lusting against the spirit." [183]

Have you ever watched a great burning furnace heaped up with ashes? Look at it some ten or twelve hours afterwards, and there will scarce be any living fire there, or only a little smouldering in the very heart thereof. Nevertheless, if you can find that tiny lingering spark, it will suffice to rekindle the extinguished flames. So it is with love, which is the true spiritual life amid our greatest, most active temptations. Temptation, flinging its delectation into the inferior part of the soul, covers it wholly with ashes, and leaves but a little spark of God's Love, which can be found nowhere save hidden far down in the heart or mind, and even that is hard to find. But nevertheless it is there, since however troubled we may have been in body and mind, we firmly resolved not to consent to sin or the temptation thereto, and that delectation of the exterior man was rejected by the interior spirit. Thus though our will may have been thoroughly beset by the temptation, it was not conquered, and so we are certain that all such delectation was involuntary, and consequently not sinful.

Footnotes:

181. The English language does not contain the precise relative terms equivalent to "sentir et con-sentir."

182. Rom. vii. 23.

183. Gal. v. 17.

CHAPTER IV - Two striking Illustrations of the same

THIS distinction, which is very important, is well illustrated by the description S. Jerome gives of a young man bound to a voluptuous bed by the softest silken cords, and subjected to the wiles and lures of a treacherous tempter, with the express object of causing him to fall. Greatly as all his senses and imagination must inevitably have been possessed by so vehement an assault, he proved that his heart was free and his will unconquered, for, having physical control over no member save his tongue, he bit that off and spat it out at his foe, a foe more terrible than the tyrant's executioners.

S. Catherine of Sienna has left a somewhat similar record. The Evil One having obtained permission from God to assault that pious virgin with all his strength, so long as he laid no hand upon her, filled her heart with impure suggestions, and surrounded her with every conceivable temptation of sight and sound, which, penetrating into the Saint's heart, so filled it, that, as she herself has said, nothing remained free save her most acute superior will. This struggle endured long, until at length Our Lord appeared to her, and she exclaimed, "Where wert Thou, O most Dear Lord, when my heart was so overwhelmed with darkness and foulness?" Whereupon He answered, "I was within thy heart, My child." "How could that be, Lord," she asked, "when it was so full of evil? Canst Thou abide in a place so foul?" Then our Lord replied, "Tell Me, did these evil thoughts and imaginations give thee pain or pleasure? didst thou take delight, or didst thou grieve over them?" To which S. Catherine made answer, "They grieved me exceedingly." Then the Lord said, "Who, thinkest thou, was it that caused thee to be thus grieved, save I Myself, hidden within thy soul? Believe Me, My child, had I not been there, these evil thoughts which swarmed around thy soul, and which thou couldst not banish, would speedily have overpowered it, and entering in, thy free will would have accepted them, and so death had struck that soul; but inasmuch as I was there, I filled thy heart with reluctance and resistance, so that it set itself stedfastly against the temptation, and finding itself unable to contend as vigorously as it desired, it did but experience a yet more vehement abhorrence of sin and of itself. Thus these very troubles became a great merit again to thee, and a great accession of virtue and strength to thy soul."

Here, you see, were the embers covered over with ashes, while temptation and delectation had entered the heart and surrounded the will, which, aided only by the Saviour, resisted all evil inspirations with great disgust, and a persevering refusal to consent to sin. Verily the soul which loves God is sometimes in sore straits to know whether He abideth in it or no, and whether that Divine Love for which it fights is extinguished or burns yet. But it is the very essence of the perfection of that Heavenly Love to require its lovers to endure and fight for Love's sake, without knowing even whether they possess the very Love for which and in which they strive.

CHAPTER V - Encouragement for the Tempted Soul

GOD never permits such grievous temptations and assaults to try any, save those souls whom He designs to lead on to His own living, highest love, but nevertheless it does not follow as a natural consequence that they are certain to attain thereto. Indeed, it has often happened that those who had been stedfast under violent assaults, failing to correspond faithfully to Divine Grace, have yielded under the pressure of very trifling temptations. I would warn you of this, my child, so that, should you ever be tried by great temptations, you may know that God is showing special favour to you, thereby proving that He means to exalt you in His Sight; but that at the same time you may ever be humble and full of holy fear, not overconfident in your power to resist lesser temptations because you have overcome those that were greater, unless by means of a most stedfast faithfulness to God.

Come what may in the shape of temptation, attended by whatsoever of delectation,--so long as your will refuses consent, not merely to the temptation itself, but also to the delectation, you need have no fear,--God is not offended. When any one has swooned away, and gives no sign of life, we put our hand to his heart, and if we find the slightest fluttering there, we conclude that he still lives, and that, with the help of stimulants and counter-irritants, we may restore consciousness and power. Even so, sometimes amid the violence of temptation the soul seems altogether to faint away, and to lose all spiritual life and action. But if you would be sure how it really is, put your hand on the heart. See whether heart and will yet have any spiritual motion; that is to say, whether they fulfil their own special duty in refusing consent to and acceptance of temptation and its gratification; for so long as the power to refuse exists within the soul, we may be sure that Love, the life of the soul, is there, and that Jesus Christ, our Lord and Saviour, is within, although, it may be, hidden; and that by means of stedfast perseverance in prayer, and the Sacraments, and confidence in God, strength will be restored, and the soul will live with a full and joyous life.

CHAPTER VI - When Temptation and Delectation are Sin

THAT princess, whom we have already taken as an illustration, was not to blame in the unlawful pursuit we supposed to be made of her, because it was against her will; but if, on the contrary, she had in any way led to it, or sought to attract him who sought her, she were certainly guilty of the pursuit itself; and even if she withheld her consent, she would still deserve censure and punishment. Thus it sometimes happens that temptation in itself is sin to us, because we have ourselves brought it upon us. For instance, if I know that gaming leads me to passion and blasphemy, and that all play is a temptation to me, I sin each and every time that I play, and I am responsible for all the temptations which may come upon me at the gaming table. So again, if I know that certain society involves me in temptation to evil, and yet I voluntarily seek it, I am unquestionably responsible for all that I may encounter in the way of temptation therein.

When it is possible to avoid the delectation arising out of temptation, it is always a sin to accept it, in proportion to the pleasure we take, and the amount of consent given, whether that be great or small, brief or lasting. The princess of our illustration is to blame if she merely listens to the guilty propositions made to her but still more so if, after listening, she takes pleasure in them, and allows her heart to feed and rest thereupon; for although she has no intention of really doing that which is proposed, her heart gives a spiritual consent when she takes pleasure in it, and it must always be wrong to let either body or mind rest on anything unworthy,--and wrongdoing lies so entirely in the heart's co-operation, that without this no mere bodily action can be sin.

Therefore, when you are tempted to any sin, examine whether you voluntarily exposed yourself to the temptation, and if you find that you have done so by putting yourself into its way, or by not foreseeing the temptation, as you ought to have done, then it is sin; but if you have done nothing to bring about the temptation, it is not in anywise to be imputed to you as sin.

When the delectation which attends temptation might have been avoided, but has not been avoided, there is always a certain amount of sin according to the degree to which we have lingered over it, and the kind of pleasure we have taken in it. If a woman who has not wilfully attracted unlawful admiration, nevertheless takes pleasure in such admiration, she is doing wrong, always supposing that what pleases her is the admiration. But if the person who courts her plays exquisitely on the lute, and she took pleasure, not in the personal attentions paid to herself, but in the sweetness and harmony of the music, there would be no sin in that, although it would be wrong to give way to any extent to her pleasure, for fear of its leading on to pleasure in the pursuit of herself. So again, if some clever stratagem whereby to avenge me of an enemy is suggested, and I take no satisfaction and give no consent to the vengeance, but am only pleased at the cleverness of the invention, I am not sinning; although it were very inexpedient to dwell long upon it, lest little by little I should go on to take pleasure in the thought of revenge.

Sometimes we are taken by surprise by some sense of delectation following so closely upon the temptation, that we are off our guard. This can be but a very slight venial sin, which would become greater if, after once we perceive the danger, we allow ourselves to dally with it, or question as to admitting or rejecting it,--greater still if we carelessly neglect to resist it;--and if we deliberately allow ourselves to rest in any such pleasure, it becomes very great sin, especially if the thing attracting us be unquestionably evil. Thus it is a great sin in a woman to allow herself to dwell upon any unlawful affections, although she may have no intention of ever really yielding to them.

CHAPTER VII - Remedies for Great Occasions

SO soon as you feel yourself anywise tempted, do as our little children when they see a wolf or a bear in the mountains. Forthwith they run to the protection of their father or mother, or at least cry out for help. Do you fly in like manner to God, claiming His compassion and succour,--it is the remedy taught us by our Lord Himself: "Pray that ye enter not into temptation" [184]

If, nevertheless, the temptation persists or increases, hasten in spirit to embrace the holy Cross, as though you beheld Jesus Christ Crucified actually Present. Make firm protests against consenting, and ask His Help thereto; and, so long as the temptation lasts, do you persist in making acts of non-consent. But while making these acts and these protests, do not fix your eyes on the temptation,--look solely on Our Lord, for if you dwell on the temptation, especially when it is strong, your courage may be shaken. Divert your mind with any right and healthy occupation, for if that takes possession and fills your thoughts, it will drive away temptation and evil imaginations.

One great remedy against all manner of temptation, great or small, is to open the heart and lay bare its suggestions, likings, and dislikings, to your director; for, as you may observe, the first condition which the Evil One makes with a soul, when he wants to seduce it, is silence. Even as a bad man, seeking to seduce a woman, enjoins silence concerning himself to her father or husband, whereas God would always have us make known all His inspirations to our superiors and guides.

If, after all, the temptation still troubles and persecutes us, there is nothing to be done on our side save to persist in protesting that we will not consent; for just as no maiden can be married while she persists in saying No, so no soul, however oppressed, can be guilty while it says the same.

Do not argue with your Enemy, and give but one answer,--that with which Our Lord confounded him, "Get thee hence, Satan, for it is written, Thou shalt worship the Lord thy God, and Him only shalt thou serve." [185] Just as the pure wife would make no reply, and cast no glance on the foul seducer who strove to lead her astray, but would straightway fly from him to her husband's side, not arguing, but cleaving to her lawful lord in renewed fidelity;--so the devout soul when assailed by temptation should never trifle with it by answer or argument, but simply fly to the Side of Jesus Christ, its Bridegroom; renewing its pledges of unchanging devotion and faithfulness to Him.

Footnotes:

184. S. Luke xxii. 40.
185. S. Matt. iv. 10.

CHAPTER VIII - How to resist Minor Temptations

WHILE it is right to resist great temptations with invincible courage, and all such victories will be most valuable, still there is perhaps more absolute profit to our souls in resisting little ones. For although the greater temptations exceed in power, there are so infinitely more in number of little temptations, that a victory over them is fully as important as over the greater but rarer ones. No one will question but that wolves and bears are more dangerous than flies, but they do not worry and annoy us, or try our patience as these do. While is not a hard thing to abstain from murder, but it is very difficult to avoid all passing fits of anger, which assail us at every moment. A man or woman can easily keep from adultery, but it is less easy to abstain from all words and glances which are disloyal. While is easy to keep from stealing another man's goods, but often difficult to resist coveting them; easy to avoid bearing false witness in direct judgment, difficult to be perfectly truthful in conversation; easy to refrain from getting drunk, difficult to be absolutely sober; easy not to wish for a neighbour's death, difficult not to wish anything contrary to his interests; easy to keep from slander, difficult to avoid all contempt.

In short, all these minor temptations to anger, suspicion, jealousy, envy, levity, vanity, duplicity, affectation, foolish thoughts, and the like, are a perpetual trial even to those who are most devout and most resolute; and therefore, my daughter, we ought carefully and diligently to prepare for this warfare. Be assured that every victory won over these little foes is as a precious stone in the crown of glory which God prepares for us in Paradise. So, while awaiting and making ready for a stedfast and brave resistance to great temptations should they come, let us not fail diligently to fight against these meaner, weaker foes.

CHAPTER IX - How remedy Minor Temptations

NOW as to all these trifling temptations of vanity, suspicion, vexation, jealousy, envy, and the like, which flit around one like flies or gnats, now settling on one's nose,--anon stinging one's cheek,--as it is wholly impossible altogether to free one's-self from their importunity; the best resistance one can make is not to be fretted by them. All these things may worry one, but they cannot really harm us, so long as our wills are firmly resolved to serve God.

Therefore despise all these trivial onslaughts, and do not even deign to think about them; but let them buzz about your ears as much as they please, and flit hither and thither just as you tolerate flies;-- even if they sting you, and strive to light within your heart, do no more than simply remove them, not fighting with them, or arguing, but simply doing that which is precisely contrary to their suggestions, and specially making acts of the Love of God. If you will take my advice, you will not toil on obstinately in resisting them by exercising the contrary virtue, for that would become a sort of struggle with the foe;--but, after making an act of this directly contrary virtue (always supposing you have time to recognise what the definite temptation is), simply turn with your whole heart towards Jesus Christ Crucified, and lovingly kiss His Sacred Feet. This is the best way to conquer the Enemy, whether in small or great temptations; for inasmuch as the Love of God contains the perfection of every virtue, and that more excellently than the very virtues themselves; it is also the most sovereign remedy against all vice, and if you accustom your mind under all manner of temptation to have recourse to this safety- place, you will not be constrained to enter upon a worryingly minute investigation of your temptations, but, so soon as you are anywise troubled, your mind will turn naturally to its one sovereign remedy. Moreover, this way of dealing with temptation is so offensive to the Evil One, that, finding he does but provoke souls to an increased love of God by his assaults, he discontinues them.

In short, you may be sure that if you dally with your minor, oft-recurring temptations, and examine too closely into them in detail, you will simply stupefy yourself to no purpose.

CHAPTER X - How to strengthen the Heart against Temptation

EXAMINE from time to time what are the dominant passions of your soul, and having ascertained this, mould your life, so that in thought, word and deed you may as far as possible counteract them. For instance, if you know that you are disposed to be vain, reflect often upon the emptiness of this earthly life, call to mind how burdensome all mere earthly vanities will be to the conscience at the hour of death, how unworthy of a generous heart, how puerile and childish, and the like. See that your words have no tendency to foster your vanity, and even though you may seem to be doing so but reluctantly, strive to despise it heartily, and to rank yourself in every way among its enemies. Indeed, by dint of steady opposition to anything, we teach ourselves to hate even that which we began by liking. Do as many lowly, humble deeds as lie in your power, even if you perform them unwillingly at first; for by this means you will form a habit of humility, and you will weaken your vanity, so that when temptation arises, you will be less predisposed to yield, and stronger to resist. Or if you are given to avarice, think often of the folly of this sin, which makes us the slave of what was made only to serve us; remember how when we die we must leave all we possess to those who come after us, who may squander it, ruin their own souls by misusing it, and so forth. Speak against covetousness, commend the abhorrence in which it is held by the world; and constrain yourself to abundant almsgiving, as also to not always using opportunities of accumulation. If you have a tendency to trifle with the affections, often call to mind what a dangerous amusement it is for yourself and others; how unworthy a thing it is to use the noblest feelings of the heart as a mere pastime; and how readily such trifling becomes mere levity. Let your conversation turn on purity and simplicity of heart, and strive to frame your actions accordingly, avoiding all that savours of affectation or flirting.

In a word, let your time of peace,--that is to say, the time when you are not beset by temptations to sin,--be used in cultivating the graces most opposed to your natural difficulties, and if opportunities for their exercise do not arise, go out of your way to seek them, and by so doing you will strengthen your heart against future temptations.

CHAPTER XI - Anxiety of Mind

ANXIETY of mind is not so much an abstract temptation, as the source whence various temptations arise. Sadness, when defined, is the mental grief we feel because of our involuntary ailments;--whether the evil be exterior, such as poverty, sickness or contempt; or interior, such as ignorance, dryness, depression or temptation. Directly that the soul is conscious of some such trouble, it is downcast, and so trouble sets in. Then we at once begin to try to get rid of it, and find means to shake it off; and so far rightly enough, for it is natural to us all to desire good, and shun that which we hold to be evil.

If any one strives to be delivered from his troubles out of love of God, he will strive patiently, gently, humbly and calmly, looking for deliverance rather to God's Goodness and Providence than to his own industry or efforts; but if self-love is the prevailing object he will grow hot and eager in seeking relief, as though all depended more upon himself than upon God. I do not say that the person thinks so, but he acts eagerly as though he did think it. Then if he does not find what he wants at once, he becomes exceedingly impatient and troubled, which does not mend matters, but on the contrary makes them worse, and so he gets into an unreasonable state of anxiety and distress, till he begins to fancy that there is no cure for his trouble. Thus you see how a disturbance, which was right at the outset, begets anxiety, and anxiety goes on into an excessive distress, which is exceedingly dangerous.

This unresting anxiety is the greatest evil which can happen to the soul, sin only excepted. Just as internal commotions and seditions ruin a commonwealth, and make it incapable of resisting its foreign enemies, so if our heart be disturbed and anxious, it loses power to retain such graces as it has, as well as strength to resist the temptations of the Evil One, who is all the more ready to fish (according to an old proverb) in troubled waters.

Anxiety arises from an unregulated desire to be delivered from any pressing evil, or to obtain some hoped-for good. Nevertheless nothing tends so greatly to enchance the one or retard the other as over-eagerness and anxiety. Birds that are captured in nets and snares become inextricably entangled therein, because they flutter and struggle so much. Therefore, whensoever you urgently desire to be delivered from any evil, or to attain some good thing, strive above all else to keep a calm, restful spirit,-- steady your judgment and will, and then go quietly and easily after your object, taking all fitting means to attain thereto. By easily I do not mean carelessly, but without eagerness, disquietude or anxiety; otherwise, so far from bringing about what you wish, you will hinder it, and add more and more to your perplexities. "My soul is alway in my hand, yet do I not forget Thy Law," [186] David says. Examine yourself often, at least night and morning, as to whether your soul is "in your hand;" or whether it has been wrested thence by any passionate or anxious emotion. See whether your soul is fully under control, or whether it has not in anywise escaped from beneath your hand, to plunge into some unruly love, hate, envy, lust, fear, vexation or joy. And if it has so strayed, before all else seek it out, and quietly bring it back to the Presence of God, once more placing all your hopes and affections under the direction of His Holy Will. Just as one who fears to lose some precious possession holds it tight in his hand, so, like King David, we ought to be able to say, "My soul is alway in my hand, and therefore I have not forgotten Thy Law."

Do not allow any wishes to disturb your mind under the pretext of their being trifling and unimportant; for if they gain the day, greater and weightier matters will find your heart more accessible to disturbance. When you are conscious that you are growing anxious, commend yourself to God, and resolve stedfastly not to take any steps whatever to obtain the result you desire, until your disturbed state of mind is altogether quieted;--unless indeed it should be necessary to do something without delay, in which case you must restrain the rush of inclination, moderating it, as far as possible, so as to act rather from reason than impulse.

If you can lay your anxiety before your spiritual guide, or at least before some trusty and devout friend, you may be sure that you will find great solace. The heart finds relief in telling its troubles to another, just as the body when suffering from persistent fever finds relief from bleeding. It is the best of remedies, and therefore it was that S. Louis counselled his son, "If thou hast any uneasiness lying heavy on thy heart, tell it forthwith to thy confessor, or to some other pious person, and the comfort he will give will enable thee to bear it easily."

Footnotes:

186. Ps. cxix. 109.

CHAPTER XII - Of Sadness and Sorrow

S. PAUL says that "godly sorrow worketh repentance to salvation not to be repented of, but the sorrow of the world worketh death." [187] So we see that sorrow may be good or bad according to the several results it produces in us. And indeed there are more bad than good results arising from it, for the only good ones are mercy and repentance; whereas there are six evil results, namely, anguish, sloth, indignation, jealousy, envy and impatience. The Wise Man says that "sorrow hath killed many, and there is no profit therein," [188] and that because for the two good streams which flow from the spring of sadness, there are these six which are downright evil.

The Enemy makes use of sadness to try good men with his temptations:--just as he tries to make bad men merry in their sin, so he seeks to make the good sorrowful amid their works of piety; and while making sin attractive so as to draw men to it, he strives to turn them from holiness by making it disagreeable. The Evil One delights in sadness and melancholy, because they are his own characteristics. He will be in sadness and sorrow through all Eternity, and he would fain have all others the same.

The "sorrow of the world" disturbs the heart, plunges it into anxiety, stirs up unreasonable fears, disgusts it with prayer, overwhelms and stupefies the brain, deprives the soul of wisdom, judgment, resolution and courage, weakening all its powers; in a word, it is like a hard winter, blasting all the earth's beauty, and numbing all animal life; for it deprives the soul of sweetness and power in every faculty.

Should you, my daughter, ever be attacked by this evil spirit of sadness, make use of the following remedies. "Is any among you afflicted?" says S. James, "let him pray." [189] Prayer is a sovereign remedy, it lifts the mind to God, Who is our only Joy and Consolation. But when you pray let your words and affections, whether interior or exterior, all tend to love and trust in God. "O God of Mercy, most Loving Lord, Sweet Saviour, Lord of my heart, my Joy, my Hope, my Beloved, my Bridegroom."

Vigorously resist all tendencies to melancholy, and although all you do may seem to be done coldly, wearily and indifferently, do not give in. The Enemy strives to make us languid in doing good by depression, but when he sees that we do not cease our efforts to work, and that those efforts become all the more earnest by reason of their being made in resistance to him, he leaves off troubling us.

Make use of hymns and spiritual songs; they have often frustrated the Evil One in his operations, as was the case when the evil spirit which possessed Saul was driven forth by music and psalmody. It is well also to occupy yourself in external works, and that with as much variety as may lead us to divert the mind from the subject which oppresses it, and to cheer and kindle it, for depression generally makes us dry and cold. Use external acts of fervour, even though they are tasteless at the time; embrace your crucifix, clasp it to your breast, kiss the Feet and Hands of your Dear Lord, raise hands and eyes to Heaven, and cry out to God in loving, trustful ejaculations: "My Beloved is mine, and I am His. 1 [190] A bundle of myrrh is my Well-beloved, He shall lie within my breast. Mine eyes long sore for Thy Word, O when wilt Thou comfort me! [191] O Jesus, be Thou my Saviour, and my soul shall live. Who shall separate me from the Love of Christ?" [192] etc.

Moderate bodily discipline is useful in resisting depression, because it rouses the mind from dwelling on itself; and frequent Communion is specially valuable; the Bread of Life strengthens the heart and gladdens the spirits.

Lay bare all the feelings, thoughts and longings which are the result of your depression to your confessor or director, in all humility and faithfulness; seek the society of spiritually-minded people, and frequent such as far as possible while you are suffering. And, finally, resign yourself into God's Hands, endeavouring to bear this harassing depression patiently, as a just punishment for past idle mirth. Above all, never doubt but that, after He has tried you sufficiently, God will deliver you from the trial.

Footnotes:

187. 2 Cor. vii. 10.
188. "Multos enim occidit tristitia, et non est utilitas in illa." Ecclus. xxx. 25.
189. S. James v. 13.
190. Cant. ii. 16.
191. Ps. cxix. 82.
192. Rom. viii 35.

CHAPTER XIII - Of Spiritual and Sensible Consolations, and how to receive them

THE order of God's Providence maintains a perpetual vicissitude in the material being of this world; day is continually turning to night, spring to summer, summer to autumn, autumn to winter, winter to spring; no two days are ever exactly alike. Some are foggy, rainy, some dry or windy; and this endless variety greatly enhances the beauty of the universe. And even so precisely is it with man (who, as ancient writers have said, is a miniature of the world), for he is never long in any one condition, and his life on earth flows by like the mighty waters, heaving and tossing with an endless variety of motion; one while raising him on high with hope, another plunging him low in fear; now turning him to the right with rejoicing, then driving him to the left with sorrows; and no single day, no, not even one hour, is entirely the same as any other of his life.

All this is a very weighty warning, and teaches us to aim at an abiding and unchangeable evenness of mind amid so great an uncertainty of events; and, while all around is changing, we must seek to remain immoveable, ever looking to, reaching after and desiring our God. Let the ship take what tack you will, let her course be eastward or westward, northern or southern, let any wind whatsoever fill her sails, but meanwhile her compass will never cease to point to its one unchanging lodestar. Let all around us be overthrown, nay more, all within us; I mean let our soul be sad or glad, in bitterness or joy, at peace or troubled, dry and parched, or soft and fruitful, let the sun scorch, or the dew refresh it; but all the while the magnet of our heart and mind, our superior will, which is our moral compass, must continually point to the Love of God our Creator, our Saviour, our only Sovereign Good. "Whether we live, we live unto the Lord, or whether we die, we die unto the Lord; whether we live therefore or die, we are the Lord's. Who shall separate us from the Love of Christ?" [193] Nay, verily, nothing can ever separate us from that Love;--neither tribulation nor distress, neither death nor life, neither present suffering nor fear of ills to come; neither the deceits of evil spirits nor the heights of satisfaction, nor the depths of sorrow; neither tenderness nor desolation, shall be able to separate us from that Holy Love, whose foundation is in Christ Jesus. Such a fixed resolution never to forsake God, or let go of His Precious Love, serves as ballast to our souls, and will keep them stedfast amid the endless changes and chances of this our natural life. For just as bees, when overtaken by a gust of wind, carry little pebbles to weight themselves, [194] in order that they may resist the storm, and not be driven at its will,--so the soul, which has firmly grasped the Unchanging Love of God, will abide unshaken amid the changes and vicissitudes of consolations and afflictions,--whether spiritual or temporal, external or internal.

But let us come to some special detail, beyond this general doctrine.

1. I would say, then, that devotion does not consist in conscious sweetness and tender consolations, which move one to sighs and tears, and bring about a kind of agreeable, acceptable sense of self-satisfaction. No, my child, this is not one and the same as devotion, for you will find many persons who do experience these consolations, yet who, nevertheless, are evilminded, and consequently are devoid of all true Love of God, still more of all true devotion. When Saul was in pursuit of David, who fled from him into the wilderness of En-gedi, he entered into a cave alone, wherein David and his followers were hidden; and David could easily have killed him, but he not only spared Saul's life, he would not even frighten him; but, letting him depart quietly, hastened after the King, to affirm his innocence, and tell him how he had been at the mercy of his injured servant. Thereupon Saul testified to the softening of his heart by tender words, calling David his son, and exalting his generosity; lifting up his voice, he wept, and, foretelling David's future greatness, besought him to deal kindly with Saul's "seed after him." [195] What more could Saul have done? Yet for all this he had not changed his real mind, and continued to persecute David as bitterly as before. Just so there are many people who, while contemplating the Goodness of God, or the Passion of His Dear Son, feel an emotion which leads to sighs, tears, and very lively prayers and thanksgivings, so that it might fairly be supposed that their hearts were kindled by a true devotion;--but when put to the test, all this proves but as the passing showers of a hot summer, which splash down in large drops, but do not penetrate the soil, or make it to bring forth anything better than mushrooms. In like manner these tears and emotions do not really touch an evil heart, but are altogether fruitless;--inasmuch as in spite of them all those poor people would not renounce one farthing of illgotten gain, or one unholy affection; they would not suffer the slightest worldly inconvenience for the Sake of the Saviour over Whom they wept. So that their pious emotions

may fairly be likened to spiritual fungi,--as not merely falling short of real devotion, but often being so many snares of the Enemy, who beguiles souls with these trivial consolations, so as to make them stop short, and rest satisfied therewith, instead of seeking after true solid devotion, which consists in a firm, resolute, ready, active will, prepared to do whatsoever is acceptable to God. A little child, who sees the surgeon bleed his mother, will cry when he sees the lancet touch her; but let that mother for whom he weeps ask for his apple or a sugar-plum which he has in his hand, and he will on no account part with it; and too much of our seeming devotion is of this kind. We weep feelingly at the spear piercing the Crucified Saviour's Side, and we do well,--but why cannot we give Him the apple we hold, for which He asks, heartily? I mean our heart, the only love-apple which that Dear Saviour craves of us. Why cannot we resign the numberless trifling attachments, indulgences, and self-complacencies of which He fain would deprive us, only we will not let Him do so; because they are the sugar-plums, sweeter to our taste than His Heavenly Grace? Surely this is but as the fondness of children;--demonstrative, but weak, capricious, unpractical. Devotion does not consist in such exterior displays of a tenderness which may be purely the result of a naturally impressionable, plastic character; or which may be the seductive action of the Enemy, or an excitable imagination stirred up by him.

2. Nevertheless these tender warm emotions are sometimes good and useful, for they kindle the spiritual appetite, cheer the mind, and infuse a holy gladness into the devout life, which embellishes all we do even externally. It was such a taste for holy things that made David cry out, "O how sweet are Thy words unto my throat, yea, sweeter than honey unto my mouth." [196] And assuredly the tiniest little comfort received through devotion is worth far more than the most abundant delights of this world. The milk of the Heavenly Bridegroom, in other words His spiritual favours, are sweeter to the soul than the costliest wine of the pleasures of this world, and to those who have tasted thereof all else seems but as gall and wormwood. There is a certain herb which, if chewed, imparts so great a sweetness that they who keep it in their mouth cannot hunger or thirst; even so those to whom God gives His Heavenly manna of interior sweetness and consolation, cannot either desire or even accept worldly consolations with any real zest or satisfaction. It is as a little foretaste of eternal blessedness which God gives to those who seek it; it is as the sugar-plum with which He attracts His little ones; as a cordial offered to strengthen their heart; as the first-fruits of their future reward. The legend tells us that Alexander the Great discovered Arabia Felix by means of the perfumes carried by the winds across the ocean upon which he sailed, reviving his courage and that of his comrades. And so the blessings and sweetnesses, which are wafted to us as we sail across the stormy sea of this mortal life, are a foretaste of the bliss of that Ever-blessed Heavenly Home to which we look and long.

3. But, perhaps you will say, if there are sensible consolations which are undoubtedly good and come from God, and at the same time others which are unprofitable, perilous, even harmful, because they proceed from mere natural causes, or even from the Enemy himself, how am I to know one from the other, or distinguish what is most profitable even among those which are good? It is a general rule, with respect to the feelings and affections, that their test is in their fruits. Our hearts are as trees, of which the affections and passions are their branches, and deeds and acts their fruits. That is, a good heart, of which the affections are good, and those are good affections which result in good and holy actions. If our spiritual tenderness and sweetness and consolation make us more humble,--patient, forbearing, charitable and kindly towards our neighbours,--more earnest in mortifying our own evil inclinations and lusts, more diligent in our duties, more docile and submissive to those who have a claim to our obedience, more simple in our whole manner of life,--then doubtless, my daughter, they come from God. But if this sweetness and tenderness is sweet only to ourselves, if we are fanciful, bitter, punctilious, impatient, obstinate, proud, presumptuous, harsh towards our neighbour, while reckoning ourselves as half-made saints, indocile to correction or guidance, then we may be assured our consolations are spurious and hurtful. A good tree will bring forth none save good fruit.

4. If we are favoured with any such sweetness, we must humble ourselves deeply before God, and beware of being led to cry out "How good I am!" No indeed, such gifts do not make us any better, for, as I have already said, devotion does not consist in such things; rather let us say, "How good God is to those who hope in Him, and to the souls that seek Him!" If a man has sugar in his mouth, he cannot call his mouth sweet, but the sugar; and so although our spiritual sweetness is admirable, and God Who imparts it is all good, it by no means follows that he who receives it is good. Let us count ourselves but as little children, having need of milk, and believe that these sugar-plums are only given us because we are still feeble and delicate, needing bribes and wiles to lead us on to the Love of God. But, as a general rule, we shall do well to receive all such graces and favours humbly, making much of them, not for their own importance, but rather because it is God's Hand which fills our hearts with them, as a mother coaxes her child with one sugar-plum after another. If the child were wise, he would prize the loving caresses of his mother, more than the material sugar-plum, however sweet. So while it is a great thing to have spiritual sweetnesses, the sweetest of all is to know that it is the loving parental Hand of God which feeds us, heart, mind and soul, with them. And, having received them humbly, let us be diligent in using them according to the intention of the Giver. Why do you suppose God gives us such

sweetness? To make us kinder one to another, and more loving towards Him. A mother gives her child a sweetmeat to win a kiss; be it ours reverently to kiss the Saviour Who gives us these good things. And by kissing Him, I mean obeying Him, keeping His Commandments, doing His Will, heeding His wishes, in a word, embracing Him tenderly, obediently, and faithfully. So the day on which we have enjoyed some special spiritual consolation should be marked by extra diligence and humility. And from time to time it is well to renounce all such, realising to ourselves that although we accept and cherish them humbly, because they come from God, and kindle His Love in our hearts, still they are not our main object, but God and His Holy Love;--that we seek less the consolation than the Consoler, less His tangible sweetness than our sweet Saviour, less external pleasure than Him Who is the Delight of Heaven and earth; and with such a mind we should resolve to abide stedfast in God's Holy Love, even if our whole life were to be utterly devoid of all sweetness; as ready to abide on Mount Calvary as on Mount Tabor; to cry out, "It is good for us to be here," whether with our Lord on the Cross or in glory.

Lastly, I advise you to take counsel with your director concerning any unusual flow of consolations or emotions, so that he may guide you in their wise usage; for it is written, "Hast thou found honey? eat so much as is sufficient for thee." [197]

Footnotes:

193. Rom. xiv. 8, and viii. 35.
194. This notion seems to have arisen from the habits of the solitary mason bee, which early writers did not distinguish from other bees.
195. 1 Sam. xxiv.
196. Ps. cxix. 103.
197. Prov. xxv. 16.

CHAPTER XIV - Of Dryness and Spiritual Barrenness

SO much for what is to be done in times of spiritual consolations. But these bright days will not last for ever, and sometimes you will be so devoid of all devout feelings, that it will seem to you that your soul is a desert land, fruitless, sterile, wherein you can find no path leading to God, no drop of the waters of Grace to soften the dryness which threatens to choke it entirely. Verily, at such a time the soul is greatly to be pitied, above all, when this trouble presses heavily, for then, like David, its meat are tears day and night, while the Enemy strives to drive it to despair, crying out, "Where is now thy God? how thinkest thou to find Him, or how wilt thou ever find again the joy of His Holy Grace?"

What will you do then, my child? Look well whence the trial comes, for we are often ourselves the cause of our own dryness and barrenness. A mother refuses sugar to her sickly child, and so God deprives us of consolations when they do but feed self-complacency or presumption. "It is good for me that I have been in trouble, for before I was troubled I went wrong." [198] So if we neglect to gather up and use the treasures of God's Love in due time, He withdraws them as a punishment of our sloth. The Israelite who neglected to gather his store of manna in the early morning, found none after sunrise, for it was all melted. Sometimes, too, we are like the Bride of the Canticles, slumbering on a bed of sensual satisfaction and perishable delight, so that when the Bridegroom knocks at the door of our heart, and calls us to our spiritual duties, we dally with Him, loath to quit our idle and delusive pleasures, and then He "withdraws Himself, and is gone," and "when I sought Him, I could not find Him; I called Him, but He gave me no answer." [199] Of a truth we deserved as much for having been so disloyal as to have rejected Him for the things of this world. If we are content with the fleshpots of Egypt we shall never receive heavenly manna. Bees abhor all artificial scents, and the sweetness of the Holy Spirit is incompatible with the world's artificial pleasures.

Again, any duplicity or unreality in confession or spiritual intercourse with your director tends to dryness and barrenness, for, if you lie to God's Holy Spirit, you can scarcely wonder that He refuses you His comfort. If you do not choose to be simple and honest as a little child, you will not win the child's sweetmeats.

Or you have satiated yourself with worldly delights; and so no wonder that spiritual pleasures are repulsive to you. "To the overfed dove even cherries are bitter," says an old proverb; and Our Lady in her song of praise says, "He has filled the hungry with good things, and the rich He hath sent empty away." They who abound in earthly pleasures are incapable of appreciating such as are spiritual.

If you have carefully stored up the fruits of past consolations, you will receive more; "to him that hath yet more shall be given," but from him who has not kept that which he had, who has lost it through carelessness, that which he hath shall be taken away, in other words, he will not receive the grace destined for him. Rain refreshes living plants, but it only brings rottenness and decay to those which are already dead. There are many such causes whereby we lose the consolations of religion, and fall into dryness and deadness of spirit, so that it is well to examine our conscience, and see if we can trace any of these or similar faults. But always remember that this examination must not be made anxiously, or in an over-exacting spirit. Thus if, after an honest investigation of our own conduct, we find the cause of our wrongdoing, we must thank God, for an evil is half cured when we have found out its cause. But if, on the contrary, you do not find any particular thing which has led to this dryness, do not trifle away your time in a further uneasy search, but, without more ado, and in all simplicity, do as follows:--

1. Humble yourself profoundly before God, acknowledging your nothingness and misery. Alas, what am I when left to myself! no better, Lord, than a parched ground, whose cracks and crevices on every side testify its need of the gracious rain of Heaven, while, nevertheless, the world's blasts wither it more and more to dust.

2. Call upon God, and ask for His Gladness. "O give me the comfort of Thy help again! My Father, if it be possible, let this cup pass from me." "Depart, O ye unfruitful wind, which parcheth up my soul, and come, O gracious south wind, blow upon my garden." Such loving desires will fill you with the perfume of holiness.

3. Go to your confessor, open your heart thoroughly, let him see every corner of your soul, and take all his advice with the utmost simplicity and humility, for God loves obedience, and He often makes the counsel we take, specially that of the guides of souls, to be more useful than would seem

likely; just as He caused the waters of Jordan, commended by Elijah to Naaman, to cure his leprosy in spite of the improbability to human reason.

4. But, after all, nothing is so useful, so fruitful amid this dryness and barrenness, as not to yield to a passionate desire of being delivered from it. I do not say that one may not desire to be set free, but only that one ought not to desire it over-eagerly, but to leave all to the sole Mercy of God's special Providence, in order that, so long as He pleases, He may keep us amid these thorns and longings. Let us say to God at such seasons, "O my Father, if it be possible, let this cup pass from me; "--but let us add heartily, "Nevertheless, not my will, but Thine be done," and there let us abide as trustingly as we are able. When God sees us to be filled with such pious indifference, He will comfort us with His grace and favour, as when He beheld Abraham ready to offer up his son Isaac, and comforted him with His blessing. In every sort of affliction, then, whether bodily or spiritual, in every manner of distraction or loss of sensible devotion, let us say with our whole heart, and in the deepest submission, "The Lord gave me all my blessings, the Lord taketh them away, blessed be the Name of the Lord." If we persevere in this humility, He will restore to us His mercies as he did to Job, who ever spake thus amid all his troubles. 5. And lastly, my daughter, amid all our dryness let us never grow discouraged, but go steadily on, patiently waiting the return of better things; let us never be misled to give up any devout practices because of it, but rather if possible, let us increase our good works, and if we cannot offer liquid preserves to our Bridegroom, let us at least offer Him dried fruit--it is all one to Him, so long as the heart we offer be fully resolved to love Him. In fine weather bees make more honey and breed fewer grubs, because they spend so much time in gathering the sweet juices of the flowers that they neglect the multiplication of their race. But in a cold, cloudy spring they have a fuller hive and less honey. And so sometimes, my daughter, in the glowing springtide of spiritual consolations, the soul spends so much time in storing them up, that amid such abundance it performs fewer good works; while, on the contrary, when amid spiritual dryness and bitterness, and devoid of all that is attractive in devotion, it multiplies its substantial good works, and abounds in the hidden virtues of patience, humility, self-abnegation, resignation and unselfishness.

Some people, especially women, fall into the great mistake of imagining that when we offer a dry, distasteful service to God, devoid of all sentiment and emotion, it is unacceptable to His Divine Majesty; whereas, on the contrary, our actions are like roses, which, though they may be more beautiful when fresh, have a sweeter and stronger scent when they are dried. Good works, done with pleasurable interest, are pleasanter to us who think of nothing save our own satisfaction, but when they are done amid dryness and deadness they are more precious in God's Sight. Yes indeed, my daughter, for in seasons of dryness our will forcibly carries us on in God's Service, and so it is stronger and more vigorous than at a softer time. There is not much to boast of in serving our Prince in the comfort of a time of peace, but to serve Him amid the toils and hardness of war, amid trial and persecution, is a real proof of faithfulness and perseverance. The blessed Angela di Foligni said, that the most acceptable prayer to God is what is made forcibly and in spite of ourselves; that is to say, prayer made not to please ourselves or our own taste, but solely to please God;--carried on, as it were, in spite of inclination, the will triumphing over all our drynesses and repugnances. And so of all good works;--the more contradictions, exterior or interior, against which we contend in their fulfilment, the more precious they are in God's Sight; the less of self-pleasing in striving after any virtue, the more Divine Love shines forth in all its purity. A child is easily moved to fondle its mother when she gives it sweet things, but if he kisses her in return for wormwood or camomile it is a proof of very real affection on his part.

Footnotes:

198. Ps. cxix. 67, 71.
199. Cant. v. 2-7.

CHAPTER XV - An Illustration

LET me illustrate what I have said by an anecdote of Saint Bernard.

It is common to most beginners in God's Service, being as yet inexperienced in the fluctuations of grace and in spiritual vicissitudes, that when they lose the glow of sensible devotion, and the first fascinating lights which led them in their first steps towards God, they lose heart, and fall into depression and discouragement. Those who are practised in the matter say that it is because our human nature cannot bear a prolonged deprivation of some kind of satisfaction, either celestial or earthly; and so as souls, which have been raised beyond their natural level by a taste of superior joys, readily renounce visible delights when the higher joys are taken away, as well as those more earthly pleasures, they, not being yet trained to a patient waiting for the true sunshine, fancy that there is no light either in heaven or earth, but that they are plunged in perpetual darkness. They are just like newly-weaned babes, who fret and languish for want of the breast, and are a weariness to every one, especially to themselves.

Just so it fell out with a certain Geoffroy de Peronne, a member of S. Bernard's community, newly dedicated to God's Service, during a journey which he and some others were making. He became suddenly dry, deprived of all consolations, and amid his interior darkness he began to think of the friends and relations he had parted from, and of his worldly pursuits and interests, until the temptation grew so urgent that his outward aspect betrayed it, and one of those most in his confidence perceiving that he was sorely troubled, accosted him tenderly, asking him secretly, "What means this, Geoffroy? and what makes thee, contrary to thy wont, so pensive and sad?" Whereupon Geoffroy, sighing heavily, made answer, "Woe is me, my brother, never again in my life shall I be glad!"

The other was moved to pity by these words, and in his fraternal love he hastened to tell it all to their common father S. Bernard, and he, realising the danger, went into the nearest church to pray for Geoffroy, who meanwhile cast himself down in despair, and, resting his head on a stone, fell asleep. After a while both rose up, the one full of grace won by prayer, the other from his sleep, with so peaceful and gladsome a countenance, that his friend, marvelling to see so great and unexpected a change, could not refrain from gently reproaching him for his recent words. Thereupon Geoffroy answered, "If just now I told thee that I should never more be glad, so now I promise thee I will never more be sad!" Such was the result of this devout man's temptation; but from this history I would have you observe:--

1. That God is wont to give some foretaste of His heavenly joys to beginners in His Service, the better to wean them from earthly pleasures, and to encourage them in seeking His Divine Love, even as a mother attracts her babe to suck by means of honey.

2. That nevertheless it is the same Good God Who sometimes in His Wisdom deprives us of the milk and honey of His consolations, in order that we may learn to eat the dry substantial bread of a vigorous devotion, trained by means of temptations and trials.

3. That sometimes very grievous temptations arise out of dryness and barrenness, and that at such times these temptations must be stedfastly resisted, inasmuch as they are not of God; but the dryness must be patiently endured, because He sends that to prove us. 4. That we must never grow discouraged amid our inward trials, nor say, like Geoffroy, "I shall never be glad;" but through the darkness we must look for light; and in like manner, in the brightest spiritual sunshine, we must not presume to say, "I shall never be sad." Rather we must remember the saying of the Wise Man, "In the day of prosperity remember the evil." [200] It behoves us to hope amid trials, and to fear in prosperity, and in both circumstances always to be humble.

5. That it is a sovereign remedy to open our grief to some spiritual friend able to assist us.

And, in conclusion, I would observe that here, as everywhere, our Gracious God and our great Enemy are in conflict, for by means of these trials God would bring us to great purity of heart, to an entire renunciation of self-interest in all concerning His Service, and a perfect casting aside of self-seeking; but the Evil One seeks to use our troubles to our discouragement, so as to turn us back to sensual pleasures, and to make us a weariness to ourselves and others, in order to injure true devotion. But if you will give heed to the above instructions you will advance greatly towards perfection amid such interior trials, concerning which I have yet one word to say. Sometimes revulsions and dryness and incapacity proceed from bodily indisposition, as when excessive watching, 1 fasting, or overwork produce weariness, lassitude, heaviness, and the like; which, while wholly caused by the body, interfere greatly with the soul, so intimately are they linked together. When this is the case, you must always remember to make marked acts of virtue with your higher will, for, although your whole soul may seem to be sunk in drowsy weariness, such mental efforts are acceptable to God. At such a time you may say with the Bride of the Canticles, "I sleep, but my heart waketh." [201] And, as I have already said, if there is less enjoyment in such efforts, there is more virtue and merit. But the best remedy under the last-named circumstances is to reinvigorate the body by some lawful recreation and solace.

S. Francis enjoined his religious to use such moderation in their labours as never to impair the fervour of their minds. And speaking of that great Saint, he was himself once attacked by such deep depression of mind that he could not conceal it; if he sought to associate with his religious he was unable to talk; if he kept apart he only grew worse; abstinence and maceration of the flesh overwhelmed him, and he found no comfort in prayer. For two years he continued in this state, as though altogether forsaken of God, but after humbly enduring the heavy storm, his Saviour restored him to a happy calm quite suddenly.

From this we should learn that God's greatest servants are liable to such trials, so that less worthy people should not be surprised if they experience the same.

Footnotes:

200. Ecclus. xi. 25, Vulgate: "In die bonorum ne immemor sis malorum." English version: "In the day of prosperity there is a forgetfulness of affliction."

201. Cant. v. 2.

PART V – CONTAINING COUNSELS AND PRACTICES FOR RENEWING AND CONFIRMING THE SOUL IN DEVOTION

CHAPTER I - It is well yearly to renew Good Resolutions by means of the following Exercises

THE first point in these exercises is to appreciate their importance. Our earthly nature easily falls away from its higher tone by reason of the frailty and evil tendency of the flesh, oppressing and dragging down the soul, unless it is constantly rising up by means of a vigorous resolution, just as a bird would speedily fall to the ground if it did not maintain its flight by repeated strokes of its wings. In order to this, my daughter, you need frequently to reiterate the good resolutions you have made to serve God, for fear that, failing to do so, you fall away, not only to your former condition, but lower still; since it is a characteristic of all spiritual falls that they invariably throw us lower than we were at the beginning. There is no clock, however good, but must be continually wound up; and moreover, during the course of each year it will need taking to pieces, to cleanse away the rust which clogs it, to straighten bent works, and renew such as are worn. Even so, any one who really cares for his heart's devotion will wind it up to God night and morning, and examine into its condition, correcting and improving it; and at least once a year he will take the works to pieces and examine them carefully;--I mean his affections and passions,--so as to repair whatever may be amiss. And just as the clockmaker applies a delicate oil to all the wheels and springs of a clock, so that it may work properly and be less liable to rust, so the devout soul, after thus taking the works of his heart to pieces, will lubricate them with the Sacraments of Confession and the Eucharist. These exercises will repair the waste caused by time, will kindle your heart, revive your good resolutions, and cause the graces of your mind to flourish anew.

The early Christians observed some such practice on the Anniversary of our Lord's Baptism, when, as S. Gregory, Bishop of Nazianzen, tells us, they renewed the profession and promises made in that Sacrament. It were well to do the like, my child, making due and earnest preparation, and setting very seriously to work.

Having then chosen a suitable time, according to the advice of your spiritual father, and having retired somewhat more than usual into a literal and spiritual solitude, make one, two, or three meditations on the following points, according to the method I set before you in Part II.

CHAPTER II - Meditation on the Benefit conferred on us by God in calling us to His Service

1. CONSIDER the points on which you are about to renew your resolutions.

Firstly, that you have forsaken, rejected, detested and renounced all mortal sin for ever.

Secondly, that you have dedicated and consecrated your soul, heart and body, with everything appertaining thereto, to the Service and Love of God.

Thirdly, that if you should unhappily fall into any sin, you would forthwith rise up again, with the help of God's Grace.

Are not these worthy, right, noble resolutions? Consider well within your soul how holy, reasonable and desirable an act it is to renew them.

2. Consider to Whom you make these promises; for if a deliberate promise made to men is strictly binding, how much more those which we make to God. "My heart is inditing of a good matter. I will not forget Thee," David cried out. [202]

3. Consider before Whom you promised. It was before the whole Court of Heaven. The Blessed Virgin, S. Joseph, your Guardian Angel, S. Louis, the whole Company of the Blessed, were looking on with joy and approbation, beholding, with love unspeakable, your heart cast at your Saviour's Feet and dedicated to His Service. That act of yours called forth special delight in the Heavenly Jerusalem, and it will now be renewed if you on your part heartily renew your good resolutions.

4. Consider how you were led to make those resolutions. How good and gracious God was then to you! Did He not draw you by the tender wiles of His Holy Spirit? Were not the sails by which your little bark was wafted into the haven of safety those of love and charity? Did not God lure you on with His Heavenly Sweetness, by Sacraments, prayer, and pious books? Ah, my child, while you slept God watched over you with His boundless Love, and breathed thoughts of peace into your heart!

5. Consider when God led you to these important resolutions. It was in the flower of your life, and how great the blessing of learning early what we can never know soon enough. S. Augustine, who acquired that knowledge when he was thirty years old, exclaimed, "Oh, Thou Beauty of ancient days, yet ever new, too late I loved Thee! Thou wert within and I abroad: Thou wert with me, but I was not with Thee." [203] Even so you may say, "Oh, Blessedness of ancient days, wherefore did I not appreciate Thee sooner!" You were not yet worthy of it, and yet God gave you such grace in your youth;--therefore say with David, "Thou, O God, hast taught me from my youth up until now; therefore will I tell of Thy wondrous works." [204] Or if you who read should not have known Him till old age, bethink you how great His Grace in calling you after you had wasted so many years; how gracious the Mercy which drove you from your evil courses before the hour of death, which, had it found you unchanged, must have brought you eternal woe.

Consider the results of this call; you will surely find a change for the better, comparing what you are with what you were. Is it not a blessing to know how to talk with God in prayer, to desire to love Him, to have stilled and subdued sundry passions which disturbed you, to have conquered sundry sins and perplexities, and to have received so many more Communions than formerly, thereby being united to the Great Source of all eternal grace? Are not all these things exceeding blessings? Weigh them, my child, in the balances of the sanctuary, for it is God's Right Hand which has done all this: "The Right Hand of the Lord hath the pre-eminence, the Right Hand of the Lord bringeth mighty things to pass. I shall not die, but live, and declare the works of the Lord" [205] with heart, lips and deeds.

After dwelling upon all these considerations, which will kindle abundance of lively affections in you, you should conclude simply with an act of thanksgiving, and a hearty prayer that they may bring forth fruit, leaving off with great humility and trust in God, and reserving the final results of your resolution till after the second point of this spiritual exercise.

Footnotes:

202. Ps. xlv. 1.; xliv. 18.
203. Conf., Oxf. Trans. bk. x. p. 203.
204. Ps. lxxi. 15.
205. Ps. cxviii. 16, 17.

CHAPTER III - Examination of the Soul as to its Progress in the Devout Life

THIS second point is somewhat lengthy, and I would begin by saying that there is no need for you to carry it out all at once. Divide it by taking your conduct towards God at one time, all that concerns yourself another time, all that concerns your neighbour, and fourthly, the examination of your passions. It is neither necessary nor expedient that you make it upon your knees, always excepting the beginning and the end, which includes the affections. The other points of self-examination you may make profitably when out walking, or better still, in bed, that is, if you can keep wide awake and free from drowsiness; but to do this you must read them over carefully beforehand. Anyhow, it is desirable to go through this second point in three days and two nights at the most, taking that season which you can best manage; for if you go through it at too distant intervals you will lose the depth of impression which ought to be made by this spiritual exercise. After each point of examination observe wherein you have failed, and what is lacking to you, and in what you have chiefly failed, so that you may be able to explain your troubles, get counsel and comfort, and make fresh resolutions. It is not necessary entirely to shun all society on the days you select for this work, but you must contrive a certain amount of retirement, especially in the evening, so as to get to bed somewhat earlier than usual, with a view to that rest, bodily and mental, which is so important for serious thought. And during the day make frequent aspirations to Our Lord, Our Lady, the Angels, and all the Heavenly Jerusalem. Everything must be done with a heart full of God's Love, and an earnest desire for spiritual perfection. To begin this examination,--

1. Place yourself in the Presence of God.

2. Invoke the Holy Spirit, and ask light of Him, so that you may know yourself, as S. Augustine did, crying out, "Lord, teach me to know Thee, and to know myself;" and S. Francis, who asked, "Who art Thou, Lord, and who am I?" Resolve not to note any progress with any self-satisfaction or self-glorification, but give the glory to God Alone, and thank Him duly for it.

Resolve, too, that if you should seem to yourself to have made but little progress, or even to have gone back, that you will not be discouraged thereby, nor grow cool or indolent in the matter; but that, on the contrary, you will take fresh pains to humble yourself and conquer your faults, with God's Help.

Then go on to examine quietly and patiently how you have conducted yourself towards God, your neighbour and yourself, up to the present time.

CHAPTER IV - Examination of the Soul's Condition as regards God

1. WHAT is the aspect of your heart with respect to mortal sin? Are you firmly resolved never to commit it, let come what may? And have you kept that resolution from the time you first made it? Therein lies the foundation of the spiritual life.

2. What is your position with respect to the Commandments of God? Are they acceptable, light and easy to you? He who has a good digestion and healthy appetite likes good food, and turns away from that which is bad.

3. How do you stand as regards venial sins? No one can help committing some such occasionally; but are there none to which you have any special tendency, or worse still, any actual liking and clinging?

4. With respect to spiritual exercises--do you like and value them? or do they weary and vex you? To which do you feel most or least disposed, hearing or reading God's Word, meditating upon it, calling upon God, Confession, preparing for Communion and communicating, controlling your inclinations, etc.? What of all these is most repugnant to you? And if you find that your heart is not disposed to any of these things, examine into the cause, find out whence the disinclination comes.

5. With respect to God Himself--does your heart delight in thinking of God, does it crave after the sweetness thereof? "I remembered Thine everlasting judgments, O Lord, and received comfort," says David. [206] Do you feel a certain readiness to love Him, and a definite inclination to enjoy His Love? Do you take pleasure in dwelling upon the Immensity, the Goodness, the Tenderness of God? When you are immersed in the occupations and vanities of this world, does the thought of God come across you as a welcome thing? do you accept it gladly, and yield yourself up to it, and your heart turn with a sort of yearning to Him? There are souls that do so.

6. If a wife has been long separated from her husband, so soon as she sees him returning, and hears his voice, however cumbered she may be with business, or forcibly hindered by the pressure of circumstances, her heart knows no restraint, but turns at once from all else to think upon him she loves. So it is with souls which really love God, however engrossed they may be; when the thought of Him is brought before them, they forget all else for joy at feeling His Dear Presence nigh, and this is a very good sign.

7. With respect to Jesus Christ as God and Man--how does your heart draw to Him? Honey bees seek their delight in their honey, but wasps hover over stinking carrion. Even so pious souls draw all their joy from Jesus Christ, and love Him with an exceeding sweet Love, but those who are careless find their pleasure in worldly vanities.

8. With respect to Our Lady, the Saints, and your Guardian Angel--do you love them well? Do you rejoice in the sense of their guardianship? Do you take pleasure in their lives, their pictures, their memories?

9. As to your tongue--how do you speak of God? Do you take pleasure in speaking His Praise, and singing His Glory in psalms and hymns?

10. As to actions--have you God's visible glory at heart, and do you delight in doing whatever you can to honour Him? Those who love God will love to adorn and beautify His House. Are you conscious of having ever given up anything you liked, or of renouncing anything for God's Sake? for it is a good sign when we deprive ourselves of something we care for on behalf of those we love. What have you ever given up for the Love of God?

Footnote:

206. Ps. cxix. 52.

CHAPTER V - Examination of your Condition as regards yourself

1. HOW do you love yourself? Is it a love which concerns this life chiefly? If so, you will desire to abide here for ever, and you will diligently seek your worldly establishment,--but if the love you bear yourself has a heavenward tendency, you will long, or, at all events you will be ready to go hence whensoever it may please our Lord.

2. Is your love of yourself well regulated? for nothing is more ruinous than an inordinate love of self. A well-regulated love implies greater care for the soul than for the body; more eagerness in seeking after holiness than aught else; a greater value for heavenly glory than for any mean earthly honour. A well regulated heart much oftener asks itself, "What will the angels say if I follow this or that line of conduct?" than what will men say.

3. What manner of love do you bear to your own heart? Are you willing to minister to it in its maladies? for indeed you are bound to succour it, and seek help for it when harassed by passion, and to leave all else till that is done.

4. What do you imagine yourself worth in God's Sight? Nothing, doubtless, nor is there any great humility in the fly which confesses it is nought, as compared with a mountain, or a drop of water, which knows itself to be nothing compared with the sea, or a cornflower, or a spark, as compared with the sun. But humility consists in not esteeming ourselves above other men, and in not seeking to be esteemed above them. How is it with you in this respect?

5. In speech--do you never boast in any way? Do you never indulge in self-flattery when speaking of yourself?

6. In deed--do you indulge in anything prejudicial to your health,--I mean useless idle pleasures, unprofitable night-watches, and the like?

CHAPTER VI - Examination of the Soul's Condition as regards our Neighbour

HUSBAND and wife are bound to love one another with a tender, abiding, restful love, and this tie stands foremost by God's order and Will. And I say the same with respect to children and all near relations, as also friends in their respective degrees. But, generally speaking, how is it with you as concerning your neighbour? Do you love him cordially, and for God's Sake? In order to answer this fairly, you must call to mind sundry disagreeable, annoying people, for it is in such cases that we really practise the Love of God with respect to our neighbours, and still more towards them that do us wrong, either by word or deed. Examine whether your heart is thoroughly clear as regards all such, and whether it costs you a great effort to love them. Are you quick to speak ill of your neighbours, especially of such as do not love you? Do you act unkindly in any way, directly or indirectly, towards them? A very little honest self-dealing will enable you to find this out.

CHAPTER VII - Examination as to the Affectations of the Soul

I HAVE dwelt thus at length on these points, on a due examination of which all true knowledge of our spiritual progress rests; as to an examination of sins, that rather pertains to the confessions of those who are not eager to advance. But it is well to take ourselves to task soberly concerning these different matters, investigating how we have been going on since we made good resolutions concerning them, and what notable faults we have committed. But the summary of all is to examine into our passions; and if you are worried by so detailed an investigation as that already suggested, you may make a briefer inquiry as to what you have been, and how you have acted, in some such manner as this:--In your love of God, your neighbour, and yourself.

In hatred for the sin which is in yourself, for the sin which you find in others, since you ought to desire the extirpation of both; in your desires concerning riches, pleasure, and honour.

In fear of the perils of sin, and of the loss of this world's goods; we fear the one too much and the other too little.

In hope, fixed overmuch it may be on things of this world and the creature; too little on God and things eternal.

In sadness, whether it be excessive concerning unimportant matters.

In gladness, whether it be excessive concerning unworthy objects.

In short, examine what attachments hinder your spiritual life, what passions engross it, and what chiefly attracts you.

It is by testing the passions of the soul, one by one, that we ascertain our spiritual condition, just as one who plays the lute tries every string, touching those which are discordant, either raising or lowering them. Thus having tried our soul as to love, hate, desire, fear, hope, sadness and joy, if we find our strings out of tune for the melody we wish to raise, which is God's Glory, we must tune them afresh with the help of His Grace, and the counsel of our spiritual father.

CHAPTER VIII - *The Affections to be excited after such Examination*

WHEN you have quietly gone through each point of this examination, and have ascertained your own position, you will excite certain feelings and affections in your heart. Thank God for such amendment, however slight, as you may have found in yourself, confessing that it is the work of His Mercy Alone in you.

Humble yourself deeply before God, confessing that if your progress has been but small, it is your own fault, for not having corresponded faithfully, bravely and continually to the inspirations and lights which He has given you in prayer or otherwise.

Promise to praise Him for ever for the graces He has granted to you, and because He has led you against your will to make even this small progress.

Ask forgiveness for the disloyalty and faithlessness with which you have answered Him.

Offer your whole heart to Him that He Alone may rule therein. Entreat Him to keep you faithful to Himself.

Ponder over the examples of the Saints, the Blessed Virgin, your guardian Angel and patron Saint, S. Joseph, etc.

CHAPTER IX - *Reflections suitable to the renewal of Good Resolutions*

AFTER you have made this self-examination, and having conferred with some holy director as to your shortcomings and their remedies, you will do well to pursue the following considerations, taking one daily as a meditation, and giving to it the time usually so spent; always making the same preparation and kindling the same affections as you learnt to use before meditating in Part I. Above all, placing yourself in the Presence of God, and earnestly asking His Grace to confirm you and keep you stedfast in His Holy Love and Service.

CHAPTER X - First Consideration--of the Worth of Souls

CONSIDER how noble and excellent a thing your soul is, endowed with understanding, capable of knowing, not merely this visible world around us, but Angels and Paradise, of knowing that there is an All-Mighty, All-Merciful, Ineffable God; of knowing that eternity lies before you, and of knowing what is necessary in order so to live in this visible world as to attain to fellowship with those Angels in Paradise, and the eternal fruition of God.

Yet more;---your soul is possessed of a noble will, capable of loving God, irresistibly drawn to that love; your heart is full of generous enthusiasm, and can no more find rest in any earthly creation, or in aught save God, than the bee can find honey on a dunghill, or in aught save flowers. Let your mind boldly review the wild earthly pleasures which once filled your heart, and see whether they did not abound in uneasiness and doubts, in painful thoughts and uncomfortable cares, amid which your troubled heart was miserable.

When the heart of man seeks the creature, it goes to work eagerly, expecting to satisfy its cravings; but directly it obtains what it sought, it finds a blank, and dissatisfied, begins to seek anew; for God will not suffer our hearts to find any rest, like the dove going forth from Noah's ark, until it returns to God, whence it came. Surely this is a most striking natural beauty in our heart;--why should we constrain it against its will to seek creature love?

In some such wise might you address your soul: "You are capable of realising a longing after God, why should you trifle with anything lower? you can live for eternity, why should you stop short in time? One of the sorrows of the prodigal son was, that, when he might have been living in plenty at his father's table, he had brought himself to share the swine's husks. My soul, you are made for God, woe be to you if you stop short in anything short of Him!" Lift up your soul with thoughts such as these, convince it that it is eternal, and worthy of eternity; fill it with courage in this pursuit.

CHAPTER XI - Second Consideration--on the Excellence of Virtue

CONSIDER that nothing save holiness and devotion can satisfy your soul in this world: behold how gracious they are; draw a contrast between each virtue and its opposite vice; how gracious patience is compared with vengeance; gentleness compared with anger; humility with pride and arrogance; liberality with avarice; charity with envy; sobriety with unsteadiness. It is one charm of all virtues that they fill the soul with untold sweetness after being practised, whereas vice leaves it harassed and ill at ease. Who would not speedily set to work and obtain such sweetness?

In the matter of evil, he who has a little is not contented, and he who has much is discontented; but he who has a little virtue is gladsome, and his gladness is for ever greater as he goes on. O devout life! you are indeed lovely, sweet and pleasant; you can soften sorrows and sweeten consolations; without you good becomes evil, pleasure is marred by anxiety and distress: verily whoso knows what you are may well say with the woman of Samaria, "Lord, give me this water," [207] an aspiration often uttered by Saint Theresa and Saint Catherine of Genoa.

Footnotes:

207. S. John iv. 15.

CHAPTER XII - The Example of the Saints

CONSIDER the example of the Saints on all sides, what have they not done in order to love God and lead a devout life? Call to mind the Martyrs in their invincible firmness, and the tortures they endured in order to maintain their resolutions; remember the matrons and maidens, whiter than lilies in their purity, ruddier than the rose in their love, who at every age, from childhood upward, bore all manner of martyrdom sooner than forsake their resolutions, not only such as concerned their profession of faith, but that of devotion; some dying rather than lose their virginity, others rather than cease their works of mercy to the sick and sorrowful. Truly the frail sex has set forth no small courage in such ways. Consider all the Saintly Confessors, how heartily they despised the world, and how they stood by their resolutions, taken unreservedly and kept inviolably. Remember what S. Augustine says of his mother Monica, of her determination to serve God in her married life and in her widowhood; and S. Jerome and his beloved daughter S. Paula amid so many changes and chances. What may we not achieve with such patterns before our eyes? They were but what we are, they wrought for the same God, seeking the same graces; why may not we do as much in our own state of life, and according to our several vocations, on behalf of our most cherished resolutions and holy profession of faith?

CHAPTER XIII - The Love which Jesus Christ bears to us

CONSIDER the Love with which our Dear Lord Jesus Christ bore so much in this world, especially in the Garden of Olives and on Mount Calvary; that Love bore you in mind, and through all those pains and toils He obtained your good resolutions for you, as also all that is needful to maintain, foster, strengthen and consummate those resolutions. How precious must the resolutions be which are the fruits of our Lord's Passion! and how dear to my heart, since they were dear to that of Jesus! Saviour of my soul, Thou didst die to win them for me; grant me grace sooner to die than forget them. Be sure, my daughter, that the Heart of our most Dear Lord beheld you from the tree of the Cross and loved you, and by that Love He won for you all good things which you were ever to have, and amongst them your good resolutions. Of a truth we have all reason like Jeremiah to confess that the Lord knew us, and called us by our name or ever we were born, [208] the more that His Divine Goodness in its Love and Mercy made ready all things, general and individual, which could promote our salvation, and among them our resolutions. A woman with child makes ready for the babe she expects, prepares its cradle, its swaddling clothes and its nurse; even so our Lord, while hanging on His Cross, prepared all that you could need for your happiness, all the means, the graces, the leadings, by which He leads your soul onwards towards perfection.

Surely we ought ever to remember this, and ask fervently: Is it possible that I was loved, and loved so tenderly by my Saviour, that He should have thought of me individually, and in all these details by which He has drawn me to Himself? With what love and gratitude ought I to use all He has given me? The Loving Heart of my God thought of my soul, loved it, and prepared endless means to promote its salvation, even as though there were no other soul on earth of which He thought; just as the sun shines on each spot of earth as brightly as though it shone nowhere else, but reserved all its brightness for that alone. So Our Dear Lord thought and cared for every one of His children as though none other existed. "Who loved me, and gave Himself for me," [209] S. Paul says, as though he meant, "for me alone, as if there were none but me He cared for."

Let this be graven in your soul, my child, the better to cherish and foster your good resolutions, which are so precious to the Heart of Jesus.

Footnotes:

208. Jer. i. 5.
209. Gal. ii. 20.

CHAPTER XIV - The Eternal Love of God for us

CONSIDER the Eternal Love God has borne you, in that, even before our Lord Jesus Christ became Man and suffered on the Cross for you, His Divine Majesty designed your existence and loved you. When did He begin to love you? When He began to be God, and that was never, for He ever was, without beginning and without end. Even so He always loved you from eternity, and therefore He made ready all the graces and gifts with which He has endowed you. He says by His prophet, "I have loved thee" (and it is YOU that He means) "with an everlasting love, therefore with lovingkindness have I drawn thee." [210] And amid these drawings of His Love He led you to make these resolutions to serve Him.

What must resolutions be which God has foreseen, pondered, dwelt upon from all eternity? how dear and precious to us! Surely we should be ready to suffer anything whatsoever rather than let go one particle of the same. The whole world is not worth one soul, and the soul is worth but little without its good resolutions.

Footnote:

210. Jer. xxxi. 3.

CHAPTER XV - General Affections which should result from these Considerations, and Conclusion of the Exercise

O PRECIOUS resolutions! ye are as the lovely tree of life planted by God's Own Hand in the midst of my heart, a tree which my Saviour has watered with His Blood. Rather would I die a thousand deaths than suffer any blast of wind to root you up--neither vanity, nor pleasure, nor wealth, nor sorrows shall ever overthrow my intentions.

Lord, Thou hast planted and nurtured this tree in Thy Bosom, but how many souls there are which have not been thus favoured, how can I ever sufficiently acknowledge Thy Mercy? Blessed and holy resolutions, if I do but keep you, you will keep me! if you live in my soul, my soul will live in you. Live ever, then, ye resolutions, which have an eternity of your own in God's Mercy, live ever in me, and may I never forsake you.

Next, you must particularise the necessary means for maintaining your good resolutions, determining to use them diligently,--such as frequency in prayer, in Sacraments, in good works; the amendment of the faults you have already discovered, cutting off occasions of sin, and following out carefully all the advice given you with this view. Then, take breath as it were in a renewed profession of your resolutions, and, as though you held your heart in your hands,--dedicate, consecrate, sacrifice, immolate it to God, vowing never to recall it, but leave it for ever in His Right Hand of Majesty, prepared everywhere and in all things to obey His Commands. Ask God to renew your will, to bless your renewed resolutions and to strengthen them. While your heart is thus roused and excited, hasten to your spiritual father, accuse yourself of any faults which you have discovered since you made your general confession, and receive absolution as you did at the first. Make your protest and sign it in his presence, and then lose no time in uniting your renewed heart to its Creator and Saviour, in the most holy Sacrament of the Eucharist.

CHAPTER XVI - The Impressions which should remain after this Exercise

ON the day you make this renewal of your resolutions, and on those immediately following, you should often repeat with heart and voice the earnest words of S. Paul, S. Augustine, S. Catherine of Genoa, and others like-minded, "I am not mine own, whether I live or whether I die, I am the Lord's. There is no longer any me or mine, my me' is Jesus, my mine' is to be His. Thou world, wilt ever be thyself, and hitherto I have been myself, but henceforth I will be so no more." We shall indeed not be ourselves any more, for our heart will be changed, and the world which has so often deceived us will in its turn be deceived in us; our change will be so gradual that the world will still suppose us to be Esau, while really we are Jacob.

All our devout exercises must sink into the heart, and when we come forth from our meditation and retirement it behoves us to tread warily in business or society, lest the wine of our good resolutions be heedlessly spilt; rather let it soak in and penetrate every faculty of the soul, but quietly, and without bodily or mental excitement.

CHAPTER XVII - An Answer to Two Objections which may be made to this Book

THE world will tell you, my child, that all these counsels and practices are so numerous, that anybody who tries to heed them can pay no attention to anything else. Verily, my dear daughter, if we did nothing else we should not be far wrong, since we should be doing all that we ought to do in this world. But you see the fallacy? If all these exercises were to be performed every day they would undoubtedly fill up all our time, but it is only necessary to use them according to time and place as they are wanted. What a quantity of laws there are in our civil codes and digests! But they are only called into use from time to time, as circumstances arise, not every day. Besides, for that matter, David, king as he was, and involved in a multiplicity of complicated affairs, fulfilled more religious duties than those which I have suggested; and S. Louis, a monarch unrivalled in time of peace or war, who was most diligent in the administration of justice and in ruling his country, nevertheless was wont to hear two masses daily, to say vespers and compline with his chaplain, and to make his meditation daily. He used to visit the hospitals every Friday, was regular at confession, took the discipline, often attended sermons and spiritual conferences, and withal he never lost any opportunity of promoting the public welfare, and his court was more flourishing and notable than that of any of his predecessors. Be bold and resolute then in performing the spiritual exercises I have set before you, and God will give you time and strength for all other duties, yea, even if He were to cause the sun to stand still, as He did in Joshua's time. [211] We are sure always to do enough when God works with us.

Moreover, the world will say that I take it for granted that those I address have the gift of mental prayer, which nevertheless every one does not possess, and that consequently this book will not be of use to all. Doubtless it is true that I have assumed this, and it is also true that every one has not the gift of mental prayer, but it is a gift which almost every one can obtain, even the most ignorant, provided they are under a good director, and will take as much pains as the thing deserves to acquire it. And if there are any altogether devoid of this gift (which I believe will very rarely be the case), a wise spiritual father will easily teach them how to supply the deficiency, by reading or listening to the meditations and considerations supplied in this book or elsewhere.

Footnote:

211. Josh. x. 12, 13.

CHAPTER XVIII - *Three Important and Final Counsels*

ON the first day of every month renew the resolution given in Part I. after meditation, and make continual protestation of your intention to keep it, saying with David, "I will never forget Thy Commandments, for with them Thou hast quickened me." [212] And whenever you feel any deterioration in your spiritual condition, take out your protest, and prostrating yourself in a humble spirit, renew it heartily, and you will assuredly find great relief.

Make open profession of your desire to be devout; I will not say to be devout, but to desire it; and do not be ashamed of the ordinary, needful actions which lead us on in the Love of God. Acknowledge boldly that you try to meditate, that you would rather die than commit a mortal sin; that you frequent the Sacraments, and follow the advice of your director (although for various reasons it may not be necessary to mention his name). This open confession that you intend to serve God, and that you have devoted yourself deliberately and heartily to His Holy Love, is very acceptable to His Divine Majesty, for He would not have any of us ashamed of Him or of His Cross. Moreover, it cuts at the root of many a hindrance which the world tries to throw in our way, and so to say, commits us to the pursuit of holiness. The philosophers of old used to give themselves out as such, in order to be left unmolested in their philosophic life; and we ought to let it be known that we aim at devotion in order that we may be suffered to live devoutly. And if any one affirms that you can live a devout life without following all these practices and counsels, do not deny it, but answer meekly that your infirmity is great, and needs more help and support than many others may require.

Finally, my beloved child, I intreat you by all that is sacred in heaven and in earth, by your own Baptism, by the breast which Jesus sucked, by the tender Heart with which He loves you, and by the bowels of compassion in which you hope--be stedfast and persevere in this most blessed undertaking to live a devout life. Our days pass away, death is at hand. "The trumpet sounds a recall," says S. Gregory Nazianzen, "in order that every one may make ready, for Judgment is near." When S. Symphorian was led to his martyrdom, his mother cried out to him, "My son, my son, remember life eternal, look to Heaven, behold Him Who reigns there; for the brief course of this life will soon be ended." Even so would I say to you: Look to Heaven, and do not lose it for earth; look at Hell, and do not plunge therein for the sake of this passing life; look at Jesus Christ, and do not deny Him for the world's sake; amid if the devout life sometimes seems hard and dull, join in Saint Francis' song, [213] --

"So vast the joys that I await,
No earthly travail seemeth great."

Glory be to Jesus, to Whom, with the Father and the Holy Ghost, be honour and glory, now and ever, and to all Eternity. Amen.

Footnotes:

212. Ps. cxix. 93.
213. "Tanto `e il bene ch' io aspetto Ch' ogni pena m' e diletto." These are the words of Saint Francis d'Assisi, which S. Francis de Sales renders-- "A cause des biens que j'attends, Les travaux me sont passe-temps."

www.ingramcontent.com/pod-product-compliance
Lightning Source LLC
Chambersburg PA
CBHW021234090426
42740CB00006B/526

* 9 7 8 1 7 7 3 5 6 0 3 0 4 *